RECOVERING

RECOVERING
HOW TO GET AND STAY SOBER

L. Ann Mueller, M.D., and Katherine Ketcham

BANTAM BOOKS
TORONTO • NEW YORK • LONDON • SYDNEY • AUCKLAND

RECOVERING: HOW TO GET AND STAY SOBER
A Bantam Book / May 1987
3 printings through March 1988

Library of Congress Cataloging-in-Publication Data

Ketcham, Katherine, 1949–
  Recovering: how to get and stay sober.

  Bibliography: p. 282.
  Includes index.
  1. Alcoholism—Treatment.   2. Alcoholics—
Rehabilitation.   I. Mueller, L. Ann, 1942–
II. Title.   [DNLM: 1. Alcoholism—rehabilitation—
popular works.   WM 274 K445r]
RC565.K44   1987   616.86'106   86-32088
ISBN 0-553-34303-3

Published simultaneously in the United States and Canada

Bantam Books are published by Bantam Books, a division of
Bantam Doubleday Dell Publishing Group, Inc. Its trade-
mark, consisting of the words ''Bantam Books'' and the
portrayal of a rooster, is Registered in U.S. Patent and Trade-
mark Office and in other countries. Marca Registrada. Ban-
tam Books, 666 Fifth Avenue, New York, New York 10103.

PRINTED IN CANADA

15   14   13   12   11   10   9   8   7   6

To
Frank and Joan Ketcham
Hollis and Helen Seat
Ralph and Blanche Mueller

ACKNOWLEDGMENTS

Our thanks and gratitude to James R. Milam, Ph.D., for guiding us all in the right direction; Doris Hutchison for her years of teaching, putting the concepts into practice, and proving that they work; Ginny Gustafson, C.A.C., for her help with the chapter on intervention.

And for their contributions, comments, and insights regarding the alcoholism recovery process, our thanks to: Mike Hobi, M.S., Gayle Hobi, C.A.C., Q.D.C., Helen Kester, M.S., Mary Joan Robbins, R.N., Joan Rabey, C.A.C., and the staff of Hughes Treatment Center, Mt. Ayr, Iowa.

CONTENTS

This book is written for *you*, the alcoholic, and for *you*, the alcoholic's mother, father, sister, brother, husband, wife, daughter, or son.

Its purpose is to help you understand your disease and exactly what you will have to do to get well again. We will take you through the progression of the disease, from its early, hidden stage through the middle stage, when the disease begins to surface and you begin to suffer from it, and into the late stage, when alcoholism does its damage so thoroughly that no cell in the body is safe from its deadly assault.

We will help you to understand the symptoms of the disease so that you will be able to recognize it in yourself or in someone you love. You will, at long last, understand why your life has been unraveling and why the disease destroys not only your health but your relationships with friends and family, your career, and even your self-respect. All the years of pent-up anger, guilt, self-hatred, and frustration will be understood, finally, not as evidence that *you* are a deficient, weak, and neurotic person but that your disease made you its victim, *without your choosing it.* Helpless within its lethal embrace, you became what every alcoholic sooner or later becomes—a slave to alcohol, unable to care about anything but your next drink.

"The devil made me do it!" joked comedian Flip Wilson. In alcoholics, there truly is a devil, and that devil is the disease. Alcoholism manipulates its victims, takes over their personalities, and reduces them to caricatures of their true selves. No devil, real or imagined, was ever so horrifying. Look at a population of drinking alcoholics and you will see a group of people who are eerily, uncannily alike: depressed, irritable, moody, guilt-ridden, and obsessed with alcohol to the point where they seem willingly to toss overboard everything of value in their lives; it seems not to matter to them that they are on a sinking ship.

But take those same alcoholics, years or even months after they stop drinking, and you will see a group of individuals with no consistent relationship to one another beyond their disease. Recovering alcoholics are, like the larger population of nonalcoholics, as diverse a group of people as one could choose randomly. Rich, poor, young, old, employed, unemployed, happy, depressed, normal, neurotic, Ph.D.s, plumbers—alcoholism has few prejudices.

Yet, prejudices about the nature of this disease abound, confusing many of us who are trying to understand alcoholics. This is why knowledge of the disease—its causes, nature, and progression—must become the cornerstone of treatment. Knowledge must be based on facts, however, not myths. For too long alcoholics have been given the wrong information about their disease, and the casualties have been enormous in number and tragic in consequence.

One particular case comes to mind, although there are thousands of such examples. Dave S., a high school teacher, was referred by his family doctor to a psychiatrist. After several months in therapy, the psychiatrist told Dave that he drank heavily because he was consumed with anger and hatred toward his father. The psychiatrist gave Dave tranquilizers to calm him down and sleeping pills to help him sleep.

For sixteen months Dave stayed away from alcohol. Then, at Christmas, he visited his family and had a heart-to-heart talk with his father. He was elated: he felt that finally they understood each other and that his frustrations were resolved. That night he started drinking again, convinced that he could now handle it.

But he couldn't. Six months later Dave had a fight with his father, who told him he never wanted to see him again and struck him from his will. Dave began to drink more heavily. His physician treated him for bleeding ulcers and advised him to cut down on his drinking. His relationship with his wife steadily deteriorated. He was stopped twice for drunken driving, but was released both times with a minimum fine.

Less than one year after he started drinking again, Dave ended up in the morgue, drunk and fatally injured, after driving his car at seventy miles per hour into a concrete highway divider.

Could Dave—and all the millions of other alcoholics like him—have been saved? Yes, absolutely. Dave looked for help and found the wrong help. He came into contact with a number of people—physicians, psychiatrists, lawyers, judges, policemen, family, and friends—who could have guided him into recovery but instead either misdiagnosed his disease or mistakenly believed that he wasn't "that bad, yet." He died not just of his disease but of the fact that his disease was never recognized or treated. Literally millions of alcoholics—"not that bad, yet"—have met a similar fate and died from misdiagnosis and mistreatment of their disease. And millions, today, continue to receive the wrong information about their disease and inadequate or inappropriate treatment.

So we have written this book for you, the alcoholic, and for you, the person who loves an alcoholic, to help you understand what you need to do to get well and to guide you to those who are best able to help.

Thank heaven (you have been long enough in hell) that you have a disease for which there is a treatment that works. Be courageous and persistent in trying to understand this disease. Insist that you receive the best and most thorough treatment available. And know that you can get well. You *can* recover. In this book, we'll show you how.

PART ONE

Alcoholism:
What It Is and What It Isn't

CHAPTER 1

Knowledge— the Crucial Foundation for Recovery

Forget everything you have ever been told about alcoholism. Everything. That includes all the information in all the books you have ever read, all the lectures you've heard, all the discussions you've had with friends, relatives, or fellow alcoholics, and all the conclusions you've arrived at yourself. Not all this information is false or misleading, but there are enough misconceptions about alcoholism to muddle your thinking and make it difficult if not impossible for you to come to a true understanding of the disease.

So, wipe the slate clean. And then get ready for a new understanding of alcoholism that will suddenly make everything clear, pulling all the scattered pieces together and forging a new reality. Psychologists refer to this experience as a "gestalt"—by reinterpreting the facts, you create a completely

3

new meaning or pattern of reality. What you will see and understand, then, will have little relation to what you've seen and understood before.

The new vision in alcoholism hinges on two words: *psychological* (mental) and *physiological* (physical). In the past when people looked at alcoholism and tried to understand the disease, they concentrated on its more obvious psychological or mental aspects. Consider the following statements:

• Alcoholics drink so much because they have deep psychological problems.

• Alcoholics have a low tolerance for frustration and are basically rebellious, unreasonable, temperamental, immature, and dependent people with strong feelings of inadequacy.

• Alcoholics are selfish people who think of nothing but themselves and their next drink.

• Alcoholics feel guilty and ashamed about their drinking, but they're too weak-willed to stop.

• Divorce, loss of a job, the death of a loved one, and other life traumas can cause someone to become an alcoholic.

• Children of alcoholics learn bad habits from their parents and often become alcoholics themselves.

• Alcoholics are typically nasty, abusive, and impossible to live with when they're *not* drunk, which proves that their problems aren't all alcohol-related.

• Drinking as much as a bottle a day is pretty good evidence that alcoholics are self-destructive and hate their lives.

Sound familiar? Of course. But every one of these common attitudes and opinions about alcoholism is upside down, based on a misperception of the disease. Let's switch things around, placing the emphasis on the solid **facts** of the disease rather than the prevailing **myths,** * and we'll finally get the horse pulling the cart.

Myth: Alcoholics drink so much because they have deep psychological problems.

Fact: Alcoholics have deep psychological problems *because* they drink so much. Their personalities, like their bodies, get destroyed by the continued drinking. One of alcohol's chief targets is the brain, and after being exposed to heavy, continu-

*For a comprehensive review of the myths and facts surrounding alcoholism, see *Under the Influence: A Guide to the Myths and Realities of Alcoholism,* by James R. Milam, Ph.D., and Katherine Ketcham, Bantam Books, 1983.

ous doses of alcohol for several years the brain becomes toxic—poisoned and sick. When you've got a toxic brain, you don't run a temperature or feel sick to your stomach—you think and behave abnormally. This psychological "sickness" (ranging from irritability to depression and from insomnia to lethargy) is the direct result—not the cause—of alcoholism.

Myth: Alcoholics have a low tolerance for frustration and are basically rebellious, unreasonable, temperamental, immature, and dependent people with strong feelings of inadequacy.
Fact: You bet they are. But, again, blame it on the sick brain. The great majority of alcoholics are psychologically normal before they start drinking; the negative personality characteristics surface *after* they become affected by and addicted to alcohol. That's not to say that some alcoholics aren't rebellious, or immature, or temperamental, before they start drinking. But these traits have nothing to do with their becoming physically addicted to alcohol. A "bad" personality never turned anybody from a nonalcoholic into an alcoholic (witness how many rude, immature, unhappy, and obnoxious nonalcoholics there are in this world).

Myth: Alcoholics are selfish people who think of nothing but themselves and their next drink.
Fact: Are alcoholics selfish? Sure. But no more so than anyone else *until they become addicted to alcohol*. This addiction (like all physical addictions) requires continual feeding. Alcoholics have no choice but to be obsessed with drinking—either thinking about it or doing it. The addiction—the physical, uncontrollable need to drink—leaves them no choice.

Myth: Alcoholics feel guilty and ashamed about their drinking, but they're too weak-willed to stop.
Fact: Guilt and shame surface because alcoholics believe they should be able to say "no" to alcohol and control their drinking. But they can't (at least not for very long); this is the nature of the disease, and no amount of willpower can change its physical demands. Put a mouse (no matter how robust and well fed) in a cage with a ravenous cat, and you'll have some idea how much fighting power your will has against your addiction to alcohol.

Myth: Divorce, loss of a job, the death of a loved one, and other life traumas can cause someone to become an alcoholic.

Fact: Life's major traumas (and minor irritations) are often used by alcoholics to rationalize their drinking ("My mother died," "My dog got run over," "The baby's crying," "The car won't start"), but such events can't suddenly turn a nonalcoholic into an alcoholic. In fact, many life traumas are actually caused by the disease. When alcoholics take too many sick days (the Monday-morning hangover), or make mistakes and bad decisions on the job because their hands are shaky, their stomachs are queasy, or they can't think straight, they get fired. Husbands and wives get fed up, too, and divorce is epidemic among alcoholics.

Myth: Children of alcoholics learn bad habits from their parents and often become alcoholics themselves.

Fact: Alcoholics can no more "learn" their disease than cancer victims can "learn" to grow malignant tumors. Alcoholism *is* inherited, but not in the sense of learning. What is inherited—passed from parent to child—is a genetic susceptibility or vulnerability to alcoholism (more on this in chapter 2).

Myth: Alcoholics are typically nasty, abusive, and impossible to live with when they're *not* drunk, which proves that their problems aren't all alcohol-related.

Fact: It's one of the sad and paradoxical facts of this disease that *not* drinking is often worse for the alcoholic than drinking. When alcoholics stop drinking, they suffer the tortures of the damned. Like a fish out of water, it's a life-and-death struggle to get back into the drink. Watch out if you're blocking the way—alcoholics literally *need* that drink to feel anything approaching "normal," and they'll do just about anything (from begging to stealing to bodily harm) to get it. A classic example is the man who drove his lawn tractor three miles to the liquor store after his wife poured out all the alcohol in the house and hid his car keys.

It's also a fact that alcohol is a poison, with long-lasting effects on the nervous system that will plague the alcoholic when he's drinking, when he's drunk, or when he's sobering up.

Myth: Drinking as much as a quart a day is pretty good evidence that alcoholics are self-destructive and hate their lives.

Fact: Drinking a quart a day is evidence of nothing other than addiction to alcohol. Alcoholics may appear to be self-destructive by drinking so much, but *not* drinking seems to them infinitely more self-destructing and insane. Drinking makes alcoholics in the active throes of their disease feel better; *not* drinking makes them feel much worse. Which choice, then, makes more sense?

If, as you read this chapter, a light bulb kept turning on in your brain and your heart started beating faster, you're catching on to this new understanding of alcoholism. If, however, you find yourself resisting with statements like, "Well, that might be true for some people, but my grandfather is just a crotchety old man whose only friend is alcohol," or, "I wish I could believe that Dad was a helpless victim, but he's shown time after time that he doesn't care about anyone but himself"— *don't be discouraged*. You're fighting a lifetime of misinformation and prejudice. Consider the image of an alcoholic as a skid row drunk, and you'll know how deeply ingrained is our disgust. Think about how you feel when you say, "I'm an alcoholic," or, "My mother is an alcoholic," and you'll know how deep is our shame.

These misunderstandings and prejudices cannot be overcome overnight. But they can and must be overcome. If our society is ever to treat alcoholics with the care and respect they deserve—Do we turn our noses up when someone tells us they have multiple sclerosis? Are we ashamed to admit that we have diabetes or high blood pressure?—then we will all have to get down to the business of trying truly to understand the nature and causes of this disease we call alcoholism.

CHAPTER 2

Alcoholism:

A Definition and a Description

What is this disease you've got (or you think you might have)? First, we'll give you our own definition, filled with complex words that only the experts understand. Then we'll try to explain what these words mean, in terms of how the disease affects your body and your mind. Alcoholism, as anyone reading this book knows, is much more than a bunch of words. So we'll try to go beyond the words in an attempt to understand the real nature and impact of alcoholism on your health and your life.

The Definition

Alcoholism: a **chronic, primary, hereditary, eventually fatal disease** that **progresses** from an **early physiological susceptibility** into an **addiction** characterized by **tolerance changes, physiological dependence,** and **loss of control** over drinking.

The Descriptions

Chronic. "Chronic" means perpetual, constant, and lasting a long time. In diseases, chronic is often contrasted with "acute," which means severe but of short duration. If you have an attack of appendicitis, it's called acute, because it occurs suddenly and it lasts just a few hours or, at the most, days. Alcoholism, on the other hand, is chronic because it never leaves you. Once you've got it, you're stuck with it for life.

Other chronic diseases include diabetes, high blood pressure, heart disease, emphysema, and arthritis. In most chronic diseases, including alcoholism, treatments are available to combat the symptoms and progression of the disease. So, while *chronic* is a scary word in the sense of "you're stuck with this thing for the rest of your life," it doesn't mean that you're a hopeless cause. Far from it.

Some people argue that alcoholism is not chronic at all, at least not for all alcoholics, and that some alcoholics can get over their dependence on alcohol. For these people, dependence on alcohol is seen primarily as psychological or learned; thus, they believe it can be unlearned. Alcoholics have a fascination with this type of research; like the victims of any chronic disease, they would like to believe that there is a quick cure or that someday their disease will go away for good. And alcoholics have other reasons, too, for wanting a "cure," since they suffer from the stigma and shame of their disease and would like to be "normal."

Many psychiatrists and counselors tend to place heavy emphasis on the psychological reasons why people drink too much. Because alcoholics show plenty of "psychological" symptoms, research into psychological and behavioral problems may seem productive and potentially enlightening.

One particularly popular line of research has been the attempt to show that some alcoholics can drink "normally" without suddenly beginning to drink out of control. "Experimental bars" have actually been created, in which the experimenters try to teach alcoholics how to drink normally and responsibly (put down your glass after each sip, say "no" after one drink, eat when you drink, alternate drinks with a glass of water, etc.). Other alcoholism experts are up in arms over this "controlled drinking" research, and heated words are tossed back and forth among the various researchers, creating hostility, anger, resentment, and bitter rivalries.

What's going on here? Why is everyone fighting? Who's right? Really, it all depends on your definition of alcoholism. If you define it as maladjusted drinking behavior, based on psychological problems, childhood stresses, and personality quirks, then you've got the stage set for fixing the supposedly temporary psychological problems and teaching alcoholics how to drink responsibly like psychologically "normal" people.

If, however, you define alcoholism as a physical addiction, then any attempt to teach alcoholics to drink responsibly or to support them in their efforts to drink in control must be seen as misguided, doomed to failure, and morally and ethically unconscionable.

Rather than slinging accusations back and forth, however, let's look at this controversy in a more constructive way. In the past, all people with alcohol problems were lumped together as alcoholics. It's time (actually, long past time) to separate alcoholics from problem drinkers. Problem drinkers should be defined as those whose cells are not physically adapted—adjusted—to alcohol and thus are *not* physically addicted, but who definitely have problems when they drink (although not necessarily every time they drink). While alcoholics have a *chronic, physical* addiction to alcohol, problem drinkers have an *acute*, primarily *psychological* need to drink that flares up at certain times and is caused by pressures from *without*, not by a physical demand and drive from within. Or, to look at it another way, problem drinkers abuse alcohol; alcohol abuses alcoholics.

It used to be thought that problem drinking was simply the beginning stage of alcoholism. A person with problems—stress, death in the family, personality deficiencies—would abuse alcohol and, because of a lack of willpower or weakness of character, would wind up addicted. But the truth is much more complicated. While some alcoholics have serious problems that cause them to abuse alcohol, the great majority begin drinking for the same reasons non-alcoholics drink: for the pleasurable and intoxicating effects. But at some point, and this point varies from one alcoholic to another, ranging from several weeks to several years after the first drink, the addiction takes over and causes the early-stage alcoholic to drink differently than his non-alcoholic friends and to experience problems caused by his drinking (see pages 32–37 for a discussion of the early stage symptoms). Unlike the true problem drinker, however, these "problems" do not precede the addiction but are actually caused by it.

Primary. *Webster's New World Dictionary* defines *primary* as "first in order of development or importance," "the condition from which all other symptoms are derived," and "original." In alcoholism, the meaning is pretty clear: the disease comes first, then the other symptoms (psychological, social, and behavioral) arise. These secondary psychological symptoms are actually caused by, or are the consequence of, the physical disease.

As we've said before, this is not the way most people see it. Most people think the psychological problems come first, causing a person to drink too much and eventually to become physically addicted to alcohol. Here again, the cart's been trying to pull the horse.

Why have so many people, including hundreds of experts, been so confused about this disease for so long? The answer is surprisingly simple: the psychological symptoms show up *before* the alcoholic *appears* to be physically addicted to alcohol. In the early to middle stages, when the alcohol-affected brain begins to show itself in distorted behaviors, thoughts, and emotions, alcoholics can still control their drinking most of the time. They're not sick, their doctors don't notice anything physically wrong with them, they can part their hair in a straight line and drink their morning coffee without spilling it all over themselves—in other words, they don't act, look, or talk the way we think an alcoholic should act, look, or talk.

But psychological problems they do have. They're often

irritable, moody, depressed, tense, and nervous. Sometimes they lie about their drinking, or they blame it on the pressures of the job, the nagging wife, the screaming kids, the barking dog, the bad weather. They promise they'll cut down, and they do for a while, but then they start right up again. All in all, these people seem immature, frustrated, dependent, weak-willed, deceptive, and basically unhappy. It's no wonder they use alcohol to try to solve their problems, and then they get hooked. Right?

Wrong. Though they may not seem physically addicted, they are. The addiction is there all along, well hidden, generally resting quietly, but gaining strength until the time comes when its power is so fierce that it can no longer disguise itself. In the beginning stages of the disease, however, the addiction causes only relatively "minor" problems—depression, irritability, insomnia, nervousness, anxiety, etc.

Unknown even to the alcoholic, the addiction is creating these discomforts and, in a sense, using them to increase its power. The alcoholic feels depressed, so he drinks; then he feels better. That's the early addiction. The alcoholic believes her husband and kids are ganging up on her, so she drinks half a bottle of wine, quickly, to relax and try to think more clearly. That's the addiction. The alcoholic has several drinks at a tavern after work and, to avoid confrontations, decides to tell his wife he had a late meeting. Why did he lie? The addiction.

The addiction known as alcoholism alters its victims' thinking, behaviors, and personalities slowly but insidiously, so that they become unknowing collaborators, using every excuse they can find to drink, blaming their drinking on others or on events outside their control and, as time goes by, becoming more and more like the image of an alcoholic.

But, of course, they were alcoholics all along.

Hereditary. Alcoholism is passed from alcoholic parents to their children, through a genetic susceptibility to alcohol. How do we know this? The best evidence comes from a series of studies conducted by researcher Donald Goodwin. Goodwin studied children who had been separated from their parents at birth and adopted by nonrelatives. He found that the sons of alcoholic parents were four times more likely to become alcoholics themselves—even though they had no contact with their natural parents and were raised in an alcohol-free environment. In twin studies Goodwin found that if one identical twin was alcoholic, the other was, too, but this was not as consistently true for fraternal twins. Since identical twins share exactly the same genetic makeup but fraternal twins do not, this is more startling evidence that alcoholism runs in the genes.

Lots of nonhereditary factors can influence the progression of a hereditary disease. You've got to drink, for example, if you're going to get the disease. But even if you don't drink, you can still pass your inherited susceptibility to your children. The "skip factor" is common in alcoholism. This is when the sons or daughters of an alcoholic shun alcohol and thus avoid the risk of becoming alcoholics themselves. *Their* sons or daughters, however, have not grown up with an alcoholic parent and therefore may not feel the same repulsion toward drinking. They still have the inherited susceptibility to alcoholism, however, and if they drink, they run a fairly high risk of becoming alcoholics. Therefore, when you look at your family tree to determine if there is any alcoholism, be sure to consider the teetotalers, too; did they avoid alcohol because their parents or other close relatives were alcoholics? If so, the inherited susceptibility may continue in your genes—even though your parents never touched the stuff.

The combination of alcohol and other central nervous system drugs (tranquilizers, sedatives, painkillers, sleeping pills) can also have a powerful effect on the progression of this hereditary disease. Someone who combines drugs and alcohol may be entering the "hyperspace" of addiction, greatly speeding up the addictive process, becoming addicted to both alcohol and drugs, with each addiction aggravating and urging on the other.

Nutrition is another factor that can influence the speed and severity of the addictive process. If you eat lots of sweets, drink cup after cup of coffee, skip meals, and in general eat poorly, you may be weakening your body's defenses and unknowingly feeding the addiction. If, on the other hand, you eat well and generally keep in good nutritional and chemical balance, you may be able to slow down the addictive process. Unfortunately, one of the symptoms of the progressing disease is that the alcoholic becomes less interested in eating and less able to keep food down. Alcohol also interferes with the use and processing of nutrients in the body, and many middle- and late-stage alcoholics suffer deficiencies of certain crucial vitamins and minerals.

If your mother drank when she was pregnant, you may also have a heightened vulnerability to alcoholism; if she drank heavily, you may have become addicted to alcohol while in the womb. This may seem incredible, but alcohol passes through the placental wall, so if your mother drank heavily and constantly, you did, too. Years later when you take your first drink you may have an "instant" reactivation of this fetal addiction. This phenomenon may account, at least in part, for those "instant alcoholics" who seem to become addicted to alcohol with their very first drink.

Finally, if your health is bad—if you've got other diseases that sap your strength and energy, if you are under a great deal of stress, if you never exercise, if you're malnourished—more fuel is being added to the fire of the addiction.

Heredity, then, is the foundation for the building of the addiction. How fast the structure goes up, however, can depend on any number of factors, in addition to the inherited susceptibility to alcoholism.

Eventually fatal. It would be nice if we didn't have to include these two words in this definition, but there's one very important reason: lots of people are fooled into thinking that only the really *bad* alcoholics (you know, those late-stage degenerate types) die from their drinking. And, in a way, that's true. Most of the rest of you drinking alcoholics will die before you ever get to the end stage of your disease. You'll die from heart attacks, or falling off ladders or down stairs, or car accidents, liver disease, strokes, choking on your own vomit, internal bleeding, cirrhosis, cancer, heart failure, lung infections, pneumonia, or overdoses of sleeping pills, tranquilizers, or sedatives. And on your death certificate your survivors won't find the word *alcoholism*, because even if your doctor knew about your disease, he'd want to spare your family the shame of the label.

But alcohol will kill you, one way or the other, if you continue to drink. It may weaken your heart or eat away your liver or make you fall asleep at the wheel. Your death will seem early, unfair, and only slightly alcohol-related. But don't be fooled—it's alcohol that cut your life short. Alcoholism is a killer. Whether you die the slow, painful way or go out suddenly in a dramatic and tragic death, you can bet that alcohol was behind you all the way, pushing death a little closer.

Disease. Why do we use the word *disease?* Why not *illness,* or *sickness,* or *affliction?* Because disease implies a *process* of destruction that has a specific cause or causes and characteristic symptoms. That definition fits alcoholism. The words *illness, sickness,* and *affliction,* on the other hand, imply a temporary condition of poor health. Alcoholism isn't temporary, and "poor health" is, obviously, too mild a description.

Progresses. Relentlessly and persistently, alcoholism progresses from its barely recognizable early stage through the ever-increasing problems of the middle stage and into the late, destructive, fatal stage. In medical terms, *progressive* means becoming more severe or spreading to other parts of the body. In layman's terms, *progressive* means that the only way alcoholism can be stopped is either by abstaining forever from alcohol or by dying from something else first.

Early physiological susceptibility. Before we ever take our first drink, we're predisposed to (or protected from) alcoholism. Something inside us is "programmed" to react to alcohol in a certain way. Heredity, as we discussed, is largely responsible for determining who will have this susceptibility or vulnerability to alcohol. But what, exactly, is inherited?

Scientists and researchers haven't worked out all the details yet, but the overall picture is coming into focus. It appears that the susceptibility to alcoholism centers in two areas of the body: the liver and the brain. Alcohol is processed in the liver, where it is first converted to acetaldehyde, a highly toxic (poisonous) and reactive substance, and then to acetate. In alcoholics, scientists have discovered a liver enzyme that breaks down alcohol into acetaldehyde at a rate up to *forty times faster* than in nonalcoholics. But the second stage of chemical conversion—the breakdown of acetaldehyde into acetate—is *slower* in alcoholics than nonalcoholics.

As a result, acetaldehyde is produced in greater quantities in alcoholics and it remains in their bodies for a longer time. What happens to this surplus is another fascinating detective story. Researchers have discovered that some of the excess acetaldehyde travels to the brain, where it reacts with certain brain chemicals to create compounds called "tetra hydro-isoquinolines" (THIQs). The THIQs are chemically similar to the addictive substance found in heroin and morphine.

So what have we here? An abnormal metabolism in the liver that produces large quantities of acetaldehyde, which then travel to the brain and interact with other chemicals to create addictive substances. This is the factual foundation for a comprehensive theory that explains susceptibility to alcoholism.

We call this susceptibility "early" because it exists before the alcoholic ever starts to drink. Marc Schuckit and colleagues at the University of California at San Diego studied the children of alcoholics and found that they, too, had the metabolic abnormality—before they had ever taken a drink. Henri Begleiter at the Down State Medical Center in Brooklyn examined brain wave tracings of children of alcoholics and found that 30 to 40 percent had brain deficits in the P3 brain waves, which control memory and emotion. The children in Begleiter's studies had never drunk alcohol, indicating a possible genetic influence on brain deficits and alcoholism susceptibility. And doctors Ryback and Eckhardt at the National Institute on Alcohol Abuse and Alcoholism (NIAAA) have developed blood chemistry tests that they believe can be used to identify alcoholics in the early stage or even before they take a drink.

To summarize in one sentence what we mean by "early physiological susceptibility": Alcoholics have a built-in, inherited, uncontrollable reaction to alcohol that causes them to become addicted when they drink.

Addiction. *Webster's New World Dictionary* defines *addiction* as "the condition of being addicted to a habit" and *addict* (verb) as "to give oneself up to some strong habit." *Habit* is defined by the same dictionary as "a pattern of action that is acquired and has become so automatic that it is difficult to break."

This is the sort of definition that has contributed to much of the confusion and controversy surrounding alcoholism. It is a definition that fits certain "addictions" (gambling or overeating, for example) but *not* drug addictions (heroin, morphine, codeine, and alcohol). Addiction to alcohol has nothing to do with "giving oneself up" or "habit." It does have to do with tolerance changes, physical dependence, and loss of control, all of which we'll define in the next pages.

It's important to understand that alcohol is a *selectively addicting drug,* meaning that not everyone who drinks will become physically addicted to it. This, too, is a cause for confusion since most addictive drugs, including heroin, morphine, and codeine, are addictive for almost anyone who uses them regularly. We seem to have no protection against addiction to these drugs. But most people do have a protection against addiction to alcohol; their bodies can process and eliminate it without becoming addicted. Only a minority of alcohol users—the estimated 10 to 20 percent of our drinking population with a physiological susceptibility—cannot use the drug without becoming addicted to it.

Tolerance changes. Remember the old days when you could drink everyone under the table? You could drink and drink, but you felt fine (high, but fine), and you acted as if you had had only a few drinks. You could walk, talk, think, and react like a sober person—you were Super Person!

Most early-stage and many middle-stage alcoholics experience this ability to drink large amounts of alcohol without getting obviously drunk. In fact, when they drink, they can function even *better.* The trick, though, as every experienced drinking alcoholic knows, is to drink just enough but not too much and to continue drinking. If you drink too much— if you overdrink your tolerance—you'll experience the unpleasant (what an understatement) symptoms of drunkenness, including nausea, dizziness, loss of coordination, inability to think clearly or logically, slurring words, etc. If you stop drinking, you'll soon begin to feel physically and mentally rotten.

What's behind this phenomenon? *Tolerance.* Tolerance is a sign that your body's cells have adapted—adjusted—to alcohol and can function normally even when you've had a lot to drink. Tolerance, as one research team described it, signals "a change in the nervous system leading to *improvement of physiological functioning* in the presence of . . . alcohol."* (emphasis added)

Unfortunately, the alcoholic's tolerance for alcohol will change over time, as he or she continues to drink. Suddenly,

*H. Wallgren and H. Barry, *Actions of Alcohol* (Elsevier Publishing Co., 1970), vol. 2, p. 496.

it may seem, you can't drink as much as you used to. You get drunk faster. You have trouble controlling how much you drink, and you often drink too much. Why? Because the same cells that had adapted to alcohol in the early stage of the disease have now been damaged by alcohol (and its byproduct acetaldehyde). These cells can no longer tolerate alcohol in large amounts—they simply can't handle it efficiently. So, as the disease progresses, your tolerance for alcohol will change, a sign that your cells have actually adapted to alcohol and then, over time, become damaged by it.

Physiological dependence. When you're physically dependent on a drug, you suffer *physically* when the drug is withdrawn. The cells in your body actually *need* the drug in order to function normally. Without it, they're in agony, and they send out severe distress signals that cause the addicted person to feel physically horrendous.

In alcoholism, this physical agony is called the withdrawal syndrome, and it gets worse as the disease progresses. In the early stage, you often feel anxious, shaky, and nervous after a drinking bout (although you usually don't relate these feelings to the physical distress of withdrawal). But even though you don't feel great, you can still get out of bed, read the newspaper, pour a cup of coffee, drink it, and go to work. Lots of nonalcoholics suffer somewhat the same symptoms—nervousness, weakness, insomnia, nausea, sweating, shaking, loss of appetite, memory impairment—which are commonly and collectively known as "the hangover."

In the early stage of the disease, the alcoholic may not get a hangover at all, or may experience only slight discomfort after a night of drinking. But as the disease progresses, the agony gets much worse and surpasses anything the nonalcoholic might experience. Now, your hands shake noticeably in the morning, and your head feels as if it is splitting apart. Your brain is fogged and you have trouble remembering little details. You can't concentrate. You forget things. Sometimes you forget whole hours or even entire days. You're moody and irritable, and it seems as if everyone in the world is ganging up against you. All the traffic lights turn red when you get to them. Everyone is on your case. The telephone rings too loudly. The screen door slams, and you jump out of your skin.

You feel better, though—much better—when you drink. After a few drinks, you calm down a little. Things aren't really so bad. Your headache miraculously goes away. After a few more drinks, your hands are steady, and you no longer get the cold sweats. You can think clearly about things. Life seems somewhat sweet, if not downright terrific.

When you're not drinking, you find yourself thinking about drinking, even craving a drink. And this, too, gets worse. Eventually, the urge to drink will become overpowering, and you'll hide bottles in your glovebox, in your desk drawer, or in your garden, next to the tomatoes. You don't always drink from them (although you will more and more as time goes by), but it's nice to know they're there.

If you keep drinking, you'll experience the late-stage symptoms of withdrawal: convulsions, hallucinations, and the DTs (delirium tremens). You'll be paranoid and fearful. The ringing of the doorbell will send you into a cold sweat. You won't be able to go anywhere without alcohol (it's no longer just "nice" to know the bottles are there when you need them; you've *got* to have them there). You'll drink and pass out or vomit, and then you'll drink again. Your craving for alcohol is irresistible and your physical need for alcohol overshadows everything else in your life.

Physical dependence—two bland words that cover a lifetime of torture.

Loss of control. You promise your wife—on the soul of your dead mother—that you'll never again get drunk. And then, a week later, you go out and get drunk. Is that loss of control?

You stop drinking for three months and then get right back into your old routine of four or five drinks* a day. Is that loss of control?

You have three double martinis at 1:00 P.M., despite the fact that you've got to finish an important report (you've been

---

*A drink for an alcoholic can be a very different entity from a drink for a nonalcoholic. Alcoholics have been known to refer to a ten-ounce tumbler filled to the brim with straight 80-proof liquor as "a drink." Or a bottle of wine, or a case of beer. As one alcoholic summed it up: "When friends ask me over for a drink, I think, 'One drink, and a weak one at that? Why bother!'"

working on it for two months) and present it to the stockholders at 4:00 P.M. Is that loss of control?

You've got the "morning shakes" so you put a little (just three or four ounces) of vodka (can't smell it) in your coffee. Is that loss of control?

The answer to all these questions is "yes." Loss of control means that no matter how hard you try, no matter how many Bibles you swear on, no matter how fervently and feverishly you want to cut down on your drinking, you go ahead and drink anyway and, as time goes by, you drink too much and get drunk. You drink at socially inappropriate times and for reasons that make no sense at all to anyone else. In short, you can't reliably make the decisions anymore; your rational, logical mind is no longer able to predictably call the shots.

Loss of control begins for most alcoholics in the middle stage, when alcohol's progressive damage to the body is becoming obvious. Your cells, particularly the cells in two of alcohol's favorite targets, the liver and the brain, are not as strong and vital as they used to be, and consequently they're not as efficient and predictable at processing and eliminating alcohol. So your "tolerance" for alcohol is fluctuating and decreasing. Sometimes you can drink a lot and sometimes just a few drinks will get you drunk.

At the same time, your body "needs" alcohol because it's physically addicted to it, and when you don't drink, you suffer from withdrawal symptoms—shakes, tremors, nausea, sweating, fatigue, insomnia, nervousness, headaches, irritability, depression, on and on, you name it. So you drink to medicate yourself, to make the agony go away. But your body is too sick now to process the large amounts of alcohol needed to subdue the withdrawal symptoms, and you're caught in the double bind of being sick without alcohol and sick with it.

Graham Chapman, alcoholic, physician, and writer/performer with *Monty Python's Flying Circus*, describes the agony of this double bind in Dennis Wholey's book, *The Courage to Change*:

> "I began to keep a bottle by the bedside because if I didn't have a couple of shots of gin in the first half-hour of waking up, I would get withdrawal symptoms, the dry heaves, cold sweats, and a really appalling nauseated feeling. I didn't want to go through that every day. It became an appalling routine, waking up in the morning,

needing to get a couple of drinks down me within the first half-hour or otherwise face the unpleasantness of withdrawal. That unpleasantness began to outweigh the supposed advantages of drinking. The pleasant side of it, the joyous side of it, was no longer sufficient to counteract that unpleasantness every morning. . . . I was weak to the point that I couldn't last a day, couldn't last the first half-hour of the day, without drinking, which restricted my life considerably. I had to go everywhere with a drink, I felt. And I did."

Loss of control doesn't happen all the time, and it's not as if you go out and drink everything in sight. Losing control doesn't mean that you'll drink vanilla extract, cough syrup, or Sterno (although anyone who does, and some alcoholics do, is obviously out of control). What loss of control does mean is that you are no longer physically able to restrict your drinking to socially acceptable times and places, that your alcohol-affected brain is inaccurately judging how much you can drink, and that your body is beginning to lose its ability to process the amount of alcohol required to control your withdrawal symptoms.

In other words, you are no longer controlling alcohol— alcohol is controlling you.

As this chapter makes abundantly clear, alcoholism is a complicated, catastrophic disease that, given enough time, will destroy your health and your happiness. How do you know for sure if you or someone you love has this disease? Read on. In the next chapter we'll give you a questionnaire designed to help you decide if you're an alcoholic, and in chapter 4 we'll describe in detail the early-, middle-, and late-stage symptoms of the disease.

CHAPTER 3

Diagnosis:

A Questionnaire for the Reader

How do you know for certain if you or someone you love is an alcoholic? This may be the most crucial question in alcoholism, for early diagnosis can literally mean the difference between life and death. But it's also an extremely difficult question to answer, for every alcoholic experiences individual and unique reactions to the progressing disease.

Diagnosis is further confused because alcoholics appear to be in good health through the early and middle stages of the disease. They are not sick or incapacitated in any obvious way. They do not develop tumors that can be felt, probed, or tested by a physician. No laboratory tests have yet been designed that can absolutely verify a diagnosis of alcoholism. A surgeon can't cut into the body, pick out a piece of tissue, and, on reading the lab report, pronounce with certainty, "This person is an alcoholic." In its late stages, of course, alcoholism is obvious, the addiction is deeply entrenched, and the alcoholic is deathly ill. But the ultimate purpose of diagnosis, as with all diseases, is to discover and treat the illness before it progresses to the point where it has caused widespread and permanent damage.

Fortunately, there are warning signs in alcoholism, just as there are in the early stages of many other diseases. A cancer victim does not have to wait until he develops a tumor the size of a grapefruit before his disease is diagnosed, and neither does an alcoholic have to develop cirrhosis of the liver or suffer the agonies of the DTs before his disease can be identified and treated.

In alcoholism, the early warning signs are generally behavioral, meaning that the physical disease causes its victims to behave in ways that can be recognized as different from "normal." This is because alcohol attacks the organ in the body that controls behavior: the brain. In the very early stages of the disease, these "brain symptoms" are subtle and difficult to pinpoint, but as the disease progresses the alcoholic's behavior becomes increasingly abnormal. Eventually alcoholism emerges from its "hidden" stage, and it becomes more and more obvious that the drinker is in deep trouble with alcohol. In the late stage of the disease, the alcoholic's physical and mental health is profoundly affected, and he begins to look and act like a chronic drunk—the stereotype of the "skid row bum."

The following questionnaire was designed specifically to help readers understand and recognize the progression of symptoms from early- to late-stage alcoholism.* Its purpose is to inform, not to frighten or intimidate. A number of specific symptoms related to each stage of alcoholism are included, allowing the reader a detailed look at the nature and progression of the disease from early stage to middle stage and finally to late stage. The questions and answers are then discussed and interpreted, in an effort to help the reader understand why a "yes" response may indicate a problem with alcohol.

This questionnaire is unusual because it includes the early

---

*This questionnaire is not intended to replace professional evaluation and assessment. If you suspect alcoholism in yourself or someone you love, and if the questionnaire confirms your suspicions, seek professional guidance.

warnings signs and early-stage symptoms of alcoholism. These signs and symptoms are often completely overlooked or confused with "prealcoholic" personality traits or drinking habits and patterns that are thought to predispose to alcoholism. These "predispositions," however, are actually early symptoms of a growing addiction—an addiction that causes its victims' behavior to change in subtle but recognizable and specific ways. Recognizing the early-stage signs and symptoms will help to identify alcoholics early in their disease, before the disease has destroyed everything of value in their lives, including their careers, family relationships, and mental and physical health. With early diagnosis and treatment, the alcoholic and those who love him are spared much misery and agony, and chances for recovery are dramatically increased.

Be sure to answer the following questions as truthfully as possible. Family members can also answer the questionnaire for their suspected alcoholic. If your answer is "sometimes," put down a "yes." Some of the questions actually ask several questions—if you answer "yes" to any one of the questions, count your answer as a "yes." After the questionnaire, we'll tell you what your answers indicate about your drinking behavior.

Are You an Alcoholic?

1. Do you have any close relatives—grandparents, parents, siblings—who are alcoholics?

2. Do you consistently drink more than your friends? Are you often the last one to leave the bar or party?

3. Do you enjoy drinking and look forward to drinking occasions? Are you known as a great "party person"?

4. Do you sometimes find that you don't want to stop drinking after just one or two drinks, even though everyone else has had enough?

5. Have you experienced any change in your drinking patterns—drinking more and more often, drinking alone, or switching to a stronger drink?

6. Has anyone close to you—your wife, husband, parents, children—ever worried or complained about your drinking?

7. Does the thought of a nondrinking occasion—a church wedding and reception with a nonalcoholic punch, for example—make you anxious or even angry?

8. Have you ever wondered why some of your friends drink so slowly or stop drinking after just an hour or two? Do you ever buy drinks for your friends in an effort to keep the party going?

9. Do you tend to gulp down your first drinks and then, when you feel the effects, slow your pace to that of other drinkers?

10. When you're sober, do you sometimes regret things you've said or done while drinking? Do you find yourself apologizing to the people you love for your drinking behavior and promising to change?

11. Have your ever tried to stop drinking for a period of time (a week, or perhaps a month) because you felt it would be good for you, or because you wanted to prove that you could do it?

12. Do you sometimes make promises to yourself about controlling or cutting down on your drinking and then find yourself breaking them?

13. Are you able to drink more now than you did a year ago? Five years ago? Do you tend to drink much more?

14. Have you ever had a blackout, when you can't recall some or all of the events that occurred when you were drinking? Do you have more blackouts now than you did a year ago?

15. Have you had any difficulties at work—regular sick days, difficulty concentrating, complaints from co-workers or supervisors—that might be related to your drinking?

16. Do you sometimes feel that you're better off when you're drinking than when you're sober? Does drinking, in fact, get rid of your headaches, tensions, anxieties, and mood swings?

17. Do you feel increasingly guilty about your drinking, and yet when someone you love mentions his concern, do you become hostile and defensive?

18. Do you tend to think that your problems are the result of tension and stress, or lack of understanding from your spouse, or unreasonable demands at work? Do you feel sorry for yourself because no one seems to understand you? Do you turn to alcohol for solace and comfort?

19. Do you find yourself craving alcohol, actually wanting a drink so intensely that you are willing to risk a fight with your wife or husband or a reprimand from your boss?

20. Do you increasingly drink more than you intended to drink? Do you have trouble stopping once you've started? Do you ever drink in the morning?

21. Do your hands sometimes shake uncontrollably the morning after you've been drinking? Do you feel physically ill (nauseated, shaky, queasy) and/or psychologically upset (depressed, anxious, tense, moody, irritable) when sober? Does alcohol make you feel better?

22. Do you have any physical diseases or disorders that might be alcohol-related, such as gastritis, recurrent diarrhea, persistent nausea, high blood pressure, pneumonias, heart palpitations, fatty liver, hepatitis, cirrhosis, DTs, seizures, or pancreatitis?

23. Have you ever been hospitalized for injuries, accidents, or traumas suffered while drinking and, perhaps, caused by drinking too much?

24. Do you ever have suicidal thoughts? Have you ever had hallucinations after coming off a drinking bout? Do you ever have unreasonable fears (for example, does the doorbell or telephone ringing make you anxious and fearful)?

25. Have you experienced any losses because of your drinking—loss of a job, divorce, alienated children or family, your driver's license suspended because of drunken driving, etc.?

26. Do you neglect eating, particularly during and just after a drinking bout? Do you neglect your body by not exercising regularly or taking showers or going to a doctor for medical problems?

27. Are you able to drink less than you once could, and when you do drink, do you tend to drink until you pass out or get so sick that you can't drink any more?

Scoring the Questionnaire

Alcoholism can, roughly, be divided into three stages: early, middle, and late. The above questionnaire includes symptoms from each of these stages, and your answers will help identify (a) if you are an alcoholic and (b) what stage you are in. Use the following grading scale to score your answers:

Question	Score
(1)	1
(2)	1
(3)	1
(4)	1
(5)	1
(6)	1
(7)	1
(8)	1
(9)	1

Early-Stage Alcoholism

The first nine questions cover the early stage of the disease, when alcoholism is "hidden" and the alcoholic doesn't even suspect he has a problem. Many of the symptoms associated with this early stage are also experienced by nonalcoholic drinkers. For example, both early-stage alcoholics and nonalcoholics may answer "yes" to the question: "Do you enjoy drinking and look forward to drinking occasions?" But not many non-alcoholic drinkers would answer "yes" to all or even most of the nine questions.

If you answered "yes" to several of these questions, you may be an early-stage alcoholic—even if your answers to the rest of the questions are a truthful "no." A "yes" answer to five or more of these questions is typical of the early-stage disease.

(A fuller picture emerges if you include your scores for questions 10–27. If, for example, your score totals 3 on questions 1–9, but you answer "yes" to questions 12 and 14, your accumulated score is 7, which falls into the category of early-stage alcoholism.)

Question	Score
(10)	2
(11)	2
(12)	2
(13)	2
(14)	2
(15)	2
(16)	2
(17)	2
(18)	2

Middle-Stage Alcoholism

Questions 10–18 cover the middle-stage symptoms of alcoholism. In the middle stage, the alcoholic's problems become more obvious, even though the great majority of middle-stage alcoholics look healthy and are generally in control of themselves and their lives. The disease has progressed significantly but not to the point where the alcoholic is destitute and deathly ill—that will come later, if the alcoholic continues to drink.

In the middle stage, the alcoholic can still exert some control over his drinking, and chances are good that he will deny or rationalize his

symptoms if he's confronted. Denials and rationalizations are actually symptoms of middle-stage
alcoholism, and they indicate that the alcoholic
knows, deep inside, that he's in trouble with
alcohol but is physically addicted and cannot
function without it, at least for very long.

The middle stage of alcoholism can last a
long time, as much as ten to twenty years, and
for that reason we've divided it into three sub-
stages. Add your score on this section to the total
score from the first nine questions:

9–15 points: early-middle stage
16–21 points: middle stage
22–27 points: late-middle stage

Question	Score
(19)	3
(20)	3
(21)	3
(22)	3
(23)	3
(24)	3
(25)	3
(26)	3
(27)	3

Late-Stage Alcoholism

Questions 19–27 deal with the final, deterio-
rative stage of alcoholism, when most alcoholics
outwardly appear to be alcoholic. The disease
has progressed to the point where the alcoholic
is physically ill both when drinking and when
sober. Medical complications such as gastritis,
cardiac problems, and liver disease seriously undermine the alcoholic's physical health.

The late-stage alcoholic can no longer deny
that he has a problem controlling his drinking,
but neither can he imagine life without alcohol.
Because he is physically unable to control his
drinking, he usually ends a drinking spree drunk
or passed out. Withdrawal symptoms become
severe and incapacitating. As he continues to
drink, he will become increasingly withdrawn,
fearful, and uncommunicative. Paranoia, hallucinations, and severe tremors are common in
this late stage.

Unless they receive effective treatment, most
late-stage alcoholics will die of medical complications caused by their disease or from accidents
suffered when drinking.

If your accumulated score from all 27 questions is 28 or more, you are definitely in the late
stage of the disease.

Accumulated Score

Early stage:	5–8 points
Middle stage:	
Early-middle:	9–15 points
Middle:	16–21 points
Late-middle:	22–27 points
Late stage:	28 or more points

CHAPTER 4

The Early-, Middle-, and Late-Stage Symptoms, Step by Step

The theme song of alcoholism is progression: if you're an alcoholic, you're going to suffer more often and more intensely from your drinking. You can't, no matter how hard you try, remain an early-stage alcoholic for the rest of your drinking days. Your addiction won't let you.

In the beginning you can tame this monster called addiction. It seems like such a sweet and harmless thing! You drink, you feel good, only rarely do you drink too much, and then you don't feel *too* bad. But the addiction will slowly take you over, destroying your will, breaking your promises, undermining your physical health, and confusing your brain, all the while blinding you to its growing power and tenacity.

This addiction develops a voracious appetite: the more you feed it, the more it needs. If you don't drink, your addiction is going to make you pay for your virtue with withdrawal symptoms like headaches, mental confusion, nervousness, anxiety, depression, tremors, sweating, and, later, hallucinations, convulsions, even death. It's true; you can die from *not* drinking. The withdrawal symptoms are the addiction's perverse way of calling you back: it won't let you alone, and the more you drink, the more it will hound you.

You still believe you can handle it, that you are in control. But the reins are slipping, the beast is off at a gallop, and you're holding on for dear life. *Dear life*: what a euphemism this becomes! Your life is anything but dear, sweet, or lovely. Your life, in fact, becomes that wild ride, the insane struggle to hang on, and the overwhelming fear that if you let go, you are truly lost. As the addiction takes control, you are no longer able to understand or to recognize that this creature you are so desperately clinging to is plunging madly into destruction and that you cannot steer it because you are out of control. You are slowly but surely dying, and there is little you can do to save yourself.

The addiction has taken you over. The insane seems comforting and secure; the rational and logical seem insane. The world becomes mad, and you are at the center of the madness, a puppet, a plaything of the addiction, a hollow shell of a human being with a demon inside.

If you doubt that the end is true insanity, consider the case of Roger, a late-stage alcoholic who found that he couldn't take a shower without falling down and hurting himself. So he tried taking baths. But baths were dangerous, too, because he kept falling asleep. So Roger stopped taking showers or baths altogether. As far as he could see, that was the only solution; he certainly wasn't going to stop drinking.

Wilbur Mills, former nineteen-term U.S. congressman, faced a similar dilemma and used the same kind of alcoholic mad logic to solve it:

> "I always wanted the alcohol cold, so I could never keep
> a bottle in my desk or in the car. It had to be cold, so I

always had to have ice cubes in it. Toward the end of my drinking, it occurred to me one night, what would happen to me if I swallowed one of those ice cubes? Might strangle. So I quit using ice cubes. I put my bottles in the icebox to keep them cold and not run the risk of swallowing ice cubes. The way I drank, I could easily have swallowed them. My mouth was wide open. I used a peanut butter glass, and it didn't take me many swallows to take it down."*

The Early Warning Signs

A man who had had a heart attack angrily confronted his physician. "Just eight months ago, you gave me a clean bill of health! Why didn't you tell me my heart was weak?" A middle- or late-stage alcoholic might have the same complaint. Suddenly, it seems, he's deathly ill and his doctor is talking about extensive treatment. But where were all the warning signs?

All chronic diseases start out in a hidden stage when it's difficult for anyone, even a knowledgeable and conscientious physician, to see the disease gaining strength and power. Early-stage alcoholics look like normal people, talk like normal people, and even appear to drink like normal people! So where's the addiction?

It's there: hiding, pulling together its resources, slowly subverting the alcoholic's body to its own uses, gradually getting stronger. The early-stage alcoholic may appear to be healthy and "normal," but the addiction is triggering little warning flags that pop up from time to time. As the early stage progresses, these warning signs will become more apparent and occur more frequently, indicating that the disease is slowly but insidiously progressing.

*From *The Courage to Change*, by Dennis Wholey (Houghton Mifflin, 1984), pp. 53–54.

Early-Stage Warning Signs

- Enjoyment of drinking
- Preoccupation with alcohol
- Changes in drinking patterns
- Drinking more and more often.

Enjoyment of drinking. Joe, a 24-year-old engineer and an early-stage alcoholic, loves to drink. A few beers make him feel great: his tensions dissolve, his insecurities fade away, and his outlook on life becomes more and more optimistic. After a few more beers, Joe concludes that his friends are great people and life is pretty wonderful. Drinking is great fun for Joe—he loosens up, he can talk openly to strangers, and he generally feels high on life.

A lot of people—most drinkers, in fact—enjoy drinking. So how could Joe or the people who love him tell when enjoyment of drinking is an early-stage warning sign and not just a normal reaction to alcohol's intoxicating effects? One important distinguishing characteristic is that early-stage alcoholics, unlike nonalcoholics, tend to enjoy drinking out of proportion to its social benefits. To an early-stage alcoholic, alcohol is more than just a beverage to enjoy at parties—it is the most important reason for having a party. Social occasions become excuses to drink; and, whenever he can, the alcoholic will create a social occasion or attempt to prolong it. When Joe buys another pitcher of beer for friends who have already decided they've had enough, he's displaying two characteristics of this early stage: first, he needs the social occasion as an excuse to drink; second, his drinking is more intense than his friends'.

Joe drinks frequently and sometimes heavily because of alcohol's "positive" effects on him. Alcohol doesn't just make him feel *good*—it makes him feel *great*. Marty Mann, one of the first women members of Alcoholics Anonymous and a founding member of the National Council on Alcoholism, claimed that alcohol does "magic" things for the alcoholic. "It performs miracles for him. It magics away his discomforts, his anxieties, his fears. It gives him instant self-confidence. And so it becomes terribly important to him." For the early-stage alcoholic, alcohol is more than a social lubricant; it seems, in fact, to be the missing cog. While drinking, a chemical connection is made and the alcoholic has a bigger-than-life experience that he is eager to repeat.

If you suspect that you or someone you love is an alcoholic, look for an enjoyment of drinking that goes beyond the nonalcoholic's pleasure at loosening up or feeling good. Look for behavior that indicates a growing *need* for alcohol—a need that is more intense than a temporary decision to get slightly drunk and forget about tensions and problems for a few hours.

Another early-stage warning sign is **preoccupation with alcohol**. Imagine that Joe is at a picnic, the beer is running out, and the party still has a few hours to go. Joe will: (1) be one of the first to notice and remark on the low supply; (2) make sure to "get his share" by drinking a few quick ones or stashing some beer in an out-of-the-way place; (3) offer to get more; or (4) leave the party disgruntled and determined that next time he'll be responsible for bringing the beer.

If he knows he's going to attend a party where no alcohol will be served, Joe will characteristically have a few drinks before the party and then leave the party early. "What kind of party is this, with no booze?" he might complain. The lack of alcohol will be felt as more than a disappointment, but as an annoyance—it may even make him mad. "Count me out when it's time to go to the Wallaces' again!" he may say.

Preoccupation with alcohol—a subtle sign of addiction—also shows itself as a desire and, increasingly, a need to have alcohol around at all times. Joe knows that his liquor supply is running low long *before* it runs out. On his shopping list, wine and beer come first. At a party, he knows exactly where his drink is and where he can get a refill. You won't see Joe walking around a room looking for his drink—chances are it will never leave his hand, except to be refilled.

Over a period of several years, Joe experiences **changes in drinking patterns**. He begins to *drink faster,* particularly his first drinks; he actually gulps them down. Every once in a while he decides to *switch drinks,* giving up beer for something stronger, like a martini or scotch on the rocks. After a few fast drinks, he tends to slow down his pace to match that of his friends, an attempt to convince both himself and others that he is a "normal" drinker. The addiction is not so strong yet that Joe can't exert some control over it. But as the changes in his drinking patterns show, the addiction is progressing and becoming more obvious.

Soon, Joe begins to **drink more and more often**. Where one or two drinking occasions a week were standard a few years ago, now he considers that an unusually sober week. He'll typically have two or three drinks before dinner, and he's beginning to drink during and after dinner. Where his cocktail hour used to start at 5:00 P.M., now it begins at 4. Where he used to say "no" to alcohol at lunch, now he says "why not?"

Joe isn't alarmed at the changes in his drinking patterns because he feels fine, he appears perfectly healthy, he can hold his liquor as well as or better than his friends, he gets drunk only occasionally, and, if he must, he can quit for several days, weeks, or even months. So he drinks a lot—what's the big deal if it isn't hurting him?

Joe's family and friends are fooled, too. Although Joe drinks a lot and alcohol seems unusually important to him, he's handling it just fine. His friends brush off their worries with statements like, "You know Joe, he just enjoys drinking," or, "He's going through some rough times at work right now; he'll slow down later when the pressure's off."

In a drinking society such as ours, where many people drink heavily and where alcoholism is still thought to be a disease of character and willpower, it's easy, even tempting, to overlook or explain away early warning signs as symptoms of tension or anxiety or just simple overindulgence. And, certainly, just because someone likes to drink and drinks often doesn't mean that he's an alcoholic. In fact, none of the early-stage warning symptoms—enjoyment of drinking, preoccupation with drinking, changes in drinking patterns, and drinking more and more often—can be taken alone as a diagnosis of alcoholism. In diagnosing early-stage alcoholism, it's important to look for three crucial factors: several signs or symptoms occurring together; progression; and the beginnings of alcohol-related problems. If all three factors are present, a diagnosis of alcoholism is a pretty safe bet.

1. Several signs or symptoms occurring together. Someone who looks forward to a martini after work; who, over a period of several years, begins to drink two, three, or even more drinks before dinner and perhaps a few after dinner; and who becomes irritable if his drinking routines are interrupted is showing several warning signs of early-stage alcoholism.

2. Progression. Progression, as we said, is the theme song of alcoholic drinking—if someone is an alcoholic, his drinking patterns will change, he will become increasingly (and more obviously) dependent on alcohol, and he will begin to suffer because of his drinking, with withdrawal symptoms becoming more obvious and more severe. Nonalcoholics, on the other hand, typically hold to a fairly routine pattern of drinking, and sticking to this routine requires little control or forethought.

The amount someone drinks isn't as important in this early stage as whether that amount changes significantly over a period of several months or years. For example, a nonalcoholic may drink a lot, say three or four drinks every night before dinner, but as time goes by, he won't increase that amount to five, six, or more drinks. An alcoholic, however, inevitably experiences an increase in the amount he drinks. And, as he drinks more and more often, his drinking will have an increasingly harmful effect on his health and on his life.

3. Alcohol-related problems. "Problems" can be defined as anything related to alcohol that interferes with the drinker's ability to live a normal, healthy, and productive life and to maintain strong, steady relationships. In the early stage, alcohol-related problems are relatively minor. Recurring bad hangovers—more than one a week—would be a cause for concern. Everyone who drinks too much will have a hangover, of course, but alcoholics tend to drink too much too often—in a sense, they're willing to pay frequent and often painful "penalties" to enjoy the substantial "benefits" of drinking.

Problems may also crop up as arguments with family and friends because of the amount the alcoholic drinks ("Why can't you have just one or two drinks like everyone else?"); because of the way he acts when he's drinking ("You were really hammering away at Tom tonight—that's so unlike you!"); or because of the way his drinking affects his relationships with others ("I don't care if you have a few drinks with the boys after work, but does it have to be every weekend? Don't you care about spending time with your family?")

The early-stage, progressing alcoholic may also be having minor problems at work: bad morning hangovers once or twice a week that interfere with getting work done; regularly leaving work an hour early to join friends for drinks; drinking wine at lunch and then finding it difficult to concentrate on work; complaints from co-workers about laziness, inconsistency, or lack of motivation.

As the disease progresses, these "problems" will get worse, eventually threatening the alcoholic's family life, career, finances, mental stability, and physical health.

The Middle-Stage Symptoms

During the middle stage, the addiction digs in its claws, a slow and insidious process that will create more and more problems—psychological, physical, and behavioral—for the alcoholic. Middle-stage alcoholics are not yet totally helpless, and they will try to fight back by cutting back on their drinking or quitting altogether; making promises that they fully intend to keep (but continually break); setting new routines; even by seeing a psychologist or marriage counselor. But all their efforts are, eventually and inevitably, in vain. The drinking goes on and the problems worsen, slashing deep wounds into the alcoholic's life and physical and mental health.

The middle-stage alcoholic will, at times, see the beast within him. He will be frightened, pretend it doesn't exist, deny it, wish it away, and attempt to ignore it. Nothing works. The addiction is there, and it's getting stronger all the time.

Middle-Stage Joe

Joe is now 32 years old, married, with two young children. He's been promoted to assistant project engineer and given a substantial raise. The job suits Joe just fine; he gets to travel to different construction sites and pretty much makes his own schedule. The "brass" trust him and consider him one of their most loyal employees. But his co-workers have a few com-

---

Middle-Stage Symptoms

Early-Middle:
- Increased tolerance for alcohol
- Rationalizations, denials
- Mood changes
- Personality changes
- Drinking more than intended

Middle:
- Marital problems
- Unreasonable resentments
- Irritability, depression, nervousness, anxiety
- Hiding bottles
- Protecting supply

Late-Middle:
- Tremors
- Elaborate alibi system
- Attempts to quit or cut down
- Broken promises
- Guilt, despair, self-pity
- Loss of self-respect

---

plaints. Joe is moody and frequently gets into arguments with the contractors. He insists that he knows what's right, and he's got a bad temper when someone crosses or disagrees with him.

Joe's best friend, Fred, refuses to drive in the city with him because he tailgates, leans on his horn, and makes obscene gestures at other drivers. Red lights drive Joe crazy; he swears the lights see him coming and turn red just to rile him.

Joe's a different man when he drinks. He calms down, relaxes, eases up. But he's drinking a lot and that's creating problems with his wife. Every night Joe has a "few" at the bar near his office—just to give the traffic time to thin out, he says. But most nights he doesn't get home until seven or even eight o'clock, and then he has a few more drinks while his wife heats up dinner. When she complains that she doesn't have any time with him, Joe becomes sullen and uncommunicative; she learns soon enough that it's better to keep quiet.

Joe's wife tries hard not to worry about his drinking. He drinks a lot, she admits to herself, but at least he never gets outright drunk. In fact, she's amazed by how much he can drink and still look and act sober: at an office party she watched him slam down six or seven drinks in less than two hours and then drive home without even swerving over the white line.

Joe is drinking a lot more than he used to: he's drinking every day, he never has just one drink, and he always keeps drinking once he's started. "I've got a problem with alcohol," he once joked to a friend. "I can't get enough of it!" Joe thinks of alcohol as a good friend, the one sure and steady thing in his life. Unlike his wife, or his friends, or his work, alcohol is predictable—it always, without fail, makes him feel better. In fact, he figures he's got more problems when he lays off the booze than when he's drinking. Drinking makes him feel normal again. If he's got a headache, alcohol takes it away; if he feels sick to his stomach, alcohol makes him feel better. Drinking gets rid of all the stress and anxiety of his job, living in a city, and dealing with "this mess of idiots and incompetents."

When his wife tells him he drinks too much, Joe gets defensive and hostile. "What does she know about it," he mumbles to himself, "she's practically a teetotaler." He remembers his mother nagging his father about the same thing, and he's convinced that's the reason his dad had a heart attack at the age of 49.

His wife's complaints, though, get to Joe. He feels guilty about spending so little time with the kids, so he decides to change his routine and come home right after work. But after a few weeks he gives up on that; the kids, he rationalizes, didn't even know he was there.

Joe's doing a lot of rationalizing and denying these days. Fred's been bugging him to cut down on his drinking because he's afraid it's affecting his work. "You're always moody and tired during the day," Fred tells Joe, "and you're starting to drink earlier all the time." He mentions the flask that Joe always keeps in the glove compartment of his car. "That used to be there for fun," Fred says. "Now I think you need it."

"The devil I do," Joe says, and later that day he dumps the contents of the flask out the door. "I can quit whenever I want for as long as I want," he tells Fred.

Joe quit that time for a month. That was proof, he figured, that he could take it or leave it. He started drinking again, he said, because he'd rather take it. But that was his choice; his efforts to control his drinking were successful, he claimed, and proved that he didn't have a drinking problem.

But Joe didn't tell anyone about the "bad" side of his drinking. He'd had a few blackouts, and they scared him to death. Once, he drove home from a party with his wife; he woke up the next morning and asked her how they got home. Another time his wife kidded him about swimming naked in the neighbor's pool. Joe blushed and laughed, but he remembered nothing about it.

Joe was also worried about the tremors in his hands. He was so shaky in the morning he could hardly sign the construction reports. And almost every day he felt nervous, tense, and headachy. *It's probably the job,* he thought, but he wondered if it might be the drinking, too. He shrugged his worries off, though, because they didn't make sense: drinking made him feel better, not worse. And he started to keep a flask beneath the seat of his car. He didn't like the idea of sneaking drinks, but he didn't want to put up with any more of Fred's sermons, either.

Joe felt terrible about the constant arguing with his wife and Fred, but even though he tried to be more understanding, he just couldn't seem to make things right. His wife was always upset or angry with him about something or other; Fred wouldn't even drive in a car with him. He felt as if his life was slipping out of control, and he didn't seem able to do anything about it. He couldn't confide in anyone, because they'd just blame the drinking.

Joe never told anyone what he felt like that month when he stayed sober. All that month, every hour of the day, he couldn't stop thinking about drinking; not a day went by that he didn't want a drink. When he finally started drinking again, it was as if a cockeyed world suddenly straightened itself out.

The Late-Stage Symptoms

Everything must come to an end; for alcoholics, the end comes soon enough. It's ironic, actually, that the late stage of alcoholism isn't always or even usually the last stage. Most alcoholics die before their disease gets this far: they die early, of heart attacks, accidents, pneumonia, cancer, or suicide. Alcohol kills early-stage and middle-stage alcoholics indirectly, and usually no one will mention the word *alcoholism*. But when a pathologist looks at a late-stage alcoholic, he knows exactly what killed him.

In the early stage the addiction is cagey and sly; in the middle stage, it starts digging in its claws; in the late stage, the addiction sinks its poisonous fangs into the heart and soul of the alcoholic, allowing for the onset of the final destruction. The addiction has shed its masquerade and is evident for all to see. It has nothing to fear now, for the alcoholic is powerless to stop it. Denials and rationalizations don't work, and the alcoholic gives them up, no longer attempting to protect himself from other people's judgments. He doesn't really care what other people call him. The word *alcoholic* doesn't bother him. He must drink; he sees no other way to survive. And when he needs that drink, when the craving becomes intolerable, he will do anything to get it. Without it, he'll die; with it, he'll die. There seem to be no choices left.

In the late stage of alcoholism, the alcoholic's body, mind, and moral integrity deteriorate. Ironically, even the one thing he could do well all these years—drink—is decaying. He can't even control that anymore. Nothing of joy is left, and the alcoholic's life becomes a cycle of pain, despair, and numbing fear.

Late-Stage Joe

Joe's wife left him on his forty-fifth birthday. She put a note next to a full bottle of gin: "I tried, but I couldn't beat it. Please don't kill yourself." Joe poured himself a drink and another and another until the bottle was gone.

He lasted another year at work, and then they gave him $1000 severance pay and a gold-embossed pen. The pen made Joe laugh for the first time in months: he'd have to be drunk to get his hands to calm down so that he could write, and the idiots fired him for drinking. He threw the pen away and reached for a drink.

Joe kept a regular daily schedule after he lost his job: he drank morning, noon, and night. On the days he had to go to the store for more alcohol, he tried to drink just enough to be

Late-Stage Symptoms

- Overpowering craving for alcohol
- Drinking despite adverse consequences (divorce, loss of job)
- Complete loss of control
- Loss of tolerance
- Morning drinking
- Prolonged binges
- Alcohol-related arrests
- Malnutrition
- Drinking alone or with social inferiors
- Financial dependence
- Lack of attention to hygiene
- Severe and life-threatening withdrawal symptoms
- Physical complications and alcohol-related disorders
- Accidents
- Hospitalizations
- Psychological deterioration (paranoia, vague fears, suicidal thoughts or attempts)
- Alcohol-related arrests
- Ethical and moral deterioration

able to walk to the store, pick up the bottle, and pay for it, but not so much that he would stumble or pass out on the street. He'd been arrested a few months before for public drunkenness and spent the night in the drunk tank. By the time they let him out, he was shaking and hallucinating, and his legs wouldn't hold him up; a policeman had to drive him home. He could barely walk up the steps to his apartment, and he was terrified that he'd die before he ever made it to the bottle. The irony of that terror escaped him.

His kids came by every once in a while with money and food, but they didn't stay long. Dirty dishes filled the sink, the apartment smelled of vomit and urine, and Joe hadn't shaved or taken a shower in weeks. A social worker kept coming by, too, but after the last time he didn't expect her to return. He threw his drink at her, ruining her hairdo and her dress. No, Joe thought, she wouldn't be back.

One day Joe fell down the stairs. His landlady found him and called the hospital. He was hospitalized for two weeks:

he'd only suffered a concussion from the fall, but the doctors also discovered a swollen liver, pancreatitis, and high blood pressure. They put him on tranquilizers to help him through withdrawal, and some Alcoholics Anonymous people came in to talk to him. He listened—there wasn't much else he could do stuck in a hospital bed—but that high and mighty religious baloney wasn't for him.

The doctors tried to scare him, too, talking about cirrhosis and heart attacks and a bad pancreas, and warning him that he'd be dead if he didn't stop drinking. He'd try, he told them, he'd see what he could do.

And when they released him, he thought about trying to stay sober. He thought about it on his way to the liquor store, and he thought about it as he drank and watched the alcohol in the bottle disappear. After a few days, he didn't think about it anymore.

Joe died at the age of 48 from the DTs. He'd run out of money, he'd run out of alcohol, and he was so sick he could barely move. He was semiconscious for four days. Then he started hallucinating, seeing rats as big as dogs and spiders with three-inch fangs. He tried to run away from his visions, but there was nowhere to go. His screams alerted his landlady, who called the police. Joe died of a brain hemorrhage, flanked by policemen, in a hospital emergency room. Nobody there even knew his name.

CHAPTER 5

The Physician's Role in Diagnosis

While this book is written to help alcoholics and their families, it would be a grave mistake to leave the impression that you should start out on the road to treatment alone and unassisted. It's not that you can't do it alone—thousands of alcoholics have. But millions more haven't. The addiction is so powerful and unpredictable that it can subvert your best efforts and make recovery seem an impossibility. Only the lucky ones make it on their own.

In theory, one of the people who can help guide you to recovery is your physician. Physicians have the tools necessary to make a definitive diagnosis and the clout and credentials required to get the point across to their patients. But in fact, most physicians lack adequate training and knowledge about the disease, and many have not escaped the common prejudices, born of ignorance and misconception, against alcoholics.

An estimated 10 percent of the average general practitioner's practice consists of alcoholics. If you include early-stage alcoholics, the number climbs as high as 20 percent. Add in the number of family members who are suffering from physical, emotional, and psychological problems caused by living with an alcoholic, and between one-third and one-half of the average physician's practice is either directly or indirectly affected by alcoholism. Yet, only one of ten alcoholics is diagnosed and treated as such. The rest cycle in and out of physicians' offices and hospital rooms without ever getting effective help for their disease.

In one survey of 242 patients in a hospital-based general practice,* 11 percent were diagnosed as "problem drinkers" and 20 percent were diagnosed as alcoholics, based on the National Council of Alcoholism's criteria for alcoholism. Yet, the physician records for these patients showed that only 12 percent were diagnosed as problem drinkers or alcoholics. The other part of the story is that these physicians discussed the diagnosis of alcoholism with only two-thirds of their patients— which is just as incomprehensible as a doctor discovering cancer in one-third of his patients but hiding the fact from those patients!

Given these facts, a chapter on the physician's role in treatment is important for several reasons:

1. To give the alcoholic's family members some direction and guidance in what to expect from their physician in providing good alcoholism treatment. As you read this chapter, you will see how complex the diagnostic process can be, and you will gain some valuable knowledge about the processes of medical diagnosis and intervention. This knowledge and insight are crucial if you are to be a helpful and willing volunteer in the physician's efforts to get your alcoholic effective help.

2. To help you locate a physician or other health-care provider who is skilled and effective in alcoholism treatment. Many medical specialties are classified by formal training and expertise. Pediatricians, for example, take care of children, obstetricians deliver babies, and surgeons operate. But who takes care of the alcoholic? Everybody and yet nobody. General practitioners have passed their late-stage alcoholics on to

*Family Practice News, January 14, 1984.

internal medicine specialists, who take care of the advanced complications of alcoholism; but early- and middle-stage alcoholics are typically misdiagnosed and rarely receive appropriate treatment for their primary disease.

Most doctors have been inadequately trained in alcoholism diagnosis and treatment; and physicians, like most people, harbor numerous myths and misconceptions about the disease and its victims. After reading this chapter, you will be better able to select a physician who is experienced in handling alcoholics, skilled in diagnosis, nonjudgmental, alert to the caginess of the addiction, and sensitive to the family's needs and concerns. You can then become an active catalyst in making sure that your alcoholic gets the care and commitment he needs and that his disease requires.

3. Finally, physicians who are either alcoholic themselves, related to alcoholics, or concerned about their alcoholic patients can use the information in this and other chapters as a guide to diagnosing, confronting, and treating the alcoholic.

The Physician's Attitude

One way to assess your doctor's attitude toward alcoholics is to ask him point blank: "What's your philosophy about alcoholism and treating alcoholics?"

If he looks embarrassed or uncomfortable or responds with a statement like, "I think they have severe psychological problems, and I refer all my patients to a psychiatrist," or, "I have great difficulty treating alcoholics because they don't follow my orders, they lie to me, and they seem to have no motivation or desire to get well," or, simply, "I don't have much success with them," look for help elsewhere. It's critically important that your doctor understand the disease concept of alcoholism, that he recognize that the alcoholic's denials, evasions, and rationalizations are symptoms of the disease, and that his attitude is not tainted by moral judgments.

Alcoholics aren't the easiest of patients to treat—they do deny their problems, they miss appointments, they even throw up on the waiting-room rug—but they can be treated with great success. In fact, most alcoholics' physical and psychological problems can be effectively reversed if they stop drinking. Relapses are not symptoms of weakness of character or lack of resolve or willpower—they are simply a complication of this chronic disease, just as insulin shock is a complication of diabetes management, and angina is a complication of heart disease.

The physician must understand, however, that the alcoholic, unlike the diabetic or the patient with heart disease, is not likely to volunteer information about his disease. In most cases, particularly in the early and middle stages, the alcoholic doesn't even know he's got a disease. The typical middle-stage alcoholic feels better when he drinks, not worse; he's not physically ill; he's surrounded by people who love him; he lives in a nice house; he holds down a steady job. It's easy for his doctor to be fooled, too, by the lack of dramatic physical evidence and by the alcoholic's continued assurances that he's "just fine, thanks, no problem, never felt better." Furthermore, as the addiction gains strength and power, it blinds its victims to their disease, making them unwitting participants in their own destruction.

The physician, then, has to do some sleuthing when it comes to his alcoholic patients. To do a good detective job he will need to be:

Nonjudgmental. Moralizing, criticizing, or disapproving is not productive in dealing with alcoholics. The angry patient gets angrier; the deceptions and denials grow even stronger. The physician must recognize that denials and rationalizations are symptoms of the disease; that the alcoholic drinks excessively because he's addicted; and that the alcoholic's expressed personality is a product, not a precursor, of the disease.

Direct. The physician should ask specific, factual questions designed to uncover the effect of drinking on the patient's life. He should avoid oblique or irrelevant questions like "How are things going at home?" or "Do you drink beer or martinis?"

Persistent. In questioning alcoholics, the physician should not accept evasive or vague answers and should try to avoid getting sidetracked when alcoholics respond to specific questions by glossing over the issue, sidestepping, or using qualified denials ("Not really," "Probably not," "Practically never," "No more than anyone else") or alibis ("I'm under a lot of stress," "My wife's driving me crazy").

Friendly but firm. Anger is an inappropriate response to the alcoholic's evasions or denials, but it's also important that the physician be directive, refusing to allow the patient to avoid questions.

Patient. A diagnosis of alcoholism takes time, and if the physician tries to rush through it, looking only at the superficial facts, the diagnosis will be missed completely or the alcoholic's complaints misconstrued as evidence of emotional or psychological problems. The enormity of the disease and its impact on both the alcoholic and his family more than justifies the extra time spent in diagnosis.

Diagnostic Aids

The Medical History and Questionnaires

In taking a medical history, the physician should always, with every adult patient, ask (1) if the patient drinks; (2) if he has any problems caused by the use of alcohol or drugs; and (3) if any relatives have problems with alcohol or drugs. It's best to ask these questions somewhere in the middle of the medical history so that the patient's responses to questions about his drinking can be compared with his previous responses. If the patient seems embarrassed, hostile, evasive, or defensive when asked about his drinking, the physician should note these reactions. It's also important, though, not to threaten or frighten the patient. One way of opening up the subject would be to say, "Now I'd like to find out about your use of alcoholic beverages. Do you drink?"

A short but useful questionnaire that can be included in the general medical history is the BAST (Brief Alcoholism Screening Test), which is reported to successfully identify 96 percent of alcoholic patients and misidentify only 10 percent. The BAST questionnaire, however, would not be definitive with early- and early-middle-stage alcoholics.

The BAST

1. Has your family ever objected to your drinking?
2. Did you ever think you drank too much in general?
3. Have others (such as friends, physicians, clergy) ever said you drink too much for your own good?

Another easy and efficient diagnostic tool is the CAGE Questionnaire, developed by John Ewing, M.D.:

Have you ever felt the need to **C**ut down on your drinking?

Have you ever felt **A**nnoyed by criticism of your drinking?

Have you had **G**uilty feelings about drinking?

Do you ever take a morning **E**ye-opener?

A nonalcoholic may answer "yes" to one or perhaps two of these questions, but alcoholic patients will typically respond with two, three, or even four positive answers.

If the physician suspects that a patient may have a problem with alcohol, he should substantiate his impressions by asking the patient to complete the questionnaire in chapter 3 and/or the Michigan Alcoholism Screening Test (MAST; see appendix 1). From these questionnaires the physician can get a good sense of whether the patient is an alcoholic and what stage he or she is in.

The physician should also be on the alert for family members who may be suffering from living with an alcoholic. Depression, nervousness, persistent anxiety, phobias, behavior problems, or hyperactivity in children can all be caused by living with an alcoholic. The physician should ask the family members if they suspect a drinking problem in a loved one and then follow up by giving them the questionnaire to fill out for the suspected alcoholic.

Questionnaires are not, in and of themselves, sufficient to definitively diagnose alcoholism, but they do help to identify those people who might have a problem. The physician can then, through skilled questioning and observation, learn more about the suspected drinking problem. The medical history can also uncover a number of warning symptoms in various areas of the patient's life.

Warning Symptoms of Alcoholism

Alcoholism affects its victims in every area of their lives. The symptoms listed below refer to those events or body conditions that can be gleaned from a careful medical history.

"Symptoms" refer to what the patient feels or reports; "Signs" (see page 54) indicate what the physician sees or observes.

Physical
- head injuries
- headaches
- loss of memory or blackouts (partial or total memory loss of events surrounding a drinking event)
- morning nausea
- impotence, inability to achieve orgasm
- past ulcer operations
- multiple GI complaints: nausea, cramping, vomiting (especially early morning), diarrhea with no cause
- indigestion
- unexplained seizures
- vomiting of blood
- frequent infections
- frequent pancreatitis
- withdrawal symptoms (tremors, seizures, abnormally rapid heartbeat)

Behavioral
- mood swings
- depression
- irritability
- aggressive behavior
- suicide threats or attempts
- anxiety
- insomnia
- regular or prolonged use of tranquilizers or sedatives
- overdose of pills
- repeated attempts to stop drinking
- history of increased tolerance to large amounts of alcohol; loss of such tolerance
- craving for sweets
- fatigue

Family
- divorce (often multiple)
- children with behavior problems
- "bad nerves," depression, anxiety, neuroses in spouse
- decreased sexual relations
- decreased social life
- financial difficulties
- child or spouse abuse
- few friends
- rarely goes out
- few outside activities or hobbies
- inappropriate use of telephone (late-night calls, long monologues, rambling conversations)
- frequent canceled appointments
- complaints from neighbors, friends

Occupational (these problems generally develop in the late-middle to late stage of the disease)
- absenteeism
- tardiness
- job-related accidents
- increased insurance claims
- poor performance
- loss of job
- complaints from superiors, co-workers
- periods of unemployment
- early retirement
- frequent job changes
- moving toward job where there is freedom to drink (house painter, traveling salesman, free-lance work, real estate salesman, etc.)

Legal
- frequent auto accidents
- citations for driving while under the influence (two or more DWIs are highly indicative of alcoholism)
- assault charges
- disorderly conduct, resisting arrest, public drunkenness citations

Physical Exam

Four out of five alcoholics can be diagnosed without ever having a physical examination. But the physical exam is important for confirming a diagnosis and determining the extent of physical damage, which will then give the physician information about how far the disease has progressed and what kinds of medical intervention might be necessary on an immediate or long-term basis.

In the case of suspected alcoholics, the doctor should perform a thorough physical examination with specific attention to the physical signs listed in the chart on page 54.

The physician should also be aware of alcohol-related diseases and disorders. (See pages 56–57.)

Other facts that can help in diagnosing alcoholism, as reported by Dr. Michael Stone in *Behavioral Medicine*, January 1982, include:

• 25–33 percent of all tobacco smokers are alcoholics
• smokers who use tranquilizers or stimulants have a 50 percent rate of alcoholism
• 95 percent of alcoholics are heavy caffeine drinkers
• Smokers with high blood pressure and high cholesterol levels have a 50 percent chance of being alcoholic, especially if they are men
• 25 percent of hyperactive children come from alcoholic homes

Laboratory Tests

A number of common laboratory tests can help to identify abnormalities that are commonly found in alcoholics. Lab tests are highly variable, however, and the absence of abnormalities should not be used to rule out alcoholism. It's not uncommon, for example, for a middle-stage alcoholic to have absolutely normal laboratory tests. It's also not uncommon for a healthy-looking, middle-stage alcoholic to show extreme abnormalities in these tests.

The Alcoholism Lab Profile (appendix 2) shows the range of normal and alcoholic values for the most common laboratory tests used in diagnosing alcoholism.

The Drinking History

The drinking history should be conducted with any patient the physician suspects may have a problem with alcohol, even in the absence of physical signs or symptoms. The physician should always keep in mind that the patient's reactions to the questions are as important as his actual answers.

The following "question and answer" drinking history is enlightening in terms of how the physician handles the patient and what the patient's responses tell about his potential disease. Stan is 42 years old, a computer programmer, married, with two teenage children. His wife is a high school teacher.

—Hello, Stan, how are you?

—Just fine, Dr. Spencer. Everything's great. Except for the little problems I mentioned to you on the phone.

—The nausea and diarrhea?

—Yeah, that's right.

—Well, Stan, I've done a thorough workup on you, and I'd like to go over your medical history and lab tests. You look like you're in pretty good shape on the outside, and your physical exam was basically normal. That's good. But I am concerned about some of the results on the other tests. For example, your laboratory studies—tests that show how things are working on the inside—are off a little. Your GGTP and SGOT—those are liver tests—and some blood fats—your triglycerides—are above normal. That indicates to me that something is amiss. Based on these lab tests, your history and physical exam, and your responses to the questionnaire, I think alcohol may be doing some harm to your body. I'd like to ask a few more questions and see if we can get to the root of these problems. Now, how old were you when you had your first drink?

—Oh, I suppose when I was fourteen or fifteen—a few beers, I guess.

—Do you recall how you felt?

—Oh, yeah. [Stan laughs.] It felt great. I was intoxicated, you know how that feels. I really had a great time.

—How much does it take to get that same feeling now?

—A few drinks. [Stan looks down at the floor.]

—And how much is a few for you?

—Oh, a couple—maybe three.

Physical Signs of Alcoholism

Skin
- cigarette burns
- decrease in hair
- gynecomastia*
- increased vascularity of face
- flushing
- multiple contusions, abrasions, and cuts in various stages of healing
- nicotine stains on fingers
- palmar erythema
- livedo reticularis
- poor personal hygiene
- spider angiomas
- unexplained edema
- minor trauma (bruises on legs or arms, small burns)

Eyes
- toxic amblyopia (particularly night blindness)
- conjunctival infections
- lateral nystagmus

Nose
- increased vascularity and puffiness of mucous membranes

Mouth
- "green tongue" (from breath suppressants)
- increased gag reflex
- odor of alcohol at inappropriate times
- poor oral hygiene

Gynecomastia: Overdevelopment of the mammary glands in the male
Vascularity: Presence of blood vessels
Palmar erythema: Redness of the skin caused by engorgement of capillaries
Livedo reticularis: Permanent reddish blue mottling of the skin of the extremities
Spider angiomas: Small, red skin blemishes made up of blood or lymph vessels arranged in a spiderlike pattern; blemishes blanch with pressure
Edema: Abnormal accumulation of fluid in the body
Toxic amblyopia: Dimness of vision resulting from a toxin or poison (i.e., alcohol)
Conjunctival: Pertaining to the delicate membranes lining the eyelids and covering the eyeball
Lateral nystagmus: Horizontal jerking movement of the eyes with gaze to the right or left

Chest
- frequent pneumonia, bronchitis, unexplained tachycardia, arrhythmia, myocardiopathy, congestive heart failure

Abdomen
- enlarged liver (tender or nontender)
- jaundice
- ascites
- GI bleeding
- nonhealing ulcers

Gonads
- atrophic testes

Extremities
- myopathies
- palmar erythema
- thin in proportion to trunk
- unexplained edema

Neurologic
- hallucinosis
- hyper- or hyporeflexia
- neuropathies
- seizures ("rum fits," DTs)
- tremors

Tachycardia: Rapid heartbeat
Arrhythmia: Abnormal fluctuations of the heartbeat
Myocardiopathy: Disease of the heart muscle
Jaundice: Yellowing of the skin
Ascites: Swelling of the abdomen with fluid
GI bleeding: Bleeding from gastrointestinal tract
Atrophic testes: Decrease in size of the testicles
Myopathies: Any disease of a muscle
Hallucinosis: Condition of seeing or hearing things not real
Hyperreflexia: Exaggeration of reflexes
Hyporeflexia: Weakness of reflexes
Neuropathies: Any disease of the nervous system, especially degenerative diseases of the nerves

Alcohol-Related Disorders and Diseases

Gastrointestinal
- esophagitis*
- esophageal carcinoma
- gastritis
- malabsorption
- chronic diarrhea
- pancreatitis
- fatty liver
- hepatitis
- cirrhosis
- ulcers
- GI bleeding
- cancer of liver or bladder

Cardiac
- myocardiopathy
- beriberi
- hypertension
- palpitations

Skin
- rosacea
- telangiectasia of face and upper chest
- rhinophyma
- cutaneous ulcers

Esophagitis: Inflammation of the digestive tube (esophagus) connecting the mouth and the stomach
Malabsorption: Improper uptake of nutrients in the digestive tract
Pancreatitis: Inflammation of the pancreas
Hepatitis: Inflammation of the liver
Beriberi: A vitamin B_1 deficiency characterized by partial paralysis of the extremities, anemia, and myocardiopathy
Hypertension: Elevated blood pressure
Palpitations: Rapid or irregular beating of the heart
Rosacea: Red, acne-type tissue proliferation
Telangiectasia: A group of dilated capillaries causing dark red blotches on the skin.
Rhinophyma: An enlarged, red nose as might be seen in a heavy drinker
Cutaneous: Of or having to do with the skin
Wernicke's: A mental derangement associated with B_1 deficiency and neurological deterioration of alcoholism marked by loss of memory, disorientation, agitation, and confusion (the acute condition is often reversible by B_1 replacement)

Neurologic and psychiatric
- peripheral neuropathy
- convulsive disorders
- hallucinations
- delirium tremens
- Wernicke's syndrome
- Korsakoff's psychosis

Muscle
- myopathy

Joints
- gout

Hematologic
- megaloblastic anemia

Vitamin deficiency diseases
- peripheral neuritis
- toxic amblyopia
- beriberi
- pellagra
- scurvy

Metabolic
- hypoglycemia
- diabetes

Korsakoff's: A psychosis associated with brain deterioration of alcoholism characterized by memory failure, imaginary reminiscences, hallucinations, and agitation

Gout: An inflammatory condition of the joints caused by an imbalance in uric acid metabolism in the body

Hematologic: Pertaining to the science and therapeutics of the blood system

Megaloblastic anemia: A deficiency of red blood cells characterized by enlarged red blood cells

Pellagra: A disease caused by a deficiency in vitamin B_3 characterized by skin eruptions, digestive and nervous system disturbances, and eventual insanity

Scurvy: A disease caused by a deficiency of vitamin C characterized by hemorrhages, bleeding gums, and extreme weakness

Hypoglycemia: A condition of low blood sugar

(Adapted and expanded from *HEW: Alcohol and Health,* December 1971, as seen in *Behavioral Medicine,* "Recognizing and Treating the Alcoholic," Michael Stone, Jan. 1980).

—And if you were to total up the amount at the end of your day, how much would you say you drink?

—[Stan looks startled; his defenses are up.] Oh, I never keep track. It's nothing to worry about.

—Has anyone else worried about it? Say your wife?

—[Stan squirms in his chair.] Well, she does get upset when I drink too much. But she gets upset about lots of things. You know women. Has she been talking to you?

—No, Stan, I haven't talked to Mary yet. Have there been any problems at home she might want to talk about?

—I really don't think this has anything to do with my problem, what I came here for. Everyone has marital problems. What are you trying to get at?

—Has drinking interfered with your marriage, Stan? Has Mary gotten fed up and been to a lawyer or threatened divorce?

—[Stan is sullen and glares at the doctor.] Yeah. But that was a while ago. Everything's fine now. She goes through these stages. . . .

—Was your drinking one of the reasons she approached a lawyer?

—I don't know. Maybe. Who knows why she does anything?

—Have your kids ever said or implied that they were worried about your drinking?

—Oh, those lazy kids, they can just drive me crazy. . . .

—Have they complained, Stan?

—Yeah, but let me tell you who has complaints. [Stan is flushed and very angry.] If you had kids like them, you'd drink, too. I come home and the house is a mess, the radio's blaring, I can't even hear myself think. I work hard, and it makes me furious to have to put up with . . .

—[Dr. Spencer interrupts.] What do your kids say they don't like about your drinking?

—They think I drink too much. So what do they know? Do you let your kids tell you what to do?

—Have you had any physical battles with your kids or your wife?

—Never. [Stan answers emphatically.] I get mad at them, sure, but I'd never touch them. I'm not that kind of guy.

—Do you get mad more often when you drink?

—No. Drinking usually makes me feel better. That's why I

like drinking, you know, because it makes things better. No problem there.

—Okay, Stan, let's talk about work. Have you been late to work or missed any work recently?

—Well, I had the flu a few weeks ago, I told you about that. And then, you know, this stomach thing.

—The diarrhea and vomiting?

—Yeah. I don't know what's the matter with me. I used to be strong as a horse. Getting older, you know. Maybe I'm getting an ulcer. I'll bet that's it; I'll bet I've got an ulcer. My uncle John has ulcers.

—Have you been laid off or let go from a job?

—[Stan is taken off guard.] Oh, years ago.

—Was drinking involved?

—No. [Stan shakes his head vigorously.] No, I just couldn't get along with the boss.

—Has anyone at your present job complained about your work?

—No. I do good work. I work hard. I like it. Nobody has any complaints.

—Okay, Stan, another area to talk about. Have you ever been arrested, including traffic violations?

—Well, yeah, I have a few tickets. Look, Dr. Spencer, what does all this have to do with diarrhea?

—Stan, I think alcohol may be causing problems in your life, and I need to find out the extent of the problem. Bear with me. Now, regarding your traffic tickets, would you tell me what the charge was?

—[Stan is acutely uncomfortable.] Oh, I got a blasted DWI last month. I was at an office party, celebrating some-body's fiftieth birthday, and this fat old cop pulled me over.

—Do you know what your blood alcohol level was, Stan?

—[Stan flushes bright red.] Yeah. It was .18. Had a little too much that night. Happens to all of us.

—Is that your only arrest?

—Yeah. [Stan hesitates.] Well, a couple of years ago I was nailed by a cop. I couldn't believe it. Two blocks from my house.

—What was the charge?

—DWI.

—Stan, do you and your wife socialize often?

—Do you mean do we have friends? Yeah, we have lots of friends.

—Do you go out often?

—No. Mary just doesn't want to go out much anymore, I think it's menopause. But that's okay with me, I'd rather stay at home. You go out and pay two, even three bucks for a drink. . . . [Stan flushes again.] You know, that's highway robbery.

—I noticed some burns on your hands.

—Oh, those, no big deal. Just got careless with cigarettes. They don't make them like they used to, have you noticed that? They burn down so fast now, I barely light one up, and it's gone.

—Okay, Stan, thanks for your patience. This information has been helpful in getting to the root of your problems. [Dr. Spencer shakes Stan's hand.] I want to review these tests with a specialist, and then go over them with you and your wife. I'd like to see you Monday, next week.

—Monday? What for? Can't you give me something now for the diarrhea? This gets expensive, you know.

—Treating chronic diarrhea isn't always simple, Stan. Sometimes it's a sign of other, more serious problems. I want to go over the lab tests, as I said, and go through the information I gathered from your medical history and the physical exam. I'm sure we can find an answer to this, but I'll need your help and cooperation.

—Well, okay. Guess I'll see you on Monday.

Dr. Spencer gleaned some valuable information from this twenty-minute interview. First, Stan admitted that he had marital problems, difficulties getting along with his kids, and legal problems associated with drinking—all symptoms of alcoholism. Second, Stan was acutely uncomfortable talking about his drinking, his emotions ranging from sullenness to anger to open hostility. Third, Stan tried to deny or minimize his drinking problem; he also attempted to pin the blame for his drinking on his wife and his children.

Given Stan's responses to the questionnaire, his medical history, drinking history, physical exam, and the results of the lab tests, Dr. Spencer was convinced that Stan was a victim of the disease of alcoholism.

What Next?

Once the physician makes a diagnosis of alcoholism, he can initiate a series of actions designed to get the alcoholic into treatment:

1. *Involve the family.* The physician should make an appointment with the alcoholic's spouse, parents, or children and at this meeting discuss openly and honestly the evidence supporting his diagnosis of alcoholism.

2. *Suggest a treatment regimen.* The physician should be knowledgeable about the various treatment programs offered in the community and be able to discuss the programs' relative strengths and weaknesses with the alcoholic's family. In-patient treatment should be strongly encouraged, particularly if the alcoholic is middle- or late-stage, and if the family has insurance or the financial security to cover the cost of three to four weeks of in-patient treatment.

3. *Endorse Alcoholics Anonymous and family support groups.* The physician should strongly recommend Alcoholics Anonymous for the alcoholic, Al-Anon for the spouse, and Alateen for the children of alcoholics. He should have immediate access to AA and Al-Anon members and phone numbers for the family members to use in contacting these organizations.

4. *Discuss intervention techniques.* The physician should discuss with the family potential problems involved in getting the alcoholic into treatment, including probable denial and promises from the alcoholic that he will try to quit on his own. Intervention strategies should be discussed, and the physician should refer family members to a nearby treatment center or a private intervention specialist where they can receive further counseling and training in intervention techniques.

5. *Emphasize the need for quick action.* The family should be helped to understand that alcoholism is chronic and progressive and that the alcoholic will only get worse if he continues to drink. Getting help early in the disease is crucial, and the physician should strongly encourage both the patient and his family to act immediately.

6. *Assure the family of his support.* The physician should assure the family that he is there to help and will do anything he can to help the alcoholic receive the best care available.

What About Antabuse?

Many physicians elect to treat the alcoholic on their own, with a drug called Antabuse. By taking the Antabuse pill every day, the alcoholic, in effect, agrees that he will not drink that day, because if he does drink he'll suffer mightily. Antabuse works by stalling the metabolism of alcohol at the acetaldehyde stage, causing a buildup of the toxic acetaldehyde chemical in the body. Just a few minutes after drinking alcohol, the alcoholic on Antabuse will experience a violent, intense reaction. The *Physician's Desk Reference* describes the reaction this way:

> [Antabuse] produces flushing, throbbing in head and neck, throbbing headache, respiratory difficulty, nausea, copious vomiting, sweating, thirst, chest pain, palpitation, dyspnea [shortness of breath], hyperventilation, tachycardia [rapid heart rate], hypotension [low blood pressure] syncope [faintness], marked uneasiness, weakness, vertigo, blurred vision and confusion. In severe reactions there may be respiratory depression, cardiovascular collapse, arrhythmias [irregular heartbeat], myocardial infarction [heart attack], acute congestive heart failure, unconsciousness, convulsions, and death.

Anyone who has had a drink while taking Antabuse can attest to the truth of this description. Antabuse is, obviously, a strong deterrent to taking a drink. It is looked on as a kind of insurance policy—if the alcoholic takes his pill every day, then he won't drink unless he's willing to endure becoming violently, horribly sick. (The effects of the Antabuse pill may actually last four, five, or more days.) Physicians use Antabuse to deter alcoholics from impulse drinking and to buy precious "sober time"; they hope that the pill will keep their alcoholic patients sober long enough to allow them to discover that they want to stay sober.

Antabuse is not necessarily a bad idea, but it's not the best idea, either. Alcoholism is simply too complex a disease, the addiction too fierce and unpredictable, to treat it successfully on an out-patient basis, particularly for alcoholics in the middle or late stages of the disease who need intensive education and involvement in a more comprehensive alcoholism treatment process.

Furthermore, Antabuse is a drug, and, in effect, it's the *drug* that makes the decisions for the alcoholic. The advocates of Antabuse argue that it doesn't really matter who or what makes the decision, as long as the alcoholic doesn't drink. The longer alcoholics go without drinking, the advocates of Antabuse assert, the stronger their inner resources will become to eventually say "no" by themselves.

But the problems with Antabuse aren't so much what it *does* as what it *doesn't* do. Antabuse is like putting a cage around the addiction. The pill doesn't do anything to tame the beast or render it powerless; it only keeps it at bay. Antabuse doesn't teach the alcoholic about his disease or encapsulate him for a period of time in a world where alcoholism is understood and where denials and evasions are not accepted; Antabuse doesn't warn the alcoholic of the potential pitfalls in recovery or teach him ways to avoid these hazards; Antabuse doesn't involve the alcoholic's family in his treatment, teach him about nutrition, require AA attendance, or offer medical care and detoxification.

In short, Antabuse is simply not enough protection against a disease as powerful, insidious, and deadly as alcoholism. At best, Antabuse is a stopgap measure; it is not, by itself, the long-term solution to the alcoholic's disease.

CHAPTER 6

Intervention

The drinking alcoholic's existence is like the slowly burning fuse at the end of a stick of dynamite. In some alcoholics the fuse is short; in others it is a long time burning. But if the fire is not extinguished, the end is inevitable. The disease eats away at the core and integrity of the alcoholic's life until it inevitably reaches the "big bang"—loss of family and friends, mental and physical deterioration, and, eventually, death.

It used to be thought that the "big bang" had to occur before the alcoholic could successfully be helped. But as the alcoholic's life and health were gradually destroyed, so were his family, career, friendships, and finances. When the final explosion came, there was often no one left to witness it or to help the alcoholic put the pieces back together again. Sometimes the explosion was so devastating that there simply wasn't anything left at all.

Intervention is the process of stopping the slow burn of the disease *before* the alcoholic and everything he loves or cares about

is destroyed. Oddly enough, however, the alcoholic is not necessarily the sole focus of the intervention. The focus must also be
on the family and friends of the alcoholic: those people who, out
of love and loyalty, have followed the alcoholic onto the death
track of the disease, unknowingly risking their own emotional and
psychological health. They need help, too. But that is not the only
reason why they must become a major focus of the intervention
process. The family has the most powerful weapon available for
stopping the disease and starting the process of health and
recovery: love. Because of their love for the alcoholic, the family
has the emotional power to break through the addiction and pull
the alcoholic back to reality and the beginning of recovery.

The family's love, however, has gone through some strange
transformations in the years of living with the alcoholic, and
their sense of reality and what is "normal" becomes thoroughly
twisted. The spouse, children, parents, and siblings live for so
long hoping that this nightmare isn't really true, that their loved
one isn't a "drunk" after all, that they build up their own denial
systems to keep the reality from hitting them. The family of a
prominent lawyer, for example, developed a "solution" for
every bizarre situation that the disease threw at them. When
the lawyer began to urinate in the closet, thinking it was the
bathroom, his wife simply removed all the clothes and shoes
and lined the closet with washable wallpaper and vinyl floor-
ing. When the lawyer fell down the stairs and broke the wooden
banister, his son replaced it with a strong metal railing.

This family, like most alcoholics' families, made the only
choice that seemed to offer any hope at all: they chose to stay
with the alcoholic, cover for him, and attempt to minimize the
damage of the disease. But in this process the family began to
lose touch with reality and with their own feelings. They, too,
developed an illness.

The primary characteristic of the family illness is *emotional
isolation*. The family members build a thick protective armor
around themselves, walling off their feelings and emotions so
that they won't hurt or feel anything. They learn to behave and
think in ways that insulate them from pain and stress and allow
them to survive emotionally intact.*

*For a detailed look at the characteristic behaviors of alcoholic families, read
Another Chance: Hope and Health for the Alcoholic Family, by Sharon
Wegscheider, Science and Behavior Books, 1980.

Survival is the key word here—and in order to survive the slow, searing destruction that is alcoholism, trust, affection, and hope are eventually abandoned. In some families, only paper-thin shreds of love hold everyone together in a sort of tenuous and uncomfortable truce. In most alcoholic families, love has been altered into an all-consuming, paralyzing variety of fears: anxiety that the alcoholic will lose his job; dread that others will find out the family "secret"; terror that the family will simply disintegrate; fear that the alcoholic will die or that, drunk, he will kill someone else. Fear governs what each member of the family says, how they behave, and even how they think. Fear consumes them and, in the process, disfigures every healthy and healing emotion, particularly love.

Living with an alcoholic is like receiving a daily dose of an emotional anesthetic. Slowly, over the years, the family members will stop feeling and caring. They have focused for so long on the alcoholic that they don't know how to focus on themselves, their needs, or their emotions. All they want is peace, and they are willing to get it at any price. So they add on the protective armor, year by year, layer by layer, insulating themselves from feeling, from emotion, from hurt. They end up not feeling very much, but they don't hurt unbearably, either. It's the price they're willing to pay for a semblance of peace.

"Peace" may even be bought at the price of allowing the alcoholic to continue to drink. In one family, the children (ten altogether) were united in their decision to finally get help for their alcoholic father. But when they asked for their mother's cooperation, she answered, "You kids can do this if you want, but I've handled your dad's drinking for years, and I guess I can keep on handling it."

The children were dumbfounded: surely she wanted more out of life than this? They called a counselor who, after many hours of talking with the mother, discovered why she was so reluctant. Several years earlier, her husband had quit drinking, on his own without treatment, for eleven months. But from the day he stopped drinking, he also stopped interacting with his wife. He withdrew sexually and emotionally, moving into a separate bedroom and barely talking to her all day. Totally isolated from contact with her sober spouse, she was secretly relieved when he began to drink again. "At least when he's drinking, he'll crawl into bed and hold me," she confessed to the counselor.

In another family, the husband continually refused to seek help for his alcoholic wife. Again, an astute counselor uncovered the reasons: he was having an affair with his secretary and feared that once his wife was sober, he would have to give up the other woman. His friends and business associates knew of the affair but didn't hold it against him. "Poor guy," they'd say, shaking their heads, "his wife's a drunk—it's no wonder he's looking for comfort somewhere else." This man liked the balance of power just the way it was, even if it meant living with all the problems of alcoholism.

During the process of intervention, the family members must be helped to understand why they behave in certain ways and feel certain emotions. They must be helped to begin working toward a new view of reality, based on a full understanding of the disease and its impact on the alcoholic and those who live with him and love him.

Turning the fear, anger, shame, and distrust back into caring and love, and allowing that love to work as the major motivator for helping the alcoholic, is a primary goal of the intervention process. Intervention can be a time-consuming process, taking weeks, even months. But without healing the family, helping them to see what the disease has done both to the alcoholic and to them, and turning the fear and anger back into love, the intervention has little chance of success. The same old resentments and anxieties will continue to manipulate the family's behavior, and the alcoholic, if he gets help, will find difficult days ahead in recovery.

In this chapter we'll go through the intervention process step by step, leading up to the actual face-off with the alcoholic. It's crucial that families understand, right at the beginning, that intervention is not something that they can hire somebody else to do for them. They must do it themselves, with a counselor as their guide, and in the process they must be willing to look at their own behavior and attitudes, and change what must be changed, if the alcoholic and all who love him are to recover from this disease.

For the majority of families, three to six weeks will elapse between the call for help and the actual intervention. If the alcoholic or a family member is in crisis—an emergency-room admission for gastritis, heart attack, or cirrhosis; an assault or drunk-driving charge; a potentially violent child-custody situation; a suicide threat or attempt—an intervention should immediately be arranged to provide emergency assistance or aid. The purpose of such crisis intervention is to get immediate help and to focus attention on the underlying cause of the crisis— alcoholism—and then to direct the alcoholic toward treatment rather than become sidetracked by mistaken diagnoses, legal entanglements, court battles, etc.

The steps described below constitute a "formal intervention," which is distinguished from a crisis intervention in that there is no immediate life-threatening situation.

Step One: Asking for Help

This is, of course, the hardest step of all. How do you just pick up the telephone, dial a number, and, to a complete stranger, sum up in several sentences your years of agony and suffering?

Before you make that call, you'll have to know whom to call. Unfortunately, at this writing there is no established network of intervention counselors; unless you know of someone skilled and experienced in conducting interventions, you'll have to do some digging. You can start by finding out what your community offers in terms of in-patient and out-patient treatment, alcoholism counselors, AA groups, Al-Anon, Alateen, etc. You will get some good ideas by calling AA or Al-Anon directly (they're listed in the Yellow Pages under "Alcoholism Information and Treatment Centers") and explaining that you are looking for a counselor skilled in intervention. Community alcoholism centers are also a good source of information and referral.

Many treatment centers have their own intervention counselors, and often there is no charge for the counseling service. After investigating the treatment philosophy and becoming educated about the type and quality of care offered (see chapter 8), you can inquire about the intervention assistance available there. Make absolutely sure that the treatment program you select considers *your* health a primary part of both the intervention and the recovery process. Does the staff inform and educate you—the family—in the process? Do they involve you in active ways in the sequence of learning and treatment?

In looking for help, it's important that you understand that the intervention can backfire, particularly if the family members disagree about the need for intervention. A skilled intervention counselor will guide you to make the right decisions. Beware, too, of the philosophy that intervention succeeds only if a "closing" is achieved—in other words, only if the alcoholic enters treatment. Every person close to the alcoholic is affected by his disease, and thus there can be many successes. If any one member in the family gets healthy through the intervention, the entire process can be counted a success—even if the alcoholic continues to drink.

The counselor you select—whether private or working with a treatment center—should be knowledgeable about all aspects of alcoholism, specifically trained in intervention techniques, and skilled in applying these techniques and working with families. Most important of all, he or she should be experienced. Intervention is an emotionally charged process that varies with each alcoholic family; during this process the family as a unit and each individual family member can be extremely vulnerable. After working with fifty or sixty families, a counselor has a pretty good idea what to expect and has the confidence and clearheadedness to deal with the unexpected.

The counselor is an educator, a therapist, and a guide, but she should not be the only contact you have in the alcoholism community. In fact, your counselor should encourage you to build up a support system that will carry you through when she is no longer working with you. As a clearinghouse for various referral sources, she should have a detailed resource list and be willing and able to "connect" you to other professionals in the community.

During the process of intervention, your counselor will encourage you to take control and, as the education process continues, allow you to become the leaders and authorities in the process. Thus, she does not actually *do* the intervention herself but leads the family members along, helping them to learn about the disease and their reactions to it until they are ready to conduct the intervention themselves. As one counselor said, "My job is not to fix everything up for the family, it's to help them learn how to fix things themselves. I'm robbing them if I'm doing the job for them. They must assume responsibility for their own well-being. I can't make them well for a lifetime; only they can do that. And that's the goal of intervention."

When you call an intervention counselor, you will be reassured that you are not crazy, that you did not cause this disease, and that your behavior and responses to the alcoholic have been normal within the abnormal context of living with an alcoholic. If the family is still together, if there is even a shred of love left, you will learn that you have done a magnificent job of surviving in a near-impossible situation.

During the initial counseling sessions, the counselor will ask if the family has approached the alcoholic first to find out if he is willing to go into treatment. Some families just assume that the alcoholic will refuse to enter treatment and never even think to ask him. Other families spend all their energies trying to solve the problems created by alcoholism and never focus on the real cause of these problems. It may seem extraordinarily odd, but in many alcoholic families the word *alcoholic* has never been mentioned. Family members may have consulted numerous counselors, physicians, and psychiatrists and still be totally unaware that the root cause of their physical, psychological, emotional, and behavioral problems is alcoholism.

As the counseling sessions continue, the family will learn that alcoholism is, in fact, the root cause of their present problems. The counselor will also work to help the family become unanimous in their decision to go through with the process of intervention. If one family member holds back— retaining doubts or fears about the process, believing that the intervention is demeaning to the alcoholic, or fearing that the alcoholic will never forgive the family—then the chances are good that the alcoholic will latch on to this weak link and use it to undermine the entire process.

Drawing the family together and helping them work as a united team is crucial if the intervention is to be successful. Family members will also have to identify their motives for intervention and discard the wrong ones (guilt, anger, resentment) in favor of the right ones (love, caring, concern). The right motive is expressed in this statement: "I love him too much to allow this to go on any longer," while the wrong motive can be found in this statement: "I'm so angry at him that I'm just not going to take it anymore." An intervention undertaken with a wish to inflict treatment as punishment or with anger and resentment used as a sort of club to beat the alcoholic into submission is on shaky ground. To be successful, the intervention should be conducted in the spirit of "We are doing this *for* him, not *to* him."

The people involved in the intervention process are called the "intervention team." This team should be neither too small (which might signal to the alcoholic a lack of interest and power) nor too large (which might overwhelm and anger the alcoholic). A group of four to eight people seems to work well. The quality of care and concern is more important, however, than the quantity of people expressing that concern. One or two people alone, with the preparation and/or presence of the counselor, can conduct an intervention and successfully begin the recovery process.

The alcoholic's immediate family members should be part of this team, although sometimes there are situations in which certain family members should *not* participate in the intervention. Right at the beginning of the process, everyone involved should understand that if their presence in any way blocks an important part of the intervention, they may be excluded. For example, if a particular person's presence at the intervention will instill hostility and resentment in the alcoholic, then it may be better to have that person's care and concern represented by a letter rather than risk the success of the intervention.

In addition to the immediate family, it's also a good idea to include one or more "outsiders" such as the alcoholic's clergyman, best friend, physician, boss, or fellow employee. These outsiders add a new dimension to the intervention, signaling that the alcoholic's problems have been noticed by those who see him for only a few hours a day and attesting to the fact that the damage has spread (and been noticed) far beyond the immediate family.

Once the team is assembled, and the alcohol problems are identified and openly discussed, the family can begin work on the most time-consuming of the steps, Step Two.

Step Two: Getting Educated

Having read this far in this book, you already know a great deal about the disease of alcoholism and the symptoms associated with its early, middle, and late stages. This knowledge is critically important to the success of the intervention. It's extremely difficult for most family members to get over the feeling that the alcoholic has "done" this to them, that he has willfully ruined their lives and chosen the bottle over them. The entire process of education is designed to help you understand that the alcoholic did not choose this disease, that he is helpless over his addiction, and that all of his behaviors are manipulated by it. In other words, his alcoholic behavior is not his own; it belongs to the addiction, and when he is freed from this addiction he will become himself again. Then you as family members will be free, too—free to take down those walls, free to feel love and pain and other emotions again, free to act and not just react—free, in other words, to be and to become yourselves.

During the counseling preparations, all the family members will be taught about the disease, its effect on their lives, and their treatment options. As you learn about the disease, you will be able to "detach" yourselves from it and understand that the disease—not the alcoholic—is your real enemy. With this detachment you will be able to recognize and deal with many of the "toxic wastes" that have built up over the years—the anger, resentments, self-pity, hatred, fears, distrust, denials—and learn how to change your behavior so that you can effectively fight the disease and help release yourself and your loved ones from its power.

The reading list at the end of this book suggests additional books that will help you learn about the disease and its victims. For the purposes of intervention, we particularly recommend *Under the Influence*, which first set forth the concept that alcoholism is a primary, physiological disease and that psychological problems are actually symptoms of this disease. It's also helpful to read about the experiences of other alcoholics and their families, and the following books are particularly insightful: *The Courage to Change; The Booze Battle; End of the Rainbow; A Sensitive and Passionate Man; The Lost Weekend;*

Broken Promises and Mended Dreams; Bill W.; Harold Hughes: The Man from Ida Grove; Where Did Everybody Go? For specific information on the family's role in alcoholism and its treatment, read Sharon Wegscheider's *Hope and Health for the Alcoholic Family* and Toby Rice Drew's *Getting Them Sober.*

Free lectures, open to the public, are offered at many treatment centers, and you should try to attend any and all you can find. You will also find it helpful to attend "open" (meaning open to the public) AA, Al-Anon, and Alateen meetings.

Step Three: Getting the Facts

Now begin the step-by-step preparations for the actual intervention. Each family member will put together a list of specific, nonjudgmental facts based on firsthand knowledge of incidents, behaviors, and personality changes related to the alcoholic's drinking and/or drug-taking. You will gain confidence and courage if you practice presenting these written statements with your counselor and other group members. It's important, too, that during the actual intervention you read from your list—don't try to memorize—and avoid opinions, criticisms, or moralizing. During the actual intervention, each family member will read from his or her list, presenting the information in a calm, loving, nonjudgmental manner.

In making up your list, it's important to keep these seven essentials in mind:

1. Give specific examples of abusive, dangerous, or embarrassing behaviors that are symptomatic of alcoholism.

2. Include the exact dates and, if possible, the times of the specific events. Make sure the events are as recent as possible; something that happened last week or last month will be a lot more effective than an event that occurred five years ago.

3. Make sure that you have witnessed these events or are sure they've happened—do *not* include speculative information.

4. Mention the actual chemical consumption (a case of beer, a quart of vodka, a bottle of wine) and the harmful consequences of this consumption.

5. Point out the contradictions or conflicts in values or behavior caused by the drinking ("You're a good father but last

Friday you got drunk and slapped Matthew so hard he still has a bruise'').

6. Comment on your feelings about these behaviors, being careful to stay nonjudgmental, while at the same time making it clear to the alcoholic that you have been adversely affected by the addiction.

7. State your concern about what is happening to the alcoholic and emphasize your love for him.

Here are a few examples:

> Dad, two months ago on the 4th of July, you went outside to try to put the flag up. It was 9:00 A.M. You fell off the ladder twice and ended up throwing the flag into the bushes. When you were sober, you could climb a ladder with your hands tied behind your back. I was so frightened for you; I was afraid you'd break a leg or worse. I want you to get well, because I care about you.

> On January 30 you insisted on driving Katie to a birthday party. You'd had six drinks that I knew about and you were slurring your words. I pleaded with you to let me take her, but you grabbed the keys from me, shoved Katie in the car, and drove off. I waited in agony for you to come home; I was sure that you would both be killed in a car accident. I love you, and I know how much you love your children and how devastated you would be if anything happened to them. We all want you to be healthy again.

> Last Monday at the football game you spilled your beer all over the woman in front of you. You didn't even apologize; in fact, you kept insisting it was her fault, that she had bumped you. You got another beer and spilled that one all over me. I was so embarrassed I wanted to crawl away; but I couldn't leave you there because I was worried about you, and you were too drunk to find your way home. I drove home that night with you passed out in the backseat. The next morning, you didn't even remember that we were at a football game.

Step Four: Making a Treatment Plan

One of the major goals of the intervention is to get help for the alcoholic—so you must be prepared to tell him exactly what kind of help is available. In the counseling sessions you will learn more about the treatment program you have selected, or you will be given information to help you select a program that fits your specific financial and geographic needs. It's important that you research the various options, ask questions of the treatment center's administration and staff, and generally get a feel for the atmosphere and underlying philosophies of the different treatment programs. Be sure, too, to find out which programs offer a family program and how extensive that program is. Then you, as a family, should make the final decision about which treatment center is right for you and your alcoholic. Chapter 8 gives specific information to help you understand the differences between the various treatment options. In this way, you accept the final responsibility for the intervention process.

You will also want to plan out as many of the details of treatment as you can, including how you will pay for treatment and whether your insurance will cover it; how much sick time or vacation time the alcoholic can take from work; and whether the specific treatment center you've selected has an opening. (For more information about admission considerations and procedures, see chapter 9.)

Finally, you will want to take care of those little details that the alcoholic might use to stall off treatment. Alcoholics have been known to argue their way out of treatment because the laundry is piled up in the basement, the carpet needs vacuuming, the bills aren't paid, the dog will die of loneliness, or the kids need rides to ballet lessons. Try to think of all potential "escape routes" that the alcoholic might try and, by taking care of them yourself, slam them shut.

Abstinence is the only realistic goal of treatment, and you cannot accept a pledge from the alcoholic to "cut down" on his drinking. Nevertheless, you should make up a "what if" plan, setting out exactly what you will do if the alcoholic refuses to enter treatment or claims that he can quit on his own. If this happens, agree that you will give him one last chance to try to quit on his own. However, he must agree, at the actual intervention, that if he starts drinking again he will immediately and automatically enter treatment. If he refuses to recognize the need for help, the consequences must be carefully laid out before him.

Each intervention team will need to develop their own set of consequences—separation, divorce, loss of custody, loss of job, expulsion from school, loss of financial help, etc.—but it is crucial to the success of the intervention that these consequences have meaning to the alcoholic, that they are presented with finality, and that he understands that they will be enforced. Empty threats are all too familiar to the alcoholic and will not motivate him to get help. Threats with serious and irrevocable consequences will break through to him and, in the great majority of cases, motivate him to accept treatment.

At this point in the intervention process you will have to squarely face a very difficult question: What if the alcoholic refuses to get treatment and continues to drink? Does this mean that the intervention has failed? No. The only failure is in doing nothing. Having gone through the process of intervention, you have given your alcoholic the ultimate demonstration of love. You have acted to save your relationship rather than let it be destroyed in apathy. You have taken a risk, because of love, and you have turned your back on fear and decided to work toward change.

What happens to the alcoholic as a result of the intervention is something you cannot control. Now it is up to him—he knows and understands now what impact his disease has had on his own health and happiness as well as his family's, and he is forced to choose life or death. Whatever his choice is, you, as the family, have made your own choice—to remove yourselves from the searing destruction of the disease, heal your wounds, and begin the process of recovery for yourselves.

Step Five: Getting Help
for the Family

People who live with alcoholics have problems that are sometimes called "codependent symptoms." We call them the "you're
sick toos," and they often manifest themselves in certain behavior types:

• *Superperson.* You're superresponsible, you're never late,
you work hard, you're constantly on the go, and you suffer
terrible guilt feelings if you can't keep up.

• *Plastic person.* You keep your feelings inside, finding it
difficult to express them to anyone or even to get in touch with
them yourself. You rarely cry, you rarely laugh, and you rarely
trust anyone else's expressed feelings.

• *Neurotic.* You're depressed, anxious, and afraid, pretty
much all the time.

• *Fatalist.* You're convinced that nothing will ever change,
that life just presents some of us with bigger challenges than
others, and that we all have to make sacrifices.

• *Shrew.* You nag, you blame, you scream and shout, and,
as the years go by, your volume and your frustration increase.

• *Martyr.* You think the family's problems are somehow all
your fault, that if you'd only done things differently, everything
would be all right. Or you may feel that the problems are
somebody else's fault, but by taking the blame yourself maybe
things will get better.

• *Rescuer.* You cover for everyone, making excuses, tidy-
ing up, and attempting to carry on.

• *Wimp.* You're afraid to do anything because nothing you've
done before works, and so you keep your mouth closed, spend
a lot of time crying, and stay out of the fray.

• *Hypochondriac.* You've got headaches, backaches, leg
pains and joint pains, you can't sleep, and you always feel like
you're coming down with something.

You may fit cleanly into one of these behavior types, you
may have the symptoms of several, or perhaps you are a little
bit of all of them. It doesn't matter what particular shape your
sickness happens to take; if you live with an alcoholic, you're

going to suffer emotionally. *You need help.* Most comprehensive treatment programs include counseling sessions for the family members of alcoholics, and many treatment centers require that you spend several days or even weeks in in-patient treatment. Whatever treatment program you choose for the alcoholic, make sure you become involved in the treatment, too. Your intervention counselor will refer you to additional sources of ongoing support, including Al-Anon, Alateen, and group or individual therapy. There are now also special groups for the adult children of alcoholics. (See appendix 3 for a self-test revealing the particular problems of this group.)

It's essential that all of the family members participate in a treatment program designed to help them cope with their own problems that stem from the disease. If any one of the family members remains stuck in the old behaviors motivated by fear, anger, distrust, disgust, shame, or guilt, the disease is still alive and well. An alcoholic coming back into a sick family will, in a very real sense, be caught up in the disease once again. Either he will drink again, or he will have to leave the family to save himself. It's as simple and awful as that.

Step Six: Rehearse

This is a full dress rehearsal, in which you will practice presenting your lists to the alcoholic. It's a good idea to have a recovering alcoholic (perhaps an AA member or a counselor from the treatment center) role-play the part of the alcoholic. The rehearsal will work out last-minute details and finalize the process of preparing the family emotionally for the actual intervention. The intervention counselor will guide the rehearsal and help you to make final plans for the date, time, and place of the intervention.

The alcoholic must be sober when the intervention takes place. Thus, it's a good idea to schedule the event in the morning or when he's at work. The intervention must be conducted in a neutral place—in the counselor's office, employer's office, or at a friend's house, but never on the alcoholic's own turf, in his home or office. Legally, the intervention counselor is a stranger and can be ordered out of the house as a trespasser. Or the alcoholic can lock himself in the bathroom, sneak out to the garage and drive away, or walk into the kitchen and fix himself a drink. An alcoholic on his own turf, with his possessions around him, can gather a good deal of power from the familiar and use that power to sabotage the intervention.

After all the details are worked out, the actual intervention can take place.

Step Seven: Confronting the Alcoholic

What follows is a composite from several actual interventions, with names and distinguishing facts changed. The entire event, which took place at 9:00 A.M. in the intervention counselor's* office, took fifteen minutes.

The people involved were:

MARGARET, the alcoholic, 47 years old, an interior decorator
PETER, the husband, 52 years old, an electrical engineer
SUSAN, their 22-year-old daughter, a mother and homemaker
JOHN, their 15-year-old son
MICHAEL, Margaret's boss
KATHY, Margaret's best friend
ANNE, the intervention counselor

[Margaret and Peter walk into Anne's office, where everyone else is gathered. Margaret is shocked to see them all together and looks as if she is ready to run from the room. Anne takes her hand, welcoming her.]

ANNE: Hello, Margaret, my name is Anne Kramer. I've heard so many special and positive things about you. Your family came to me with some concerns, and we've chosen today to share those concerns, as well as their love for you. Would you be willing to just listen for about twenty minutes?

*Interventions are sometimes conducted without a counselor's presence. In an intervention class, the family rehearses the process exactly, as from a script, reading from their written lists and working out all the details beforehand. While these interventions can be successful, the presence of a skilled and compassionate counselor adds clarity and direction. Because the counselor is not emotionally involved, she can help to maintain control and make sure that the family's highly charged emotions do not short-circuit the process.

MARGARET [looks around her apprehensively]: Well, I guess so; I don't know what else I can do. [Margaret sits down on the couch between Michael and Kathy; the others sit on chairs arranged in a circle.]

ANNE: It seemed to come up quite often, Margaret, that the drinking was behind some of the fears and concerns your family and friends were having. Michael, would you start by telling Margaret about some of your concerns?

MICHAEL: Margaret, I'm here because I care about you as a friend, and I'm concerned about you and what's happening to you at work. When you came into work last Thursday you were in very bad shape. Your hands were shaking, you could barely hold on to your coffee cup. You told me you were upset because of an argument with Peter. You went out for lunch, early, and came back two and a half hours later, obviously under the influence. I told you to leave early because you obviously couldn't put in any productive time.

MARGARET: I could have stayed; I told you I'd stay if you needed me. . . .

MICHAEL: Margaret, you promised you'd listen to me. Please listen. After I sent you home, Mr. Jenkins came by to check on your progress on the Carson home. I lied to him, to cover up for you. I've done that so many times, and every time I feel guilty. Margaret, I can't do it anymore. I can't cover up for you anymore. [Michael stops and looks down at the floor.]

ANNE: Peter, would you like to share your love and concern with Margaret?

PETER: I love you, Margaret. That's the reason I'm here and the reason for everything I'm going to say. [Peter begins to cry; the tears roll down his cheeks as he talks, trying hard to keep his voice under control.] When I came home from work last Monday and found you trying to fix dinner while stumbling around the kitchen, I wanted to break down and cry. But I couldn't. I've been keeping all this pain inside and it's about to break me apart. I'm so worried about you, so concerned about you and your drinking. Honey, don't you see what the drinking has done to you? What it's done to us? I want you to get help, for you, for all of us. . . .

MARGARET: I don't need any help! I don't want any help!

PETER [calmly]: That's what you said three months ago when you tried to quit. And you did try. You tried so hard. But you couldn't do it by yourself. A week after you tried to quit you went out to dinner on your birthday and got rip-roaring drunk. . . .

MARGARET [indignant]: Peter! That was my birthday; I was celebrating. You were drinking, too, so was everyone else. . . .

PETER [continuing]: . . . And a month after that a policeman stopped you for weaving on the road. He drove you home. He protected you because he didn't want to put you through the ordeal of a drunk-driving citation. I've been so afraid . . . afraid that you would drive into a tree, afraid that I'd get a call from the emergency room. . . . [Peter covers his face with his hands and cries.]

KATHY [takes Margaret's hands in her own, smiles at her]: We've been friends a long time, haven't we? I'm worried about you, too. I'm here because I love you. Do you remember three weeks ago, Saturday when you brought your granddaughter over? You were babysitting. You'd had a few drinks before you came over—you were slurring your words—and you had three more at my house. When I tried to suggest that you were drinking too much, you became very defensive and cynical; finally, you left in a huff. I had to put the baby in her carseat because you kept getting the seatbelts all confused. I pleaded with you to let me drive but you refused. So I followed you home, just to make sure that you made it safely.

SUSAN: Mom, when Kathy first told that story, I was so angry and upset. I couldn't understand why you would put my daughter's— your only granddaughter's—life at risk. But I understand now— it's the addiction. You can't control it, Mom. You need help. Please, please, for all of us, Mom, won't you please get help?

JOHN: Mom, it took me a long time to agree to come to these meetings. I felt it would be a betrayal of you, of my love for you. I thought you'd never forgive me. But now I know why I came—we want you back. We want our mother back. I love you. Please, Mom . . .

MARGARET [breaks down, sobbing uncontrollably; the family gathers around her, hugging and crying]: Yes, yes, oh my God, what have I done? I'm sorry, I'm so sorry. . . .

ANNE [after things calm down a bit]: Margaret, everyone here loves you. We are all very proud of you. Your family has selected a treatment center and they want you to go into treatment today, right now. Michael has arranged for you to take the time off from work. Your bags are packed, a room is waiting for you, Peter is ready to drive you there. Are you ready?

MARGARET [crying softly]: Where is the treatment center?

ANNE: Your family has selected a center just fifteen minutes from your home. It's a beautiful center, with a skilled and caring staff.

MARGARET: Michael, what about my clients?

MICHAEL: Everything has been arranged with Mr. Jenkins. I've called the Carsons, and they agreed to a slight delay. Everything is taken care of at work, Margaret. Your job will be waiting for you when you get back.

MARGARET: But what about my cat? Who will take care of her? She can't be alone all day. . . .

SUSAN: Mom, I'm going to take Samantha home with me while you're in treatment. I'll take good care of her.

MARGARET [smiles slightly]: I guess there's nothing to worry about, then.

PETER [reaching out for Margaret's hand]: Are you ready, Margaret?

MARGARET [takes Peter's hand, squeezes it, and tries to smile]: As ready as I'll ever be.

CHAPTER 7

Choosing a Treatment Center

It would be wonderful if there were a treatment center practicing the general principles outlined in this book in every town in this country. But there isn't. If you live in the outback of Minnesota, you may not have alcoholism treatment available within three hundred miles. Or you may live in a city of thirty thousand people and your only immediate treatment options are a state mental institution or detoxification at a county facility. Big-city residents have the problem of choosing between dozens of facilities, some in specialized hospitals, others in general hospitals, and still others in community mental health centers.

No matter where you live, it's essential that you choose the best possible care; even if this involves a plane trip and dipping into your savings. Shopping around for alcoholism treatment, however, isn't like shopping around for a new car, with the cost and the extras being the only negotiable factors. If you buy a Buick Skylark at any dealer in this country, you'll get the same basic machine every other dealer offers. But your money buys very different things when it comes to alcoholism treatment. You may think you're buying the Cadillac of treatment when, in fact, you're paying thousands of dollars for a Jacuzzi, roses on your bedside table, uniformed staff members—and outdated and ineffective treatment. There are a lot of lemons among the options now available for alcoholism treatment.

This chapter is designed to help you sift through the various treatment programs, learning what they offer, how much they cost, and their specific advantages and disadvantages. Our goal is not to single out one specific treatment option as the "best" or "only" choice, but to give you a guide to choosing between the options available to you and making the choice that will best ensure a stable and enduring recovery.

Nevertheless, this is necessarily a directive guide, based on the firm and unshakable concept that alcoholism is a physiological disease and that most if not all of the alcoholic's psychological problems are a direct result of the addictive process. With this theoretical foundation in mind, we offer the following recommendations:

• Do not, under any circumstances, accept psychotherapy (in-patient or out-patient) as your sole treatment for alcoholism. Psychoanalysis or psychotherapy may be helpful for the small percentage of alcoholics who have psychological problems *apart from their drinking,* but such treatment must not be considered alcoholism treatment per se. For the rare patient who is actively psychotic, psychotherapy can be offered simultaneously with intensive alcoholism treatment.

• Do not, under any circumstances, enter a program that offers tranquilizers or sedatives as standard, ongoing treatment. Sedative and tranquilizing drugs can safely be used *only* during the initial detoxification period. Likewise, recovering alcoholics under a physician's care must not accept prescriptions for tranquilizers or sedatives. Not all physicians are aware of the dangers of these drugs for recovering alcoholics, so you will have to be your own guardian, avoiding any and all prescriptions for such drugs.*

*During surgery or in emergency medical treatment, drugs often cannot be avoided. Appendix 6 p. 270—explains how to manage drugs in crisis situations.

• Do not, under any circumstances, consider a treatment program that even subtly suggests that alcoholics can return to "normal" drinking. *Abstinence* from alcohol and all other drugs that affect the central nervous system must be the permanent cornerstone of any treatment program you choose.

• For certain alcoholics, a treatment center with medical facilities and a physician on staff is essential. These include alcoholics with longstanding multiple addictions (to both alcohol and other addictive drugs), including sedatives, tranquilizers, sleeping pills, narcotics, or other painkillers, heroin, or cocaine; late-stage alcoholics or alcoholics who have a history of seizures or delirium tremens; and alcoholics with other medical problems or diseases that require intensive care and supervision.

• Nutritional therapy should be an integral part of the treatment program you choose and actively employed in the treatment process.

• Family treatment and/or counseling should be offered, and family members should be strongly encouraged to take an active part in the alcoholic's recovery.

• An aftercare plan, including out-patient counseling, and follow-up care should be included as part of the treatment regimen.

Your Choices

In-patient and out-patient treatments are the basic treatment choices, but within these two categories are a number of very different types of treatment. The following descriptions are not intended to be exhaustive but simply to give you an idea of "what's out there" and what, in general, each treatment option offers. Once again, our recommendations are based on the concept of alcoholism presented in this book. Due to financial, geographic, or other personal factors, you may decide on a program that does not specifically endorse this concept yet still offers comprehensive and effective care. The important points to remember are these: be informed, consider your choices carefully, and make the best choice based on what is available to you.

In-Patient (Short-Term)

Short-term, residential treatment programs range in duration from several days to several months, with four weeks the usual length of stay. These programs are offered in (1) specialized alcoholism treatment facilities, with or without medical services; and (2) psychiatric treatment facilities in state-run medical institutions, private psychiatric hospitals, and psychiatric wards of general hospitals.

Alcoholics also get "treatment" in general (acute care) hospitals for the medical complications of their disease. In the general hospital, however, the focus is on fixing the immediate complaints and then releasing the patient. The treating physician might recommend a social service evaluation in an attempt to initiate a treatment plan; but without specialized attention, knowledge, and a uniform approach to alcoholism, such a plan is characteristically lost or forgotten about when the patient is discharged.

Suicidal, abusive, or mentally deranged alcoholics are sometimes "treated" in psychiatric hospitals. Here, the diagnosis is "depression," "schizophrenia," or some other mental disorder. Alcoholism is only a peripheral, and often unmentioned, concern.

Neither of these options—acute care in a general hospital or psychiatric treatment for an alcoholism-related mental disorder—can be considered alcoholism treatment. Years ago these were the only options for alcoholics; but years ago, most alcoholics died of their disease.

Specialized Alcoholism Treatment Facilities

These programs range from highly sophisticated facilities, staffed by physicians, nurses, and specially trained alcoholism counselors and featuring gourmet food, hot tubs, and strolls on the ten-acre grounds; to hospital-based programs with a designated alcoholism unit; to mom-and-pop-type operations run on a shoestring, with cramped facilities and a small staff of recovering alcoholics as counselors.

Strip off the outer trappings, however, and most of these treatment programs offer essentially the same components:

1. education (lectures, discussions, reading, educational films)

2. counseling (individual and group)
3. occupational guidance
4. family involvement
5. AA introduction and participation
6. aftercare, including out-patient counseling and followup.

Hospital-based programs and many of the independent centers specializing only in alcoholism treatment include medical services in addition to intensive rehabilitation. These services consist of a detoxification unit, with intensive round-the-clock medical care, a medical director, nursing staff, etc. Such facilities are classified as "hospitals" and are, at this writing, more likely to receive insurance coverage for treatment.

Costs for specialized alcoholism treatment programs vary widely, with a range of $1,000 to $10,000 for a three-to-four week stay. Alcoholism treatment "hospitals" are generally more expensive than programs not offering intensive medical care.

Recommendations: Specialized alcoholism treatment cen ters are, we believe, your best overall treatment choice, because they are set up specifically for alcoholics, with staff trained in alcoholism theory and treatment (many are recovering alcoholics themselves).

But don't be fooled into thinking that all of these centers offer exactly the same thing and therefore one is as good as another. The real differences (besides the "look" of the places) aren't readily discerned from reading the treatment brochures or even from walking around the centers. These differences are based on a philosophy that is often difficult to pinpoint, and this philosophy (or lack of it) can have a dramatic impact on a program's effectiveness. The most common example is that while virtually all programs acknowledge the disease concept of alcoholism, the treatment emphasis in many of these centers is geared toward "treating" the supposed psychological causes of the disease.

It's essential, therefore, that you do a little research before deciding on a particular program. These are some of the questions you should be asking: What is the underlying philosophy about the nature and causes of alcoholism? What tools are offered to help the patient maintain sobriety in the future? How long is recovery expected to take? How long will it take for the alcoholic to act and feel "normal"? Does the staff look for psychological causes for drinking?

If treatment is offered in a general hospital, look at the physical setup of the alcoholism ward. The program should include group rooms for patients to mingle and interact, lecture facilities, and indoor and/or outdoor recreational facilities. These physical modifications to the normal atmosphere of a general hospital will not necessarily make or break treatment, but they will certainly enhance the alcoholic's enjoyment of a three-to-four-week stay there.

It is also a good idea to visit the treatment center and observe the interactions between patients and staff. How do the staff members interact with the patients: are they autocratic and dictatorial? patronizing? buddy-buddy? An atmosphere of hope and optimism should be apparent, with the staff firmly in control but sensitive and caring. Patients should look and act like "normal" people: friendly, alert, and interacting with one another. They should not, as a group, appear sullen and hostile, or sit in their rooms staring out the window. Some patients will, of course, "look the part," but most should appear happy to be where they are. Don't worry about the occasional patient who looks zonked out or somehow not all there. But make sure that not all the patients look that way.

Your visit to the treatment center should be welcomed and your questions answered patiently and directly. You should get a feeling of being with people who are kind, knowledgeable, and obviously in control. Meeting and talking with members of the staff is important, because these are the people who will be directing the alcoholic's recovery, and their attitudes and opinions will directly influence him.

A sense of humor means a lot to alcoholics, and it's generally a good sign if you see patients laughing and jovial, interacting informally with one another and with staff members, playing cards and enjoying other recreation during free time. Patients should also be out of their rooms *doing* something, either scheduled or unscheduled activities, in a dynamic, alive, busy environment.

For more information about the kinds of questions you should ask and questions you can expect to be asked when contacting a treatment center, see chapter 9.

Alcoholism Units in Psychiatric Hospitals

Alcoholism "treatment" really began in psychiatric hospitals at the beginning of this century. Most general hospitals wouldn't admit alcoholic patients (they were viewed as hopeless, mentally ill, and disruptive for other patients) and automatically referred them to psychiatric facilities. In general, these institutions were state-run; by the time most alcoholics made it into treatment, they couldn't afford to buy alcohol let alone pay for private psychiatric care.

At most psychiatric hospitals, alcoholics were grouped with other "mentally ill" patients, usually in a large ward. Their treatment consisted of strapping them to a bed while they sweated and shook their way through withdrawal ("cold turkey" detoxification), followed by either short- or long-term efforts at counseling. No general rules governed how long the alcoholic patient stayed in the psychiatric hospital—some were released immediately after detoxification; sicker alcoholics sometimes stayed for months.

Because state-supported psychiatric hospitals were a favorite dumping ground for alcoholics, specialized wards were eventually established to house them. Private psychiatric hospitals also began to update their services and establish their own alcoholism "wards." These public and private alcoholism wards continue to be one of the major treatment options available to alcoholics.

In recent years, psychiatric treatment for alcoholism has become much more humane and specialized to the particular needs of the alcoholic. Today, many psychiatric programs offer the basic components available in specialized and hospital-based alcoholism units. The philosophical orientation in the psychiatric hospital, however, is geared to the psychological reasons why alcoholics drink, with heavy emphasis on psychoanalysis and psychotherapy. Even more dangerous is the regular and prolonged use of tranquilizers and sedatives at many of these psychiatric treatment facilities.

Costs for private treatment can be exorbitant, running as high as $10,000 for two to three weeks of treatment. Success rates tend to be very low (10 to 15 percent), but can vary dramatically from one hospital to the next.

Recommendations: The effectiveness of any treatment program depends to a large extent on what the patient learns about the nature of addiction to alcohol. Given the correct knowledge and insight, he will learn how to live with the addiction and protect himself from it. A program based in a psychiatric hospital is at high risk, obviously, for focusing attention on the emotional and psychological conflicts of the alcoholic rather than on the physical nature of the addiction. Psychoanalytical treatment not only confuses the issue, but confuses the patient, who ends up thinking that his psychological and emotional makeup is responsible for causing his disease.

The quality of a particular psychiatric program will depend on your doctor's training in alcoholism and how much of his psychological orientation he can suspend in order to truly support the disease concept of alcoholism. If you are considering a psychiatric hospital, we suggest a thorough interview with the treating physician in order to determine his or her specific theories about alcoholism and strategies for combating the addiction.

In addition, be sure to inquire about the use of drugs and the place and priority of psychoanalysis in treatment. It would be useless for you to try to modify treatment if drugs and psychoanalysis are routinely used. Instead, pursue other treatment options that are known to have better results in treating alcoholics.

In-Patient (Long-Term)

In the past, facilities for long-term treatment (several months to several years) provided shelter and minimal "treatment" for alcoholics who had nowhere else to go. Late-stage "skid row" alcoholics (also called the "public inebriate"), and alcoholics with illicit-drug addictions (heroin, morphine) were the most common patients in long-term facilities. Many of these alcoholics belong to a subculture for most of their adult lives and may never have learned (or may have completely forgotten) the skills necessary to living in society: skills as basic as shaking hands, using a knife and fork, driving a car, depositing money in a bank, or boiling water. Thus, "resocialization"—the process of teaching alcoholics attitudes and skills that help them to become accepted and accepting members of the community—has become an important feature of long-term programs.

Today, long-term treatment is considered a necessity for many alcoholics who have progressed into the later stages of their illness as well as for those alcoholics who have no family or emotional support network and who need ongoing protection and healing in a sheltered environment. The goal is to provide a protective environment, friendship, and support in recovery, eventually enabling the alcoholic to make a smooth return to community life. The general atmosphere is friendly and loving, with the residents helping in the day-to-day running of the home.

In general, long-term programs are less "intense" than short-term programs, with medical, psychological, and social expertise less immediately available. These programs are often called "halfway homes." Private long-term programs range from a fairly structured setting in a specialized center to apartment complexes where the landlady is a recovering alcoholic and cooks for the residents. State- or county-supported homes are often staffed with recovering alcoholics, and the ten to twenty residents help with cooking and other chores. Many of the residents work and pay for whatever they can. These are true "homes," with a low level of treatment and in-house AA meetings. The average length of stay is two to six months, but some alcoholics (those with chronic brain damage, for example) may stay permanently. Because of demand for beds, however, a permanent arrangement is often impossible, and the recovering alcoholic might be placed with a family member, friend, or other reliable person for ongoing "custodial" care.

Long-term recovery homes offer a supportive and protective environment for late-stage alcoholics suffering from physical deterioration or permanent brain damage and for alcoholics with other drug addictions. They are also an ideal choice for homeless alcoholics and alcoholics who shouldn't return home: battered wives (or battered adolescents), and spouses or children of drinking alcoholics. Alcoholics who live alone or in situations where their recovery may have difficulty getting established, such as near bars or in rooming houses with other alcoholics, can also benefit from the care and support found in long-term facilities.

Recommendations: Long-term programs are excellent choices for alcoholics who need additional help and support *after* they've been through intensive in-patient treatment. Of course, it's not

always possible for an alcoholic to go through in-patient treatment, due to the expense of such programs. But just because
that's the way things are doesn't mean that's the way they
should be. If federal and state governments were to support
in-patient treatment for those alcoholics who can't afford it on
their own, the eventual payback would far surpass the cost of
such treatment. Given effective and comprehensive treatment,
the majority of these higher-risk alcoholics can recover, returning to productive lives in the community and becoming responsible citizens and reliable taxpayers.

Out-Patient Rehabilitation

Out-patient treatment is, basically, ongoing counseling on an
hourly basis with the alcoholic usually reporting once a week
for an hour or two of counseling. Many areas provide community alcoholism centers (C.A.C.s), which are assisted by public
funds. In addition to education and counseling, referral is an
integral part of the out-patient service. The out-patient counselor will have on file a list of community resources including
physicians, counselors, ministers, and other helping professionals who are both knowledgeable about alcoholism and experienced in treating alcoholics. The counselor should also have a
well-used listing of AA and Al-Anon contacts and the places
and times of meetings.

   Out-patient clinics can also be part of an established alcoholism treatment center (residential treatment centers, psychiatric hospitals, or general hospitals), part of a private or community
mental health clinic (and thus not alcoholism-specific), housed
in a free-standing facility staffed by one or more alcoholism
counselors, or offered by independent therapists or counselors.
Out-patient programs are often publicly funded; private counseling can range anywhere from $10 to over $100 per hour for
private psychiatric counseling.

   Recommendations: For the middle- and late-stage alcoholic, out-patient counseling should, whenever possible, follow in-patient treatment and should not, by itself, be considered
adequate treatment. It is extremely difficult to get a recovery
program started on an out-patient basis because counseling a
sick alcoholic just won't work—he can't understand his predicament, the addiction is still in control, and the chances are

good that he will drink again. Another danger is that having tried counseling and failed, the alcoholic may convince himself that treatment in any form won't work for him. Thus, getting such a patient into a specialized in-patient treatment program may be more difficult after an abortive attempt at out-patient counseling.

It's not that middle- and late-stage alcoholics can't get sober in out-patient treatment, it's just that the odds are stacked much too heavily against them. The risks are too great, the personal costs too high, and the consequences of failure too devastating. As a follow-up to in-patient, intensive treatment, however, out-patient counseling can be an important benefit, particularly for the first two years of recovery. In fact, out-patient counseling should be offered by all in-patient treatment programs, as an essential and required part of the aftercare program. Counselors should be available to both alcoholics and their families to discuss anything from AA to nutritional therapy to marital problems.

Having commented on the limitations of out-patient treatment, we'd like to add a sort of "future note." Today, the majority of alcoholics in treatment are in the middle or late stages of their disease. Early-stage alcoholics are rarely diagnosed until their disease progresses to its more obvious and undeniable stages. In the near future, we believe this will change, and early-stage alcoholics will become a major part of the treatment population. Our optimism is based on exciting developments now taking place in research laboratories around the country. Laboratory tests capable of identifying alcoholics in the early stages of their disease are in the process of being developed. The actual test itself may be five or ten years away, but when developed and perfected, the impact of these tests on alcoholism treatment will be enormous. It will be possible to accurately and easily diagnose alcoholics in the early stages of their disease, before the addiction becomes overpowering. It may even be possible to diagnose alcoholics before they ever take a drink.

When this happens, out-patient counseling will become a viable treatment option by itself. The alcoholic may not require in-patient treatment if his addiction is weak and easily combated. Knowing that the disease is physiological—having the physical proof of a laboratory test—will knock denial out cold. Early diagnosis will allow early treatment. And early treatment will save thousands of lives.

How Many Paths to Recovery?

In this chapter a strong appeal has been made for a specific type of treatment. Serious deficiencies in many treatment programs now available to alcoholics have been cited. Many people will disagree with our recommendations and warnings. In general, their arguments can be summed up like this: "There's no one way to get well. Each person has individual and unique needs. Do what works for you."

The thinking behind this argument is that alcoholics can be separated into any number of groups—rich or poor; male or female; early, middle, or late stage; aggressive or timid; professional or blue collar—and that each of these different "types" of alcoholics may respond to treatment in different ways. Thus, a shy or introverted alcoholic may not do well in AA; a psychotic alcoholic may require intensive psychotherapy; a late-stage alcoholic may require three to four months of treatment, while an early-stage alcoholic may need only out-patient counseling; and so on.

All of this may be true, but it does not change the fact that the essentials of treatment must remain the same regardless of who the alcoholic is, how much money he makes, what his personality is, whether "he's" a man or a woman, or what color his skin happens to be. The essentials must remain the same because the disease is the same for each and every alcoholic. Alcoholism progresses in specific, identifiable stages. Some alcoholics are sicker than others, but they're simply in a later stage of the same illness. Their disease may take longer to heal, but its nature is exactly the same as the early-stage alcoholic's disease.

An alcoholic's "individual and unique needs" should be taken into account during treatment, but should not require a wholly separate type of treatment. Would a cancer victim be sent to a specific type of treatment center because she was divorced, or shy, or had emotional problems connected with her disease? Would a physician recommend that a diabetic receive psychotherapy instead of insulin shots because his moods fluctuated wildly? Would someone who had just had a massive heart attack receive the blessing of his physician if he decided to come in for weekly checkups rather than receive intensive and immediate treatment?

Alcoholics, like the victims of other diseases, are individuals, and individual problems may require special handling. These problems—financial, emotional, psychological, career, marriage, living skills—may require specific attention and understanding in treatment or referral to additional sources of help during the recovery period. (For more detailed information on this, see chapter 13.) Nevertheless, the general format and direction of treatment must be the same for all alcoholics. This format must be based on an understanding of the nature of addiction to alcohol and the proven techniques necessary to combat it.

In the next section, we'll give the details of these treatment techniques and explain how they can be used to weaken and eventually overpower the addiction.

PART TWO

Treatment

Most alcoholics enter treatment with a great deal of fear and trepidation. What's behind this fear? Why would someone be afraid of getting well? Wouldn't it be "normal" to want to recover from a disease that threatens to destroy your life and everything you love?

Let's get something straight right from the start. When alcoholics come into treatment, they are *not* normal. They may look normal, they may talk as if they're normal, they may even smell normal. But they're not normal. Inside that normal-looking body are millions of sick and dying cells. Inside that normal-looking head is an alcohol-poisoned brain that is incapable of thinking clearly or reacting rationally.

It takes *time* for the body and the brain to heal and become normal again. During that time, alcoholics are in a precarious position: they want to make decisions, to take care of themselves, but they are still sick and not yet capable of directing their own recovery. They need help, guidance, understanding, and expert care. Without help during this crucial healing period, they will invariably make the wrong decisions, and their disease will claim them back.

James R. Milam, Ph.D., alcoholism expert, author, and lecturer, tells a fable about caterpillars and butterflies that illustrates how crucial the concept of *time* is to successful recovery. Trying to teach a caterpillar how to fly, Milam says, is like trying to teach a sick alcoholic how to be a normal person. The caterpillar listens, he watches butterflies fly, maybe he's so enthusiastic that he even takes flight lessons. But when he tries to fly, no matter how hard he flaps his little legs, he'll crash. He's not ready. The physiological transformation that will allow him to fly has not yet taken place.

Milam's point is this: just as it's impossible for a caterpillar to fly until it goes through the necessary physical metamorphosis, so is it impossible for an alcoholic to think, act, or feel like a "normal" person until his body has had a chance to transform and recover. The word to remember is *transform,* not *reform.* You can't expect normal behavior from a sick person; you must wait for the necessary physical healing to take place. In time it will happen—just as it is natural for caterpillars to become butterflies, so it is natural for alcoholics to become normal, well adjusted, happy, productive people as physical recovery progresses.

But it does take time. For most alcoholics, it takes one to two weeks for the brain to clear and thinking to become even halfway rational. It may take another week for the brain to be able to accept and understand information. This timetable holds true even for early- and middle-stage alcoholics; late-stage alcoholics may need additional weeks or even months of healing before they can think straight, walk without stumbling, or look at people, see them clearly, and understand what they're talking about.

The time it takes for an alcoholic to "become normal" determines the sequence of events that occurs in treatment. Just as it would be useless, even catastrophic, to try to teach caterpillars how to fly, so it is an abortive, even dangerous exercise to attempt intensive counseling of alcoholics in the first weeks of treatment or to expect them to make normal decisions.

This is why in-patient treatment is so crucial for a sound and lasting recovery. An in-patient program of at least three weeks' duration will protect you from the weakening but often tenacious addiction. The controls are taken out of your hands until you are physically capable of taking them over for yourself. For the first week or two, you will be told when to eat, when to sleep, and when to get up in the morning. No one should try to counsel you during this early recovery period or dig out any deep-seated "psychological" problems. You won't be expected to understand everything that you hear in the lectures or read in books.

No one even expects you, in the beginning, to want to get well or to be enthusiastic about the treatment program. You don't have to want to be in treatment, you don't even have to believe you should be there. At first, all you have to do is *be there*.

In the first week or two of treatment, what you think doesn't really matter because your thinking is still manipulated by your addiction. Your body is sick, your brain is toxic, you don't really believe that you're an alcoholic, and, if you had the choice, you wouldn't be in treatment at all. But you don't have a choice. Your husband has threatened to divorce you if you don't get help. Your boss says he'll fire you. Your kids have had it. Your friends are no longer friendly.

For most of you, treatment is the only choice left (unless you consider drinking yourself to death a choice). Even so, you come into treatment thinking that "they" are all wrong—that you are not an alcoholic, that a mistake has been made. But right now there's nothing you can do about it. So you figure you'll sit tight, wait out these four weeks, and then get on with your life.

You may be furious. You may be embarrassed. You may want to cry. You may be determined to prove them all wrong. You may be convinced that you don't have a problem. You may look around you, turn up your nose, and say "I'm not like these people; I'm not a drunk."

None of this matters. What matters is that you are in treatment, and the process of recovery can begin. In the beginning, the only requirement is that you are there, in body if not in spirit. The spirit will come later.

CHAPTER 8

Getting There

Getting into treatment is the first and most important step. It sounds so easy—just walk through the door and ask for help. But for most alcoholics it's the hardest thing they've ever done. Asking for help may be seen as an admission of defeat—an admission that the alcoholic can't do it on his own and is therefore somehow weak and despicable. The alcoholic may fear what his friends will say—how can he face them again? And what about his career—now everyone will think he's a no-good drunk. And, underneath it all, he's scared to death about quitting drinking; he can't imagine how he will get through even a day without alcohol, let alone a lifetime.

Joan and Harold's situation is typical of the events leading up to admission into treatment and of the emotions accompanying those events. This process can be divided into five steps: the Last Straw; the Phone Call; the Confrontation; the Interview; and Admission.

The Last Straw

Joan had had it. That morning Harold rolled over in bed, moaning that he was too sick to go to work. "Call in for me," he groaned, "I just can't go in today."

It had happened a hundred times before, but this, she told herself, was the last time she would be part of it. Bills were piled high, pipes were leaking, the garbage disposal had quit working, and Harry, their son, had stormed off to school, still fuming about his dad's absence at the Friday night football game. Beer cans were strewn all over the bedroom floor, and the room reeked of urine because in the middle of the night Harold had wet the bed.

Joan stirred her coffee and tried to figure out what to do. A few months ago Harold had promised to do better. In fact, he went "on the wagon" for a few months, and, for a while, life was much better. But, as always, he had started drinking again. Still, he had kept his drinking under control, getting home on time, and not missing any work. But in the last month, life had really gotten rotten again, and Joan knew she couldn't go on this way and keep her sanity. She searched frantically through her purse to find the telephone number her friend Betty had given her six months ago. She'd kept it just in case she might need it. She needed it now.

The Phone Call

When Joan picked up the telephone she felt sick to her stomach from fear. Harold had warned her that he would have nothing to do with treatment. He didn't need it, he said; he could handle any problems on his own. Anyway, he went on, he certainly wasn't as bad as "those poor slobs who go in for the cure."

"Good morning, this is Maplewood Recovery Center. May I help you?"

"Yes." Joan was very nervous and had to fight the urge to hang up. "I'm calling about my husband."

"Are you inquiring about treatment for him?"

"Yes." Joan took a deep breath to steady her voice. "I think he needs some help. He's been drinking all weekend and can't get out of bed this morning to go to work."

"I'm sure we can help you and your husband. I'd like you to talk to Jim, one of our counselors. But before I transfer you, could I have your telephone number in case we get disconnected."

(The switchboard operator at the treatment center knew how crucial it was that this call was completed; she also knew that the caller might hang up or not follow through on the phone call. So, she asked for the telephone number so that a follow-up call could be made if, for any reason, the connection was broken.)

"Well, I guess so. It's 555-5873." Joan sounded nervous. "But you won't call here, will you? Harry would be furious with me. . . ."

"No, if you don't want us to. But is there another number where we could contact you?"

"Yes, my mother's house would be safe. Harold wouldn't set foot in her house. The number there is 555-4943."

"I have one more question—is your husband—could you tell me his name, please?"

"Harold. Harold Becker."

"Is Harold in any physical danger right now? Is he breathing okay? Is he able to talk to you and get out of bed?"

"He's okay, I think. He just says he's too sick to get up and wants me to call his boss and tell him he has the flu." Joan began to cry softly. "I just can't do it one more time."

"I understand. Hold on for just a moment, and Jim will talk to you."

"Hello, Mrs. Becker, this is Jim. I'm a counselor here at Maplewood. I understand you're calling about your husband, Harold, who appears to have a drinking problem. Is that right?"

"Yes."

"Are you free to answer a few questions right now so I can see how we can help you?"

"Yes."

"Is Harold home now?"

"Yes, but he's upstairs."

"Would he be upset with you if he knew you were making a call about his drinking?"

"Yes." Joan hesitated. "Well, I don't know. The way he's feeling this morning, I think maybe he'd welcome relief from anywhere."

"Do you think he might come down to the center to talk with us today if you asked him?"

"I don't think so. He's always refused to even talk about treatment."

"Well, it's important to act while the iron's hot, you might say. Would you be able to come down to the center today and talk, even if Harold won't?"

"I suppose so."

"Let me get some more information from you now, to get a better idea of your situation. How long have you been aware of Harold's drinking problems?"

"Well, he's been a heavy drinker for years—maybe ten years. But he seemed to handle it all right until this last year. He got really bad about six months ago and swore off it, but gradually he slipped right back into it. The past month he's been drinking as much as ever. He's missing a lot of work, and I'm afraid he's going to get into trouble soon if something doesn't happen."

"Where does he work?"

"At Clancey Motors, in the parts department."

"Has he had other medical problems that you know of?"

"Oh, his blood pressure is a little high, but nothing too bad. And his doctor mentioned something about wanting to do liver tests. . . ."

"Mrs. Becker, how old is Harold?"

"He'll be forty-four in three weeks."

"Does he have company insurance to cover health problems?"

"Yes, he has complete coverage."

"Do you know if his insurance policy covers alcoholism treatment?"

"No, I don't. I didn't even think about that." Joan started crying again. "How are we going to pay for this?"

"Most insurance policies cover alcoholism treatment. If you have an insurance card handy, I'll copy down the policy number and we can find out exactly what your coverage is.

Then we can discuss it further when you come in. Would it be convenient for you to drop by the center at two o'clock this afternoon?"

"Yes, I guess that would be okay. Do you want me to ask Harold to come, too?"

"Yes. It would be good to talk with him. It sounds like he might be willing to come with a little prodding. Just tell him you've really been concerned about him and decided to call and get some advice about how to help him. Tell him you have an appointment at two o'clock, and you want him to come along. By his agreement, you'll call his boss and tell him that Harold will be absent today and has a doctor's appointment. If Harold won't cooperate, then tell him he can call his boss himself and tell him whatever he wants to. Then, come on in yourself and we'll arrive at a plan of action to get Harold some help as soon as possible. I'm sure you have lots of questions that we can discuss later. But are you clear on what you should do right now?"

"Yes, I think so."

"Good. I'll see you at two o'clock. Also, you might pack a bag with overnight things in case we can get Harold into treatment right away. Good luck, and hang in there. We'll take it one step at a time."

The Confrontation

Persuading Harold to go into treatment, even just to talk, seemed to Joan an impossible task. But this time she wasn't going to nag. She didn't feel desperate; she felt strangely at peace, because she knew now that the "thinking" was over and finally she was "doing" something.

Before she walked into the bedroom to talk to Harold she took a few deep breaths. *You know,* she thought to herself, *I'm doing this as much for me as I am for him. I need help, too. If he refuses to go, there's nothing I can do for him. But I can do something for me.* That calmed her down, and she walked into the bedroom.

"Harold," she said to the crumpled figure on the bed, "we

have an appointment to talk to a counselor at the Maplewood Recovery Center at two o'clock this afternoon.''

"What are you talking about?'' Harold looked at her with bloodshot eyes. He looked, Joan thought, like an old man.

"I called the treatment center, and we're going down there this afternoon to talk to a counselor.''

"The hell we are.''

"I'm going whether you go with me or not.''

"What are you going to talk to this guy about?''

"How to help you. And how to help me.''

A minute went by, while Harold just stared, open-mouthed, at his wife. Then, to Joan's amazement, he started to cry.

"Will you come with me?'' she asked gently.

"No. I feel too bad. I can't even get out of bed.''

"I told him that you were sick. He wants you to come.''

"What else did you tell him?'' Harold asked miserably.

"I told him how bad things have gotten in the last few months. I told him that you tried to quit drinking six months ago and now you're drinking more than ever. I told him that you've been missing a lot of work lately, and I'm scared that you'll be fired. I told him that there are beer cans all over the house, and I can't take it anymore. I told him that I want you to be well again, to be yourself again.''

Harold started crying again. "Oh, my God, what am I going to do?''

"Come with me, Harold. I think they can help us.''

"What about work?''

"I'll call in for you and tell them that you have a doctor's appointment.''

"Joan, I just can't do this. I can't walk into a treatment center. I can't talk to some stranger. I promise I'll quit. I won't touch another drop.''

"No, Harold. I've heard those promises before. You can't quit by yourself. You've tried. We've got to get help. If you won't go with me, I'll go by myself. But you'll have to call into work, then. Tell them anything you want. But I won't cover for you anymore.''

The Interview

"Hello, my name is Jim. I'm a counselor here at the center. Harold, Joan, please have a seat." They all sat down. Harold, looking tense and shaky, sat on the edge of his chair, as if he might bolt at any minute. The tears of the morning were gone; Harold was obviously angry, uncomfortable, and hostile. He sat with his back to Joan and refused to shake Jim's hand.

"Joan called me this morning, Harold, because she's concerned about you and your drinking. I assume this has been a concern of yours, or you wouldn't be here. We only spoke briefly this morning, so it would be helpful if I could find out a little more about it. Harold, how long have you been aware that alcohol has been causing troubles for you?"

"It hasn't been so much a problem for me," Harold said bitterly, looking at Joan. "Just for her."

"Well, let's back up a little bit and see if alcohol is affecting you in ways that might be harmful to your health. Do you remember when you had your first drink?"

"Yeah, I was about sixteen."

"Was there anything particularly significant about that time?"

"No. I did it on a dare to see how much beer I could drink before I got sick or passed out."

"And how much was that?"

"Eight beers, I think."

"You mean, all at one time?"

"Yes."

"That's quite a bit of beer for a first-timer. Has anyone ever remarked on your ability to drink a lot?"

"Well, I don't usually drink the hard stuff. Just beer. But, yeah, I'm usually going strong while everyone else is hanging it up."

"At what age could you put away the most?"

"I suppose five years ago."

"And how much a day was that?"

"I don't drink during the day."

"Okay, during a twenty-four-hour period, how much beer could you put away if you really worked at it?"

"A few years ago I'd drink a case and a half, maybe two cases a day on the weekends."

"Did that interfere with your life in any way?"

"No."

"Did Joan complain about it at all?"

"Oh, she didn't like all the beer cans lying around."

"Was that all?"

"Well, she said I was loud and bossed her around a lot."

"Is that the way you usually act?"

"No," Harold said emphatically. "Usually she's the one who bosses me around. That's why I'm here today. She thinks she knows what's best, and she's always nagging at me. No wonder I drink so much."

"Has anyone else ever commented about your drinking?"

Harold was sullen. "My boss has called me on it a time or two."

"What happened there?"

"He just told me I'd better knock off the drinking, or he'd have to do something."

"Did he see you drinking, or what?"

"No, there were some guys behind the desk who reported me. I came in late a few times and missed some work. That's all. They probably drink more than I do."

"Have you ever just decided it wasn't worth all the hassle and tried to swear off it for a while?"

"Well, I like drinking, you know. It's just that everyone else bugs me about it. So I've tried to quit. But I guess I like it too much."

"For how long did you quit?"

"A couple of months."

"Do you mean that you went two months without any alcohol at all?"

"Well, no, I'd have a beer or two now and then, nothing regular."

"And then it built up to more and more, like every day?"

"Yeah, I guess so."

"Does that concern you?"

"She worries about it." Harold gestured at Joan but refused to look at her. "I don't."

"Do I understand you correctly, that at times you drink more than you intend to?"

"Well, I suppose so."

"When was the last time that happened to you?"

"I don't know. Well, I guess I got a little carried away this weekend. Got too excited about the Tigers . . . got carried away, you know."

"When was your last drink?"

"Last night about midnight."

"How much did you put away last night?"

Harold looked at Joan.

"Nineteen beers," she said. "I counted the empties."

"You don't look like you feel too well this afternoon," Jim said.

"No," Harold admitted. "I woke up sick to my stomach this morning. I feel pretty rotten."

"Has alcohol affected your health in any way?"

"No."

"Has your doctor ever commented about any liver problems?"

"No."

Joan interrupted. "On your last physical he said Harold showed a little change in his liver, um, hormones, is that what you call them?"

"Liver enzymes."

"Yes, that's the name."

"Did he have any advice for you, Harold?"

"He said I should cut back on my drinking or the liver tests might get worse."

"When you stop drinking, do you experience any ill effects?"

"What do you mean?"

"How do you feel when you stop drinking?"

"I feel better when I'm drinking, if that's what you mean."

"Have you ever had the DTs or seizures?"

Harold looked shocked. "No," he answered emphatically.

"Ever had any blackouts?"

"She says I can't remember some things sometimes, but I don't remember having any blackouts."

Jim was silent for a moment. Then he sat forward in his chair. "Harold, from the descriptions you've given me about what happens to you when you drink and what happens when you stop drinking, it's clear to me that alcohol is working on you in harmful ways. If you can look at it squarely, I think you'll see it, too. More than likely, you've known it for a long time, down deep inside. If you're like I was, it's just hard to face it.

"Five years ago, I had to come to grips with my alcoholism. It wasn't an easy thing. In fact, at the time, it seemed the hardest thing I had ever had to do. I fought it tooth and nail. But alcohol was tearing me up, and my family, too. I was on the brink of losing my job. In fact, it was my boss who finally pulled the rug out from underneath me. I either had to stop drinking, or I was fired. That got my attention. It sounds like you're getting to that point yourself. And let me assure you, it won't get any better. It's clear that you've tried to stop drinking—probably several times—and haven't succeeded in the long run.

"Alcohol works on you in ways that are not normal. You drink more than you intend to; you've developed a tolerance, sort of an immunity, to alcohol, where you need more and more. You kick yourself for promising your wife that you'll stop after just a few drinks, then you guzzle down a whole case of beer. Alcohol is robbing you of your best—you know it—and pretty soon it will be clear to others around you, besides your wife.

"Alcoholism is a disease; there are new and effective approaches to its treatment, and you don't have to scrape the bottom before you can do something about it. We've seen thousands of people, just like you and me, find help through effective treatment. This morning Joan and I discussed the possibility of your coming into the treatment center and getting started on your program of recovery. We've already checked out your insurance, and you have eighty percent coverage. Joan tells me you still have two weeks' sick leave. This, plus two weeks of vacation, will give you enough time to complete the program without cutting into your pay.

"Joan is behind you all the way, and so are we; there isn't a reason in the world why you can't come in right now, today. Let's go and walk through the unit; the patients are listening to a lecture right now, but in five or ten minutes someone will be around to tell you how it was for them. Joan will go down to the business office to get things underway there."

Admission

Harold looked slightly bewildered, but he didn't object. Jim could tell that Harold was nervous and was doing his best to keep all the pieces together, to stay in control. Gently, he guided Harold around the treatment center, introducing him to staff members, describing the various facilities, and telling him a little about the daily routine. Then he asked Harold to fill out some admission papers.

Harold felt bamboozled: how in the world had it gotten this far? But he saw no way out. What was he going to do, walk home? Joan had the car keys, this guy Jim was standing over him all the time, he needed a drink but he'd left his wallet at home. So Harold signed the papers. *I'll sign this stuff,* he thought. *It'll keep Joan off my back for a while.*

After Harold signed the admission forms, Jim took him to his assigned room. Harold looked around and felt strangely comforted. There were flowers on the bedside table, a view from the window, and regular beds rather than the hospital beds he'd always imagined in places like this. From his room, he could see patients walking around in regular clothes, not hospital gowns. And they weren't zombies at all—they were laughing, talking, even telling jokes!

Then Jim explained to Harold that he would have to go through the bag Joan had packed. "We have to make sure that there's nothing in here that will be harmful to anyone in the center," Jim said as he sifted through Harold's things. Jim held up some shaving cream, aftershave, and a razor. "These could all be dangerous. The lotion and aftershave both contain alcohol—patients have been known to drink this stuff. We'll keep these things at the counseling center, and you can ask for them when you need them. You can start to unpack your things if you want," Jim said, putting a hand on Harold's shoulder. "I'll be right back."

When Jim left, Harold sat down on his bed and ran his hands through his hair. He wanted to run, or to wake up and find out that it was all a bad dream. *What happened to put me in here, in an alcoholism ward?* he wondered. *What's my boss going to say? What about my friends? Why did I let Joan talk me into this?*

Jim knocked on Harold's door and introduced Patrick, an "old-timer" who had been in treatment for three weeks.

"Bet you feel a little overwhelmed," Patrick said. "I know how I felt my first day."

The two men talked for three hours. That night Harold cried himself to sleep. He wasn't sure if they were tears of joy, or fear, or failure; but he felt oddly elated. This was the first time he had cried in many, many years.

CHAPTER 9

Detoxification

"We're going to take you to detox now," the nurse said, gently leading George, age 47, along the treatment-center corridor.

"Where you takin' me?" George asked suspiciously.

"To the detoxification ward," the nurse replied calmly.

"Detoxification!" George stopped dead in his tracks and frantically began pulling his arm away from the nurse. "What the devil is that?"

Of all the parts of treatment that cause alcoholics anxiety, detoxification seems to be the scariest of all. The word is linked, in many minds, to an agonizing, humiliating, and harrowing drying-out. They fear, consciously or subconsciously, such events as being strapped to a stainless steel table, left alone in a dark room, poked and prodded at by unsmiling nurses, and injected with sedatives to make them zombielike.

Alcoholics being treated today in modern, specialized facilities have nothing to fear from "detox." The drying-out process should not be threatening, painful, or traumatic. Years ago, however, things were very different—drying out *was* agonizing and, in far too many cases, death-dealing. Just thirty or forty years ago, doctors and alcoholism researchers believed that the alcoholic withdrawal syndrome was psychological—all in the alcoholic's mind. Alcoholics were considered crazy people, but somehow worse than crazy because their insanity was self-induced. Tremors and shakes were thought to be a mental and emotional reaction to being without alcohol. Alcoholic patients were viewed as nervous, irritable, and temperamental. They were treated (when they could find treatment) with disgust and disdain. In fact, most general hospitals refused to care for alcoholics at all, carting them off instead to state-supported psychiatric institutions.

Given the obvious and profound physical symptoms associated with withdrawal from alcohol (see pp. 125–129 for a complete description of the stages of withdrawal), this treatment seems incredible. But so fierce was the prejudice against alcoholics and so deeply imbedded the belief that they were somehow moral and spiritual degenerates that even the obvious was misunderstood and ascribed to character defects or psychological breakdown.

Before describing detoxification as it is now, it's important to describe how it used to be. Perhaps you've heard some stories about detox—and they may be true, detail by unforgivable detail—but things have changed drastically in alcoholism treatment. The following passage describes the way it *was*, not the way it is now. Why dwell on the past? Because it's important to exorcise any lingering demons, by looking straight and square at the way it used to be, not so very long ago.

It's also important for you to know that alcoholism wards still exist where alcoholics are made to feel that their personality or character is a cause of their disease, where staff members are clinical, crude, and disdainful of their patients, and where fear and dread accompany each withdrawal tremor. Such treatment is as unforgivable as Don Birnam's experiences, described in the 1944 novel *The Lost Weekend*, by Charles Jackson, in an alcoholic ward of a New York City hospital.

It was a long, high-ceilinged room with a concrete floor bare of anything but beds, most of them so low they

were little more than pallets. Only three or four were of
normal height, and these were boarded up at the sides like
babies' cribs. The idea, he supposed, was to keep you
from falling out; or, in the case of the low beds, from
hurting yourself if you did fall.

On the mattress next to his, a man who looked like
some kind of crank messiah (but only because of the gaunt
and hollow face) lay staring at the ceiling. He had a three-
or four-days' growth of beard, his cheeks were sunken, his
eyes large and sad. His white legs stuck out below the
pathetically short gown like a cadaver in the morgue. He
might have been dead, but that his entire frame—all over,
all of it at once—quivered. It shook with tiny tremors,
regular, precise, constant, as if a fine motor operated
somewhere beneath him, in the mattress itself.

Farther off, a middle-aged Negro babbled God knows
what at the top of his lungs, and no one paid enough
notice to find out what he was complaining about. In the
bed across the way another Negro got up on his knees,
lifted his gown, and urinated on the floor. No one seemed
to notice or mind that, either, least of all the intelligent-
looking man who leaned against the wall a few feet away
in a stiff faded robe held together by a safety-pin, looking
about as casually as he could and being very careful to
avoid every returning glance. . . . Other men in faded
robes or short gowns open at the back moved restlessly up
and down the aisle or went in and out of the two rooms at
the end where most of the shouting seemed to be coming
from. There was a strong smell of disinfectant and dirty
feet.

Worse, perhaps, than the stench, the lack of supervision,
and the seedy and desolate atmosphere of the ward is the way
the alcoholics were treated by the staff: clinically, detached, as
if they weren't people at all. In the following passage a doctor
and his visitor tour the ward and stop by the bedside of the
patient next to Birnam:

The doctor pointed out first one patient and then another, not troubling to lower his voice. "Now that one
over there—" And even as the alarmed patient began to
respond in excited fearful apprehension, the two men slowly
turned their backs and began to regard and discuss another.
They might have been visiting a picture-gallery or admiring
impersonally the various blooms and plants in a hothouse.

They came forward and stood between his mattress and the one next to it. "Now this fellow"—indicating the staring messiah—"came in last night. He says he'd had only one glass of beer."

As the gaunt skinny man awoke to the fact that he was under study, the invisible motor somewhere within the mattress speeded up at once, accelerating the tremors that rippled throughout the whole body. Sweat began to stand out above the apprehensive eager eyes, eager to please, eager to prove he was master of himself. The sweat broke and ran down his face as the doctor addressed him. . . .

"You can see," the doctor said, "how he's beginning to perspire. The whole bed will be soaked in a minute or two. That's because we're talking to him, of course. And notice the feet and legs—well, the whole body, for that matter. The tremors are getting worse. He'll be shaking himself right off that mattress onto the floor if we stand here long enough. It's the effect of the concentration, plus self-consciousness. If we turned our backs, the shaking would die down very quickly."

The patient watched and listened with passionate anxious concern, hanging on every word, and the tremors quickened even more as the doctor addressed him again. . . . The shaking had become violent now. The hands and arms pumped up and down, the legs danced like a puppet's, the entire trunk jumped and bounced on the bed.

The two men watched this in silence for a moment, regarding the struggle almost without interest. . . .

"Doctor! Doctor!" the patient called out. "Won't you give me something?"

"No no, not now. You can have all you want of those things in the hall. They're in the jar on the desk. Go help yourself. You know where they are. Take as many as you like."

"What does he want?" the man in the business-suit said.

"Medication. A sedative. I tell him he can help himself to the salt-tablets. We encourage that as much as possible. No sedatives in the daytime. We try to maintain or restore the normal sleep-cycle, you see—make them stay awake during the day. Put them to sleep now and they'll be raising hell all night."

Then and Now

It used to be thought that if the alcoholic suffered through the hell of withdrawal without any drugs or medical help, without even the tender solicitations of a kindly nurse or doctor, then perhaps he would think twice about drinking and suffering again. Alcoholics were treated like naughty children, their crime a mighty one considering its devastating effects on sanity, family, and life itself, and their punishment, also mighty, self-inflicted. It was believed that they did this to themselves: their misery, however real and profound, was *of their own choosing*. So, in the age-old tradition of strict discipline for bad behavior, the punishment—suffering the shakes and the sweats, the cravings and the visions without help—was thought to fit the crime of overindulgence and self-abuse. You got what you asked for.

The last thirty years of research and clinical work with alcoholics have proved beyond any doubt that alcoholism is a physical disease, which the alcoholic cannot control by force of will or strength of character. But the pernicious belief that alcoholics somehow "choose" their fate hangs on. Everyone reading this book must, in truth, admit to some remnant of this belief: perhaps you see a wino panhandling on your way to work and, without even thinking about it, turn away in disgust; or you remain convinced that if it hadn't been for your domineering mother or your absent father or your good-for-nothing husband, *you* never would have started drinking so much; or you take sedatives or tranquilizers, believing that your problem is really tension and stress; or you refuse to forgive your father because when he should have been loving and caring for you, he was caressing and jealously protecting his bottle.

It goes on and on—the anger, the resentments, the inability to forgive—and it all relates to that deeply and seemingly endlessly rooted belief that alcoholics are alcoholics *because they choose to be*. "If they would only take a good look at themselves!" "If he'd just put the bottle down!" "If I were really a good and decent human being, I would have quit long ago!"

While these mistaken beliefs are deeply knotted into the average person's conception of alcoholism and alcoholics, they have absolutely no place in treatment. You will undoubtedly encounter prejudice against alcoholics in your dealings with friends, business associates, even your relatives. But you should not have to deal with it in your treatment. What you learn in treatment will protect you in your life of sobriety; if what you learn is moth-eaten by prejudice and misconception, your entire sobriety could be threatened.

"The way it is now" is not necessarily the best it can or will be. Prejudice is a stupid and stubborn beast. But treatment has come a long way from Don Birnam's living nightmare in *The Lost Weekend*. And with vigilance from all of us who care for and love alcoholics, no alcoholic need ever endure such supervised hell again.

The Beginning of Recovery

Recovery begins with abstinence, but, as one alcoholic put it, "If that's part of getting well, I'd rather die first." It is one of the bizarre facts of this bizarre disease that the torture is not in drinking but in *not* drinking. So it's no wonder that alcoholics are filled with fear and apprehension when they hear the word *detoxification*. They've tried quitting time and time again, and always they fled back to alcohol, their medicine, the tried and true cure for their suffering. What, the alcoholic wonders, can a treatment center do to make quitting easier? And how long can the hours without alcohol be endured?

Don Birnam's "morning after" ordeal will ring true for every alcoholic:

> He died a thousand deaths—aaah! Worse by far than a thousand, it was *one* death drawn out in endless torture, a death that didn't die. You kept on dying, and dying; you died all day and all night; and still there was dying yet to do, and more dying ahead—it simply did not end and would never end. It was more than the human heart could bear, or the brain: it was conscious insanity—any moment now his brain would burst with terror and he would go mad. But it didn't burst, he didn't go blessedly mad, he crouched there raw and alive, his eyes staring to see if the familiar room would go blank in breakdown, his ears straining to hear the first crack or rattle of total collapse.

You will not experience such suffering in modern-day alcoholism treatment facilities. One of the purposes of detoxification, which is the process by which your body is allowed to dry out and become accustomed to living without alcohol, is to help you through withdrawal with as little pain and discomfort as possible. The other major goals of this first part of the recovery period are: (1) to prevent the progression from early withdrawal to the more serious withdrawal stages; (2) to prepare the alcoholic for abstinence without dependence on other drugs; and (3) to correct underlying medical problems and nutritional deficiencies.

In general, the more you drink and the longer you've been drinking, the more severe your withdrawal syndrome will be and the more intensive medical attention you will require in the first days of treatment. If you drank seven or eight beers a night and binged on weekends, your withdrawal syndrome will, in general, be less intense than if you've been drinking a quart of whiskey day in and day out for six months prior to treatment. But other factors figure into the severity of the withdrawal syndrome, including how much and what you normally eat in a day and when you ate your last meal; what prescription medications and illicit drugs you take; other health problems or diseases you might have; previous history of delirium tremens or seizures; infections, head injuries, and other traumas.

Every alcoholic comes into treatment with a specific history and special problems of his own. Nevertheless, alcoholism makes all of its victims act in stereotypical ways. The disease creates its own particular set of symptoms, which progress from the early to the middle and late stages. Thus, it is possible to talk about a "typical" middle-stage alcoholic coming into treatment and describe a typical treatment during detoxification. Later in this chapter, the less common, later-stage withdrawal events (including seizures, hallucinations, and delirium tremens) will be described.

The Typical Patient

The "typical" patient enters treatment on his own two feet. He's probably been drinking within twenty-four to forty-eight hours of admission, but he's not stumbling drunk or unpleasant. He doesn't smell bad, his beard is shaved, he probably even brushed his teeth just before he came into the treatment center.

But if you lean close, you can smell alcohol on his breath. His responses to questions are slightly "off." He may talk loudly, or he may be withdrawn and uncommunicative. He's fuzzy on exact dates, and he gets irritable if he's asked too many questions. When questioned about his alcohol history, he becomes defensive.

He looks around him somewhat fearfully. He's suspicious of just about everyone he sees, but he seems comforted by seeing patients walking around freely and seemingly content. He also seems happy to discover that there are no steel bars on the windows and that the staff members don't carry nightsticks.

Soon after the admission papers are signed, this typical patient will be seen by an admitting counselor, nurse, or staff physician.* The treatment staff will assess the patient's medical history and physical condition, looking for signs or symptoms that would indicate a potentially difficult withdrawal, including:

- elevated blood pressure or pulse
- previous history of seizures or delirium tremens
- history of heavy drinking (a fifth of whiskey a day, for example) over a long period of time
- regular use of sedatives, tranquilizers, or illicit drugs
- pronounced and obvious malnutrition
- liver disease or other diseases or disorders (pancreatitis, gastritis, ulcers, bleeding or hemorrhaging, etc.)
- recent major injuries or surgeries

When asking questions, staff members will be aware that the alcoholic is still under the influence of his disease and that his answers may not be totally accurate. Thus, the treatment staff should routinely review family members' histories and the patient's past medical records. All of this information will give a pretty good idea what to expect during withdrawal, and the staff can then draw up an individualized treatment plan. In

*If the treatment facility provides medical detoxification services, the patient will be assessed by a nurse upon admission and within twenty-four hours by the attending physician. In facilities without medical services, the patient will be "screened" at entry and referred for necessary medical evaluation and treatment.

general, treatment during the detoxification period, which lasts
one to ten days, consists of three crucial elements (the three
S's):

1. Secure environment
2. Sedation
3. Supplements

Secure environment. Alcoholics in withdrawal have a frazzled and hypersensitive nervous system. Their bodies need
alcohol to function properly—this is the nature of the addiction—
and every cell will cry out and complain when alcohol is
withdrawn. A calm, controlled environment with trained and
knowledgeable staff who have a secure hold on the situation
and continually relay their caring, compassion, and competence to the patient helps tremendously in calming the agitated
patient and taking the "edge" off the withdrawal experience.

Think back to the description of the alcoholism ward at the
beginning of this chapter, and the "staring messiah" who sweated
and shook uncontrollably when threatened by the doctor's
questions. The physical experience of withdrawal is influenced
dramatically by emotional and psychological distress. This is
not to imply that withdrawal is, at bottom, a psychological
experience—it is a true physiological response to the lack of
alcohol in a system that has been accustomed to it. But physical symptoms can be provoked by emotional stress and psychological tension. A feeling of warmth and security, of love
and caring, on the other hand, can make physical pain easier
to manage and endure.

Sedation. Patients are given sedatives for two major reasons: (1) to prevent the progression of the withdrawal syndrome
by replacing alcohol with steadily decreasing amounts of sedatives or tranquilizers; and (2) to calm the anxious, hallucinating, or delirious patient. In some treatment centers, sedatives
are used routinely for every patient, while in other centers only
the sickest patients are sedated.

Using sedatives, some people believe, conflicts with one of
the goals of the detoxification period: to prepare the alcoholic
for abstinence without dependence on any kind of drug. Another argument against sedation is that it can lengthen the
period required for detoxification and interfere with the patient's alertness and early participation in treatment (this is

particularly a problem if the treatment program is restricted to less than two weeks). Finally, because sedatives and tranquilizers are pharmacologically similar to alcohol, there is always a danger of addiction if the sedatives are continued for more than a few days.

Yet, the benefits of using sedatives, particularly for symptomatic middle- and late-stage alcoholics, far outweigh the risks. Sedation calms the patient and dramatically reduces fear and suspicion. Sedated patients are much less likely to leave "AMA" (against medical advice) in the early days of treatment. Sedation prevents the withdrawal syndrome from progressing into the later withdrawal stages of seizures, hallucinations, and DTs. If carefully controlled, the risk of addiction is negligible. Finally, very few patients are sedated to the point where they can't think straight or begin participating in treatment—and patients who need heavy sedation are generally sick enough that they should remain in treatment an extra week or two.

Nevertheless, sedation should be viewed as a temporary help through the first days of withdrawal and should not be approached as a universal answer to problem patients. Each patient should be carefully evaluated for sedative needs: early-stage alcoholics may require little or no sedation; middle-stage alcoholics with no history of seizure disorders or DTs may need sedatives for only a day or two; and late-stage alcoholics or drug-dependent individuals may require slow sedation withdrawal for a week or longer.

A final note: every patient should be told exactly why he is being given sedatives, why sedation is continued for only a few days (usually not for more than three or four days), and why the use of any kind of mood-altering, central nervous system drug after the initial detoxification period must be strictly avoided. There should be no doubt left in the alcoholic's mind that sedative drugs, after the initial detoxification period, are not only dangerous but potentially lethal.

Supplements. Alcoholics are malnourished. That's a fact, and there are numerous causes. When you drink a lot you tend to neglect nutritious food, concentrating instead on snacks and fast or frozen foods. Stomach and intestinal upsets such as nausea, vomiting, diarrhea, and stomach pain from ulcers, gastritis, pancreatitis, or a swollen liver will destroy your appetite for food and tend to make you vomit any food that is eaten.

Furthermore, chronic and continuous use of alcohol produces changes in the digestive system that interfere with the absorption and use of nutrients in the body. So, even if you do eat, you're not going to get the full benefit of the nutrients.

How long and how much you've been drinking will influence how malnourished you will be. Early-stage alcoholics may have only marginal nutritional deficiencies and experience minor symptoms such as lack of energy, insomnia, and nervousness. Middle-stage alcoholics tend to have more pronounced nutritional problems, including behavioral symptoms such as irritability, depression, anxiety, loss of appetite, weight loss, and a decreased ability to fight infections. Late-stage "skid row" alcoholics who have been drinking heavily for years frequently suffer from severe malnutrition and may develop some of the classic deficiency diseases such as scurvy, pellagra, or beriberi, or nutritional disorders of the nervous system such as polyneuropathy, Wernicke's encephalopathy, or Korsakoff's psychosis.*

During the detoxification period, substantial doses of vitamins and minerals are needed to speed the healing process and combat the effects of malnutrition. For the "typical" middle-stage patient, a daily dosage schedule† would include:

1. multivitamin and mineral (such as Theragran M, Centrum A-Z, or Myadec)
2. B-complex (25–50 mg supplement)
3. vitamin C (1–2 grams)
4. calcium (500–1000 mg)
5. magnesium (250–500 mg)

Sicker patients might require additional B-vitamins, including injectable B_1, increased amounts of pantothenic acid and folic acid, and additional vitamin C.

Nutritional supplements should be continued on a permanent basis, but at lower dosages, for all recovering alcoholics. As a general rule of thumb, we recommend daily use of (1) a complete multivitamin that includes a broad spectrum of vitamins and minerals, and (2) 500–1000 mg of vitamin C. In addition, a

*These are nervous system disorders influenced by B-vitamin deficiencies, including symptoms of numbness and tingling in the extremities (polyneuropathy) and, in Wernicke's and Korsakoff's diseases, symptoms of confusion, disorientation, memory loss, and agitation.

†These dosages should be administered only under medical supervision.

standard B-vitamin-25 supplement, 500 mg of calcium and 250 mg of magnesium may be beneficial for the first three to four months of recovery.

For specific details about nutrition and nutritional supplements, we refer the reader to *Eating Right to Live Sober,* by Katherine Ketcham and L. Ann Mueller, M.D. (Seattle: Madrona Publishers, 1983; also available in paperback from New American Library), particularly chapters 8, 9, and 10.

The Stages of Withdrawal

The withdrawal syndrome progresses through four stages, with each successive stage more severe than the previous one. Many alcoholics, particularly early-stage alcoholics, will experience only Stage One symptoms; middle- and late-stage alcoholics typically progress into Stage Two. Only a small percentage of treated alcoholics will experience the more serious and life-threatening symptoms of Stages Three and Four.

The care you receive during the first day or two of your treatment will have a profound effect on both your subjective experience of withdrawal (how agitated, anxious, or frightened you might be) and the progression of withdrawal from one stage to the next. An estimated 5 to 15 percent of *untreated* alcoholics will have seizures (Stage Three) and as many as 8 percent of *untreated* alcoholics will go into full-fledged delirium tremens. With proper care and treatment—sedation, a secure environment, and nutritional supplementation—these numbers can be reduced to less than 1 percent. Furthermore, with adequate treatment, these patients will be easier to control and less agitated and frightened by the experience.

Stage One Withdrawal

Symptoms. Tremulousness; nervousness; anxiety; loss of appetite; nausea; vomiting; insomnia; sleep disturbances (increased awakenings; vivid dreaming; nightmares); abnormally rapid heart rate; high blood pressure; profuse perspiration; diarrhea; fever; hand tremors; unsteady gait; difficulty concentrating; tendency to startle easily; craving for alcohol and/or sedatives.

Time duration. Symptoms begin six to eight hours after the last drink and resolve, for most patients, in twenty-four hours.

Incidence. Early-stage alcoholics may experience little or no distress when they stop drinking. Middle- and late-stage alcoholics will predictably suffer from several or even all of these symptoms. Approximately 20 to 30 percent of patients admitted to treatment units require sedative intervention for withdrawal symptoms and signs. Almost all of those alcoholics who have been drinking an equivalent of one pint to a fifth of whiskey per day for four to six weeks prior to admission will manifest withdrawal signs and symptoms.

Treatment. (1) Well-lit room; (2) frequent observation; (3) frequent assurances and staff contact; (4) nutritional therapy (supplements and diet); (5) sedation for more agitated or distressed patients.

Stage Two Withdrawal

Symptoms. Stage One symptoms increase in severity. Heartbeat continues to be abnormally fast and respiration becomes rapid, with quick, shallow breathing. Shakes develop into a sustained tremor. Twenty-five percent of alcoholics in Stage Two withdrawal develop auditory or visual hallucinations (seeing or hearing things that aren't there). Auditory hallucinations are particularly anxiety-producing; visual hallucinations are usually less threatening.

Time duration. Stage Two symptoms usually appear within the first twenty-four hours after the patient stops drinking or reduces alcohol intake and last for two to four days. (It seems odd, but a reduction in alcohol intake with a consequent fall in blood alcohol level can lead to withdrawal symptoms. Thus, the withdrawal syndrome can actually begin when the alcoholic is still drinking.) In some cases, however, Stage Two symptoms can take up to six to eight days to develop. This is especially true for patients whose alcoholism is complicated by regular use of other sedative-type drugs.

Incidence. In a treatment setting, less than 5 percent of patients will progress to Stage Two (increased blood pressure, pulse, and sustained tremor).

Treatment. Stage One treatment is continued, with more frequent observation and medical attention. Sedation may need to be increased or changed to a different kind.

Stage Three Withdrawal

Symptoms. Onset of seizures. These are major motor seizures, resembling grand mal convulsions, although generally without loss of bowel or bladder control. Attacks may be single or multiple, but rarely will a properly sedated patient experience additional seizures.

Time duration. Over 90 percent of seizures occur within seven to forty-eight hours after the patient stops drinking or reduces intake.

Incidence. Five to 15 percent of untreated patients will experience seizures. If seizures are left untreated, 30 to 40 percent of patients will develop DTs, some immediately after the seizure and others anywhere from twelve hours to five days after the seizure. Seizures can be prevented by adequate sedation, which is why it is so crucial to find out which patients are at risk. Alcoholics who have experienced either alcohol withdrawal seizures or other seizure disorders are at high risk, as are patients who have been drinking heavily (a pint to a fifth of whiskey daily) for a long period of time. Sustained tremors are another warning sign. Patients with marked nutritional deficiencies and general physical deterioration are also at higher risk for seizures.

Treatment. Once a patient experiences a seizure, treatment should include (1) constant medical supervision and (2) sedation to arrest seizures and calm the patient. With proper sedation, further seizures can be prevented. Adequate sedation will also prevent most seizure victims from progressing into the last, life-threatening stage of withdrawal: the DTs.

Stage Four Withdrawal

Symptoms. Stage Four is characterized by the development of delirium tremens (DTs). DTs is a true medical emergency with a mortality rate of 10 to 20 percent. The cause of death is not always clear, but death is sometimes preceded by uncontrolled seizures; respiratory insufficiency; irregular heartbeat or heart failure; dehydration; electrolyte* disturbance; and/or hyper-

*Sodium, potassium, magnesium, chloride, and phosphate are the chief electrolytes in the body. These minerals play an essential role in the workings of the cells and in maintaining fluid balance and a normal acid-base balance. Magnesium and potassium levels are particularly subject to imbalance when a patient is in DTs.

thermia (high fever). The mortality rate is greatest for patients with high fever, abnormal heartbeat, dehydration, and associated illnesses such as pneumonia, pancreatitis, hepatitis, etc.

Symptoms of delirium tremens include (1) *extreme autonomic hyperactivity* or hypersensitivity (The autonomic nervous system controls blood pressure, pulse, temperature, sweating response, and muscle tone and tremor, and helps govern adrenaline activity. The patient in DTs has an overactive and hyperresponsive system, leading to marked and sustained tremors, profuse sweating, rapid heartbeat, high fever, extreme anxiety and fear, insomnia, and agitation); (2) *perceptual disorders* (illusions and hallucinations); and (3) *global confusion* (disorientation to time, place, and people).

Time duration. DTs usually begins between the third and the fifth day of withdrawal but may begin as late as the tenth to twelfth day. For 15 percent of alcoholics who develop DTs, the delirium resolves in twenty-four hours; for 80 percent, in less than three days. The disorder can continue for as long as seven to fourteen days. The longer DTs continues, the more life-threatening the condition becomes.

Incidence. Less than 8 percent for untreated alcoholics and less than 1 percent for alcoholics who receive prompt and adequate treatment.

Treatment. Once begun, delirium tremens cannot be reversed and must run its course. It is crucial, then, to prevent the disorder if at all possible, with sedation, proper treatment, and medical supervision.

Once a patient is in DTs, however, much can be done to control the intensity of the disorder and to reassure, comfort, and protect the alcoholic from harming himself or others. Treatment should include (1) a well-lit and quiet room; (2) constant attendance and observation by staff, with frequent vital signs (temperature, blood pressure, pulse rate, respiration) taken; (3) continual attempts to orient, reassure, and comfort the patient; (4) gentle physical restraint to protect the patient from harming himself or others; (5) physical examination to detect and treat other medical complications; (6) IV fluid replacement including high-potency B-vitamins and injectable magnesium (particularly important for malnourished patients with vomiting and diarrhea); and (7) adequate sedation to keep the patient calm and manageable. Patients with DTs sometimes require high doses of intravenous sedatives such as Valium or Librium.

The Detox Ward

Most alcoholism treatment programs separate the "detox" ward from the "rehabilitation" ward for the following reasons:

Economic. Because of staffing and medical costs, detoxification can be very expensive. With a separate ward set aside specifically for detox, the treatment center can sometimes receive additional compensation from insurance companies to pay for these costly medical services.

Functional. Patients in withdrawal are sicker than patients who have been in treatment for several days or weeks, and a separate detox ward allows the medical staff to concentrate their attention where it is most needed. Grouping patients in withdrawal together also makes it easier to take and record vital signs, administer medicines, and ensure adequate and prompt attention.

Environment. Sick alcoholics need a quieter environment with more control from the staff. Patients in the later phases of treatment are more stable physically, more active, and prone to loud joking, laughing, and backslapping—behaviors that may be both physically and emotionally distressing for a patient in withdrawal. Furthermore, a specialized ward firmly establishes the message that "you are sick and in need of medical attention." This message lays down a line of defense against the alcoholic's innate denial that "I'm not an alcoholic," or "I'm not as bad off as these other creeps." The medical activity of taking blood pressure and temperatures also gives a subtle message about the chain of command, letting the alcoholic know exactly who is in charge.

In most centers, the patients are kept on the detox ward for the duration of time that they are on sedative medication and/or physically unable to participate in the program activities. Different centers have different philosophies regarding whether the detox patient should participate in lectures, therapy groups, and AA meetings. A general rule is that patients can (and should) participate when they are physically able to, even if they are on medication. This establishes right off that patients are expected to take part in all treatment activities and takes away the patient's option of deciding whether he "wants" to participate.

In the first week or two of treatment, what a patient "wants" to do may not be what is best for him. The treatment staff, right from the beginning, should let the patient know that they are in control and will guide him through these early stages of recovery. The addiction, as we will discover in the next chapter, is cunning, clever, and capable of controlling the alcoholic's behavior without his being aware of it. Detoxification only begins the process of bringing that addiction under control; the battle has really just begun.

Taking Control of the Addiction

The second stage of treatment, like the first stage, begins immediately after the alcoholic enters treatment. This entire stage can be characterized as a battle, with the treatment staff ganging up against the addiction. And it's a battle with very high stakes. If the staff doesn't succeed in separating the alcoholic from the addiction—if the addiction is allowed to stay in control—the alcoholic will be lost to treatment and will sooner or later drink again.

Sometimes the battle is over quickly; sometimes, as with Sandy, the fight is hard won.

> Sandy was 31 when she came in to treatment, and she was livid. Her boss was "a mean son of a bitch" who forced her to come to treatment, and she was determined not to stay in "this trumped-up prison."
>
> When the staff withheld the antidepressants she'd been

taking for more than five years, she went over the edge, screaming that she couldn't live without them and would simply walk out the door if she didn't get them back. She refused to get out of bed in the morning because, she said, she was too depressed. The food, she raved on, was horrible; she wouldn't feed it to her dog. She had an appointment to have her hair styled the next week, and she was going, she didn't care what the staff said, nobody was going to stop her.

The staff saw through every one of Sandy's complaints and refused to give in. The addiction, they realized, was asserting itself; deprived of alcohol and drugs, it was fighting back with everything it had. The battle for control had begun with a vengeance.

The staff's strategy was to explain to Sandy, firmly and authoritatively, exactly what the principles of recovery were at the treatment center. The staff physician sat down with Sandy and explained that continuous use of sedatives, tranquilizers, and antidepressants was strictly prohibited because of their addictive qualities; that attendance at daily scheduled activities was required; and that she would be given no passes for at least two weeks. He discussed her alcohol and drug history and ended by saying, "There is only one way to start unraveling the numerous knots in your life, and that is to get you free from the controls of your addiction. We must separate you from what is taking your life slowly but surely. If you could have done it on your own, you would have; I'm sure you don't like the way things are going in your life. But you didn't because you couldn't; you needed help in fighting this addiction. That's why you're here."

Sandy's addiction counterattacked. "I've been to specialists," she said, "who have better credentials than you have, and they say my problem is depression and that I must be on medication. This center is a sham," she continued. "It's not what I thought it would be at all. The floors are dirty, the food is awful, the nurses and counselors are incompetent. I want out."

The staff continued to fight back with a firm and steady approach, telling Sandy over and over again that her addiction was attempting to take control, and they couldn't allow that. She would simply have to let them guide her until she and her addiction were "separated" and she could make rational decisions on her own.

But Sandy held fast; her addiction, fed by her long use of both alcohol and prescription drugs, was firmly entrenched and continued to manipulate her thoughts, emotions, and behavior. She refused to sign a consent form that would allow the staff to talk to her former doctors. She threatened to sue the treatment center. She stayed in bed until 10:00 A.M. She wouldn't eat. She disrupted lectures by talking loudly and refusing to stay seated.

After three days of constant skirmishes, Sandy's employer was called in. Coached by the staff, he laid it all out for Sandy: if she left treatment, he'd had it with her and nothing she could do would make him change his mind. Sandy's husband was also asked to talk with her, and he, too, reinforced the staff's decisions.

On the fifth day of her treatment, Sandy was sullen, but she went to the morning lecture. She started eating more, although she continued to complain about the "starchy" food. In the second week, she began to open up to her counseling group and talked about getting hooked on prescription drugs. She was sleeping better and no longer suffering from the constant nightmares that had plagued her in the first week of treatment.

On the thirteenth day of treatment, Sandy broke down and cried, hugging her counselor. "I've been so scared," she sobbed. "Do you really think you can help me?"

The Master Manipulator

In the first days of treatment, the addiction *is* the alcoholic—it manipulates what the alcoholic says and does, controlling her thoughts and behavior. The addiction is a master puppeteer, pulling the alcoholic's strings while making it appear that the alcoholic is, in fact, in control.

Sandy had to be separated from this overpowering addiction. In a sense, she had to be "jailed" for the first two weeks of treatment, with no chance of parole. All escape routes were slammed shut by the staff, who formed an ironclad fence around her, protecting her from the addiction. If there had been any holes in the fence—if Sandy had been allowed to continue taking prescription drugs; if she had successfully manipulated the staff to feel sorry for her and allow her to stay in bed or change her diet; if she had been permitted to leave the center to have her hair done—the addiction's power would have solidified, threatening Sandy's chances of recovery.

The most devastating mistake that can be made in the early days of treatment is to assume that the alcoholic is, in fact, in control and can be trusted to act in her own best interests. She cannot. The addiction is too strong, the alcoholic too weakened by her disease, and recovery may be destroyed.

As can be seen from Sandy's treatment, separating the alcoholic from the addiction requires several critical skills:

Firmness, steadiness of purpose, and *a posture of authority.* The purpose of this stage is to isolate the addiction and render it powerless, and the staff must not be swayed from this goal. Staff members must treat the alcoholic firmly but gently, refusing to give the addiction any ground. Patients' pleas, tears, and threats must be understood as the expressions of a struggling addiction.

X-ray vision. Every member of the staff must be able to "see through" the alcoholic, understanding that she is being controlled by something that she can neither recognize nor understand at this point in treatment, and that her actions, her thoughts, and even her feelings are not truly her own, but are expressions of an active and powerful addiction.

Sometimes it's easy to recognize the addiction; sometimes, however, the addiction hides itself with masterful ease and even the well-trained professional can be fooled. It doesn't take x-ray vision, for example, to recognize the addiction in the 250-pound lumberjack who picked up a fire extinguisher and threatened everyone who came near him. (A staff nurse who had been working with alcoholics for fifteen years walked up to this patient and in a steady, firm voice said, "Give it to me," at which point the lumberjack did so, literally, spraying chemical foam from her head to her toes and then letting loose on the nurses' station and everyone else standing around.)

But it does take special vision to see the subtle signs of addiction in patients who seem to be adjusting well and who are not openly rebellious. The alcoholic's behavior may appear to be normal when in fact the addiction is still pulling the strings. Forty-year-old Elizabeth, for example, convinced her counselor that she absolutely had to attend her daughter's piano recital. "We've had a difficult time lately," she explained, "and my daughter would never forgive me if I missed her recital. It's so terribly important to me," she pleaded. The counselor, reasoning that a good relationship with her daughter was essential to Elizabeth's recovery, gave her a pass for the evening. But Elizabeth never made it to the recital—she stopped at the first bar she saw to have "just one" and stayed until she passed out.

Recognizing the Addiction

The staff must not be taken in by the addiction's cunning. It helps if staff members can use their imaginations, thinking of the addiction as *alive,* which indeed it is, just as a cancer victim's tumor is alive. While it can't be felt, x-rayed, or surgically removed, the addiction does show itself in a number of ways, affecting the way the alcoholic looks, the way she talks, and the way she behaves.

The Faces of Addiction

The alcoholic's expressions and demeanor are often a mirror of the strength of the addiction and can alert the staff to keep up their guard. Some of the "faces" of addiction include:

• *Boredom.* A bored patient—one who shows no interest in the lectures, who forms no friendships or allegiances with other patients, who yawns and fidgets during discussions—is probably still under the power of the addiction. Boredom, in most cases, is a cover for an addiction that refuses to allow its victims to think seriously about sobriety.

• *Arrogance, cockiness, superiority, and aloofness.* The patient who feels that she is above it all—who looks down on the other patients as somehow "beneath" her, who claims that she's not as bad off as the other patients, or who sets herself apart from the others—hasn't accepted the fact that alcoholism has no sexual, racial, or class barriers. She hasn't, in other words, accepted the fact that she is an alcoholic. An alive and strong addiction should be suspected as preventing this acceptance.

The Speech of Addiction

The staff must listen to the alcoholic and learn to "hear" the whisperings of the addiction in what she says. Certain standard sayings or ways of talking can be a clue to whether the addiction is still in control. For example:

• *The Nitpicker.* "This is a terrible program"; "The staff aren't trained"; "This is just a bunch of brainwashing"; "The food here is horrible."

• *The know-it-all.* "I don't know why they keep repeating this stuff, it's so obvious"; "These people don't have anything to teach me"; "I could give these lectures myself."

• *The independent.* "I came in of my own accord, I can leave of my own accord"; "You can't keep me here"; "If I want to go, I'll go, and you can't stop me"; "If I don't get my way, I'll sue you."

• *The "gotta go."* "I gotta go feed my cat, no one knows about her, she hasn't eaten in three days"; "I gotta go take care of my sick wife, she'll be in real trouble without me"; "I gotta go clean my house, it's a mess, and the refrigerator repair man is coming next week"; "I gotta go get my hair done, I can't go one more day looking like this."

• *The helper.* This can be any number of types: the motherly type focusing on "poor Jimmy's family problems" in group but denying any serious problems of her own; the doctor or dentist in treatment who is constantly giving advice while refusing to accept his own role as someone in need of help; the self-proclaimed "counselor" who directs attention away from himself by trying to solve everyone else's problems.

The Behavior of Addiction

How the alcoholic acts and feels should be carefully watched for signs of the addiction attempting to reassert its control. Common behaviors seen in patients with a struggling and still active addiction include:

• *Feelings of being caged or in jail.* These are common complaints of patients in the first days of treatment and indicate a strong need to drink and thus an active addiction. The alcoholic says she misses her independence, but, in fact, her addiction is calling out for its regular alcohol feedings.

• *Mood swings, depression, anxiety, nervousness, insomnia,* and *paranoia.* These are all fairly common complaints in the first weeks of treatment and are caused by two related factors: central nervous system damage and the "protracted withdrawal syndrome." The central nervous system (the brain, spinal cord, and branching nerves) is the body area most severely affected by progressive use of alcohol and drugs. Healing takes time. The initial withdrawal—including shakes, sweats, tremors, and changes in blood pressure and pulse—is a vivid sign of an acutely disturbed brain and body system. These symptoms typically require up to a week to stabilize.

The protracted withdrawal syndrome is a continuation of the central nervous system distress and shows up in persistent symptoms of depression, nervousness, anxiety, irritability, and insomnia. In most patients, these complaints ease up in the first weeks of abstinence, medical attention, and comprehensive nutritional therapy.

Some patients, however, need more time to heal because the addiction is so firmly entrenched and takes longer to subdue. These patients typically include late-stage alcoholics with a long and hard drinking history; alcoholics with medical complications such as heart and liver disease; patients who are addicted to other drugs, either prescription or illicit; and alcoholics who have severe, long-term nutritional deficiencies.

Subduing the Addiction

In order to subdue the addiction, the body must heal; for proper healing to occur, three essentials must be emphasized from the very beginning of treatment. These three essentials can be remembered by the acronym TNT: *T*ough love, *N*utritional repair, and *T*otal abstinence.

Tough love. Technical competence from the staff isn't enough; alcoholics must receive love, understanding, patience, and persistence, in an overall atmosphere of optimism and hope.

No matter how sick they might be, alcoholics can feel it when someone cares about them and truly understands their disease. They also know when someone thinks they're "that

kind of person": a drunk, a bum, a degenerate, an obnoxious
SOB (there are lots more labels, but you alcoholics know them
well enough). Even in withdrawal, alcoholics are extraordinarily sensitive to the way they're being handled. A nurse or a
counselor who believes, consciously or subconsciously, that
alcoholics are somehow responsible for their illness or who
loses patience when alcoholics become belligerent or defensive will only feed into their denial system, triggering more
anger and resistance and making recovery more difficult.

If the alcoholic perceives that his caretakers have little
empathy for him or his complaints, he will feel confused,
lonely, and misunderstood. If he senses that someone on the
staff thinks he's lacking in self-control or that he's just a depressed, unhappy, and difficult person to handle, then he will
feel guilt, shame, and despair. All these emotions will corrode
his potential recovery.

Caring, compassion, and concern will go a long way toward breaking down the alcoholic's resistance and renewing
his sense of himself and his self-worth. But this caring comes
with strings attached. It is not the soft, passive "I'll stand by
you even if you drink yourself to death," or the "I'll take care
of you no matter what" kind of love, but "tough love"—the
kind of caring that says "I love you; you're sick and need help;
I'll do whatever it takes to see you through treatment."

Tough love means refusing to coddle, cover up, or make
excuses for an alcoholic who won't commit himself to the
recovery program; treating the recovering alcoholic as a human
being who can make decisions, admit mistakes, and heal his
own wounds; allowing him to look at the painful consequences
of his disease; and trusting him to work through his guilt and
his grief.

Tough love is caring enough about the alcoholic to help
him understand that he must take responsibility for his recovery
and, ultimately, for his life. Tough love offers him the privilege
of that responsibility.

Nutritional repair. Most middle- and late-stage alcoholics
have been "eating" alcohol for years, meaning that alcohol is
no longer just a beverage but the main (and in the late stage,
often the only) course. Alcohol is a food in the sense that it
contains calories, but in terms of nutrition, it's a total bust—
you'd have to drink forty quarts of beer or two hundred quarts

of wine just to meet your daily nutritional requirements for vitamin B_1! But that's not all: the body has to use up valuable nutrients to process alcohol; alcohol interferes with the stomach's ability to absorb and use nutrients, and alcoholism directly affects those organs—the digestive tract, liver, pancreas, adrenal glands, and the brain—that are involved in the processing, use, and storage of nutrients.

If you're an alcoholic, then, you're going to be malnourished to one degree or another, and even marginal nutritional deficiencies can affect the way you feel and your ability to stay sober. You don't have to have pellagra, scurvy, or beriberi to suffer from the effects of malnutrition. The most common symptoms of marginal nutritional deficiencies are precisely those that plague many alcoholics in early withdrawal and sometimes weeks or months into sobriety: depression, irritability, mental confusion, memory loss, mood swings, nervousness, anxiety, inability to concentrate, insomnia, lethargy, and fatigue.

An often overlooked but valuable "treatment" for these lingering problems is to straighten out your nutrition. While it takes some planning and commitment, excellent returns come from:

1. Eating three good meals a day. "Good" means nutritious, which means a diet rich in natural, whole, unprocessed, and unrefined foods balanced in fat, and wholesome vegetables, grains, fruits, and protein.

2. Eating three nutritious snacks—midmorning, afternoon, and evening—every day. Snacks are important because they keep the blood sugar on an even keel, which keeps energy high and improves the brain's functioning.

3. Eliminating caffeine from your diet, which means cutting out caffeinated coffee, teas, and cola beverages. Caffeine is a powerful stimulant capable of upsetting blood sugar control, causing restlessness, irritability, insomnia, and headaches, and aggravating stomach disorders.

4. Cutting out all sweets from your diet, including table sugar, desserts, candy, and sugar-sweetened drinks. Sugar can stress the weakened organs involved in controlling and regulating blood sugar and contribute to depression, fatigue, anxiety, mood swings, and so on.

Total abstinence. Think of recovery as a building and abstinence as its foundation. Without abstinence, the entire structure will collapse. Abstinence must come first, before anything else is attempted. You can't productively counsel a drinking alcoholic or an alcoholic in withdrawal; he'll shake his head, try to look serious, and not hear a word you say. (The best you can do is make him feel guilty about drinking.) You won't be able to cram facts into his head, because his head isn't working right, and the facts will just get chewed up in the confusion of his brain. You can't try to make him understand his disease if he's still drinking, because he'll deny it or cover it up, lie about it, or blame it on you. You can't pump good food into a drinking alcoholic and expect to make him better, nor can you start him on the road to recovery by having him swim twenty laps a day or jog ten miles. All the nutrition, all the counseling, all the facts, all the exercise and fresh air will collapse into the sink hole of the disease—because the alcoholic is still drinking.

Alcoholics cannot drink if they hope to recover from their disease, nor can they take central nervous system (CNS) drugs such as tranquilizers, sedatives, and certain painkillers. Being addicted to alcohol, which is a CNS drug, the alcoholic will soon also be affected by other CNS drugs that he takes. This is a process called *cross-addiction,* which means an alcoholic can substitute one drug (like Librium or Valium) for alcohol, with similar effects upon his nervous system. Tolerance to one CNS drug means tolerance to the other CNS drugs (cross-tolerance), and severe withdrawal can occur when the drugs are stopped.

A sober alcoholic who regularly takes tranquilizers, sedatives, or painkillers is in danger of becoming addicted to them and in serious danger of reawakening his alcohol addiction. Given the choice between alcohol and pills, the alcoholic inevitably chooses alcohol. It works fast, and it works miracles. Every alcoholic knows that, and the memory can be rekindled by using CNS drugs even after ten months or ten years of sobriety.

Tranquilizers and sedatives are often used in treatment in the early days of recovery to lessen the severity of the more dangerous and life-threatening withdrawal symptoms, but after that they *must not* be prescribed for or used by alcoholics, even if the alcoholic has been sober for years. If these drugs cannot be avoided, as in surgery or major trauma, the alcoholic must recognize the dangers and make plans with her doctor and family to protect herself following the use of these drugs. (Suggestions for this protective plan can be found in appendix 6).

Abstinence from alcohol and other CNS drugs is the cement that walls off the disease and allows the process of controlling the addiction to begin. This cement usually takes a few weeks to harden, and in that time the addiction will try to break out of its new cage. Everyone caring for the alcoholic must respect the power and cunning of this addiction.

The first few days of abstinence are the toughest, in one sense, because the addiction is still strong and powerful and the alcoholic is sick and shaky. But in another sense, everyone is prepared for the fight and knows what to expect. Days or weeks later, when the addiction appears to be weak and quiet, the alcoholic and the staff can be caught off guard, as in the case of Elizabeth described on p. 143. This is why it's so crucial to have *time* in treatment, first to let the cement of abstinence harden, and then to build, step by step, a protective system that is strong and solid and able to withstand any and all threats, internal or external, to the alcoholic's sobriety.

Keeping the Real Enemy in Mind

With these three TNT essentials—*tough love, nutritional repair*, and *total abstinence*—the addiction's power will gradually weaken as the alcoholic's body and brain heal and grow strong. During this healing process, it's essential to keep in mind that the staff is fighting the *addiction*, not the patient, and that the nature of the addiction is essentially the same for every patient.

It's also important to remember that alcoholics who appear to be in control and having an easy time of it are not necessarily those who will have a rapid and complete recovery. In fact, the subtle signs of the addiction's attempts to reassert its control are perhaps even more dangerous than the obvious signs, because they can go unheeded. The lumberjack with the fire extinguisher was quickly wrestled to the ground and subdued; the staff kept a close eye on him and after a week he was, in the words of the nurse he sprayed with chemical foam, "as gentle as a 250-pound lamb." Elizabeth, on the other hand, appeared to be completely in control: she looked healthy, she ate well, her speech was clear and intelligible, her thinking "rational." A trained and skilled nurse believed that Elizabeth was well on the way to recovery. Such is the addiction's cunning.

For most patients, the addiction will lose its strength dramatically in the first few days of abstinence, and then its power will slowly diminish over the next few weeks. The staff's protective control can be loosened gradually, and most patients are able to recognize the signs of the addiction and begin asserting their own control after a week to ten days in treatment. Isolating and protecting alcoholics from their addiction, however strong or weak it appears to be, is a necessary and crucial foundation for the next stages of recovery, in which the alcoholic is slowly given back her independence and taught how to protect herself against the addiction.

CHAPTER 11

Breaking Through Denial

If the theme song of alcoholism is progression, denial is its recurring note. All alcoholics experience denial, and the sicker they are, the more vehemently they will deny their disease. Of all the confusing aspects of alcoholism, this is the most confusing of all—why would a person deny he was deathly sick and repeatedly refuse help? To everyone else, the alcoholic's denials seem to prove that he is deceitful, stubborn, belligerent, and psychologically unbalanced, with a death wish so strong that there's little or nothing anyone can do to help him.

Why Deny?

There is reason to the madness of denial. Denial is actually common to all chronic, devastating diseases. Cancer victims deny that they are sick by pursuing any number of unproven treatments in an effort to get well, switching doctors, seeking new opinions, or discontinuing treatment—all in the hope of discovering that they are not really victims of this dread disease or that they will suddenly, miraculously be cured.

Heart attack victims deny their disease by going right back to high-stress jobs, loading their food with salt or butter, or shrugging off others' concerns with statements like "Now that they fixed it, my heart's as good as new." Diabetics deny their disease by cheating on their diet and eating sweets on the sly. People with pains in their chest who ignore them and hope they go away, who cough up blood and keep it a secret, who put up with excruciating pain and refuse to see a doctor to discover the cause, are denying that they are sick and need help.

Denial is an inborn, automatic protective system that shields us from the emotional trauma of being sick, debilitated, or somehow "abnormal." Denial is a way of masking fear and handling stress by pretending that the disease is not there or that it is not *that* serious, or by hoping that it will simply go away.

The disease of alcoholism, however, has its own special set of denials, and the nature of these denials changes as the disease progresses. Early-stage alcoholics deny their disease for the same reasons that their families don't see it and their doctors don't comment on it—they look healthy, they act "normal," they're not sick or crazy or out of control or passed out in a gutter. How, then, could they be alcoholic?

Before someone comes down with obvious symptoms of the flu, the virus incubates for a few days. The victim will eventually get sick, but at this stage he doesn't feel sick, and he has no obvious symptoms. Suppose a conscientious physician conducted some tests and discovered the virus. If he tells his seemingly healthy patient that he's got the flu, he'll be in for a lot of head shaking and denials like "How can I be sick when I feel fine?" "What kind of a quack are you?" or even "You think I'm paying for this visit, you're crazy!"

People who get the flu, however, don't have to deal with labels like "drunk," "bum," or "degenerate." People with the flu are just sick. People with alcoholism have some extra garbage to carry around with them. The label "alcoholic" is synonymous, for most people, with "lacking in willpower," "screwed up," and "hopeless." Who in his right mind is going to admit to being a voluntary derelict and degenerate? Alcoholics, of course, aren't in their right mind (the addiction having taken it over), so they continue to deny their disease long after it becomes obvious to everyone else.

Denial is simply a symptom of alcoholism, just as vomiting is a symptom of the flu. The sicker the flu victim, the higher his fever and the more he'll vomit. The sicker the alcoholic, the louder and stronger his denial. This is because the brain—the center of judgment, perception, memory, and behavior—is hard hit by alcohol, with numerous chemical and electrical signals misfiring or missing connections. The alcoholic literally cannot "see" his disease, because his brain is not working right. Thus, his denial is not a lie, based on an attempt to deceive, but a misperception, based on his physical inability to accurately comprehend his condition.

Denial is, in fact, the addiction talking. When you hear an alcoholic denying that he's sick, insisting that he can control his drinking, or blaming his problems on stress, tension, unhappiness, or loneliness, you're hearing the addiction. In the early stage of the disease, denial is only a whisper; in the middle stage, it's a barely controlled conversation; in the late stage, it is a demented, persistent scream. As the disease steadily progresses, perception is distorted, memory is fogged, emotions are way out of whack, and the entire system of rational thought and perception short-circuits.

In trying to understand the alcoholic's denial, it's crucial to keep these two aspects in mind: the psychological process, common to all chronic diseases, of using denial to handle stress, mask fear, and protect against emotional trauma; and the physical changes in the brain, caused by long exposure to large doses of alcohol, that inevitably destroy the alcoholic's ability to "see" the disease that is so obvious to everyone else.

Lillian

The first thing the doctor noticed about Lillian was her smell—she reeked of urine. When he examined her, he discovered that her buttocks and inner thighs were raw and bleeding. Her underclothes were soaked with urine, and even her dress was stained.

"You're having problems with bladder control, Lillian," he said calmly.

Lillian shook her head and looked confused.

"You haven't noticed any problems?"

"No," she answered.

The doctor consulted his notes. "Lillian, your daughter tells me you've been drinking too much. You've been calling her at three in the morning, drunk. She found you passed out on the bathroom floor yesterday. And your garbage can was stuffed full with wine bottles."

"That's all a lie," Lillian said, getting angry. "I never call her in the night, and I've never passed out."

"We want you to get well. I'm going to admit you to the hospital treatment center today."

"Treatment for what?" Lillian asked suspiciously.

"For alcoholism," the doctor said.

"I don't need treatment!" Lillian was incensed. "You can't keep me here. I don't need your help." She got out of her chair, took a few steps, stumbled, and fell flat on her face.

The doctor picked her up and gently smoothed her dress.

"Get your hands off me!" Lillian shrieked. "You're the one with the problem; you wait and see, I'll sue you for this. Who told you you could examine me?" Lillian was trying to open the office door and began kicking at it. The door opened, and she stumbled into the waiting room. Seeing her daughter, she lurched toward her.

"You always hated me," Lillian screamed at her daughter. "How could you do this to me?"

"Mother, you're sick," her anguished daughter cried. "You need help." Lillian started laughing hysterically and then began sobbing.

"You hate me!" Lillian cried.

"Mother, I love you."

"Lies, it's all lies," Lillian shouted over her shoulder as the doctor and a nurse guided her into the hospital.

Four weeks later, a different Lillian sat in the same chair in the doctor's office. She talked quietly about her disease, how well she felt, and how grateful she was to her daughter and to the doctor for getting her into treatment.

"Lillian," the doctor said, "do you remember our meeting here four weeks ago?"

"Not much," she said. Then she smiled and added, "But enough."

"Do you remember denying that you had a drinking problem?"

Lillian hesitated before answering. "You know, I really don't think that I knew I had a problem. That sounds crazy, but I have no recollection of drinking anything before I came here, although you said I was drunk. I never knew I'd lost control of my bladder. I believe you now when you tell me I did, but I didn't know it then, at least not in the sense that I know and understand things now. I don't remember the early morning phone calls to my daughter, and I can't recall passing out on the floor. I think I was just too sick to realize what had happened to me. I just didn't know how bad it was."

Breaking Through to Reality

It's no use attacking denial when the alcoholic is still sick, because denial is a symptom of the sickness—as long as he's sick, he'll deny that he's sick. Around and around it goes, with the spouse or the doctor or the parent trying to make the alcoholic admit that he has a problem and needs help, and the alcoholic continually and vehemently denying it.

A mistake often made in treatment is the attempt to get the alcoholic to "see" his predicament when he's still toxic or in the later stages of withdrawal. The fact is that he can't see anything until his addiction is manageable and under control and his body has begun to heal.

When the alcoholic drinks, his denial is a thick wall that is extremely difficult to penetrate. The more he drinks, the stronger and more impenetrable this wall becomes. In treatment, the goal is to weaken the wall and let the outside light shine through so that the alcoholic can begin to see his real enemy. Then he can be taught how to take his own wrecking ball to the remains of denial.

Abstinence is the first step toward this goal. The alive and raging addiction erects the fortress of denial, and only by attacking and weakening the addiction, through abstinence, can the walls come tumbling down. But time, persistence, and a thorough understanding of the disease are also essential. The walls of denial can quickly be built up again, even if the alcoholic is sober, if he is somehow mishandled or misunderstood.

Tom

One week into treatment, Tom's counselor confronted him. "You're being stubborn, Tom, you're not cooperating with us."

I don't feel good, Tom thought, *my head throbs, my hands shake, I'm depressed, and my nerves are on edge.* But he said, "Well, what do you want from me, anyway? I'm here, aren't I? So fix me!"

"We want you to act like a grownup and stop playing games."

Games? Tom thought. *My wife's left me, my house is for sale, I don't have a job anymore, and nothing in my life makes sense.* But he said, "You think I'm playing games? What about you guys with your rational emotive therapy garbage, your AA lingo, and your vitamin and mineral malarkey. You tell me who's playing games!"

Tom stomped back to his room and slammed the door. He was shaking with anger and frustration. *I hate this place,* he thought. *I hate these counselors. I don't belong here.* Deep down, he felt a sense of guilt and failure: here he was screwing everything up again. He wanted to cry, but at the same time he was terrified that he'd break down in front of his counselor.

As the days went by, Tom began to think that he'd never get better. He was just a drunk, a selfish bastard

whom no one liked. Tom's "stinkin' thinkin'," as AA members so succinctly put it, began to generalize to everything else. *This treatment center is like a jail,* Tom thought, *and the staff treat me like I'm a criminal. The counselors are idiots. The other alcoholics are Goody Two-shoes and Caspar Milquetoasts. The whole rotten mess stinks. I'm gonna show them I can do it on my own.*
Tom left treatment the next day.

Tom's defensive walls, which were only partially disassembled when the counselor confronted him, were built up quickly, choking off the real world and making a nice, snug, dark place for the addiction to come back, nestle in, and grow strong again. Tom's defenses were actually anticipating the return of the addiction—they were preparing him to drink again.

The treatment staff must be able to recognize the symptoms of a still-active addiction—stubbornness, belligerence, mood swings, violent or aggressive behavior—and "nip them in the butt," as one patient aptly put it. These are not expressions of the alcoholic's personality, but warning signs that the addiction is still alive and kicking. In the first two weeks of treatment, denial is to be expected. But as the days go by, the alcoholic's denials should weaken and go through a sort of evolutionary process, from the angry and belligerent "I'm not an alcoholic," to the sullen "I'm not as bad as the rest of these drunks," to the reluctant "I've got a problem, but maybe I can control it myself," and, finally, to the initially faltering but nevertheless clear admission that "I'm Tom, and I'm an alcoholic."

The Addiction Talking

Ongoing denial can be heard in these statements:
• "I can't handle my roommate anymore, she's dirty, she smells, she snores at night, and she's got the shakes." *Translation:* "She looks like an alcoholic; I'm not like her. I can't relate to her."
• "AA meetings don't do anything for me." *Translation:* "I don't really need them anyway; I'm not a drunk like the rest of these creeps."

- "I'm too shy for this AA business." *Translation:* "I'm not ready to admit that I need help."
- "This counseling session isn't getting me anywhere." *Translation:* "I don't belong here."
- "I've been here a week already, and I'm ready to leave." *Translation:* "I don't need any more of this stuff, I'm cured."
- "I miss my coffee and doughnuts, and anyway, what's wrong with white bread?" *Translation:* "This nutrition stuff isn't really all that important, and anyway I'm young and healthy and don't need it. Those late-stage types are the ones who have to watch their diet, not me."

Each of the above statements shows a half-hearted acceptance of the disease. The speaker is balking, in one way or another, against the treatment regime and the general principles set forth by the staff and considered necessary for permanent recovery. These patients are giving lip service to treatment and blaming their basic nonacceptance on any number of people or things: the staff, the food, the other patients, AA, etc. Such a patient has *submitted* to the treatment program but hasn't yet *surrendered* to it. This inability to surrender is a sign that the brain and body are not completely healed. As a result, the alcoholic is unable to completely understand or embrace the concepts of treatment.

When the alcoholic is finally capable of accepting his disease, he will at the same time renunciate denial. With acceptance comes an almost visible *surrender,* a giving up of tension, strain, and conflict. Anyone who has witnessed it, knows that the alcoholic who surrenders to his disease looks and seems at peace. He is quiet in his actions, cooperative, and receptive. He can laugh at himself, he can cry with the other patients. He feels joy in the world, and at times he feels fear, but he has confidence that he can do what must be done to stay sober. Harry Tiebout, M.D., an expert on the concept of surrender in alcoholism, writes:

> After an act of surrender, the individual reports a sense of unity, of ended struggles, of no longer divided inner counsel. He knows the meaning of inner wholeness and, what is more, he knows from immediate experience the feeling of being wholehearted about anything. He recognizes for

the first time how insincere his previous protestations actually were. ("Surrender Versus Compliance in Therapy," *QJSA* 14, no. 1 [March 1953] pp. 58–68.)

Surrender doesn't mean that the alcoholic becomes an emotional dud, that all his personal fire and individuality are erased. Surrender simply means that the alcoholic sees his disease, realizes the depth of his predicament, and determines to do whatever he must to recover. This is not a weakening but a strengthening of the individual, and it is wholly essential if the alcoholic is to stay sober.

How Does Surrender Come About?

In the first week or two of treatment, as we've said, most alcoholics are not yet physically or emotionally capable of surrender and will hold part of themselves back from treatment. It takes time for the brain to heal, for the alcoholic to relax, make friends, and open up to strangers. He may be feeling the lingering effects of withdrawal, or he may simply be afraid to trust these strangers with his future. He may also be unwilling, usually at a subconscious level, to admit that he is powerless over alcohol and can never drink again. The label "alcoholic" scares him and turns him off. He doesn't want to be an alcoholic, and he doesn't feel he deserves this disease, either. He wants to be "normal," like everyone else.

All these emotions and thoughts are natural, but they should pass after a few weeks of treatment. If the alcoholic continues to be defensive and hostile—outwardly complying with the program by following the rules and attending daily functions but inwardly rebelling by acting in disruptive or inconsiderate ways, refusing to attend AA meetings or actively participate in treatment functions—a different approach may be required.

For some alcoholics, the walls of denial are thicker and take more time and energy to dismantle. Late-stage alcoholics frequently have a tougher time breaking down denial because their brains are still poisoned, even after weeks of abstinence, and withdrawal symptoms may be persistent and disturbing. All that may be required is time: time to allow the continued healing of the brain and nervous system. Remember: if the brain is still sick, the alcoholic can't be expected to accept and control his disease, because he can't yet understand what it is.

Polydrug users are also characteristically sicker than the alcoholic who is addicted only to alcohol, their withdrawal symptoms are more severe, their defenses are buttressed by two addictions, and, their denials are often more tenacious. These patients typically require extra time, patience, and careful handling. (See chapter 13, which describes the treatment needs of these and other "special" alcoholics.)

Denial is a common and expected stronghold of the addiction. The more firmly entrenched the addiction, the stronger the fortress of denial. But with effective treatment and a firm understanding of the disease, denial will cease to be an active part of the alcoholic's thoughts by the end of three to four weeks of in-patient treatment.

For the rare alcoholic with a particularly fierce addiction, who remains resistant to treatment and is unable to surrender to the recovery process, special measures may be needed to break down the remaining walls of denial. For these alcoholics, a mini-intervention, following the same rules and procedures described in chapter 6, can be arranged at the treatment center. The patient's employer, spouse, girlfriend, boyfriend, children, parents, or close friends—whoever has the most emotional "pull" with the patient—can be brought in to talk to the alcoholic and calmly but forcibly present him with the facts of his disease.

Any intervention should be carefully worked out with a counselor beforehand, with the specific facts of the disease and its impact on the alcoholic's life spelled out. The consequences of the alcoholic's leaving treatment or starting to drink again must be decided on, with a firm commitment to enforce them. The alcoholic's boss, for example, might say, "If you leave treatment, Ted, your job won't be waiting for you"; or the alcoholic's spouse might say, "I'm not going to argue with you. I mean what I say: If you don't work this program, I can't have you come home." This kind of forceful intervention (another example of tough love) is often the final weight needed to break the addiction's back.

Given time and effective treatment, the recovering alcoholic will come to understand the nature of his disease and what will happen if he drinks again. With this understanding, he can accept the responsibility for his future and once again be the guardian of his own life.

CHAPTER 12

Building the House of Sobriety

Your addiction is under control, your denial system has collapsed, you're free of the shakes and the sweats, and you're sleeping well and feeling good. Right about now, you wonder why treatment has to continue. You're ready, eager, and full of enthusiasm and confidence. There's so much to do to put your life back together, and you want to get started.

But there's plenty of work—hard work—left to do. In this last part of treatment you'll have to lay the groundwork of an invisible but essential structure that will protect your sobriety for the rest of your life. We call this structure "the house of sobriety," and it contains four distinct rooms or levels: mental, physical, emotional, and spiritual. As in all houses, each of these separate sections is dependent on the construction of the other parts of the house to maintain overall structural integrity. If one room is allowed to become dusty and moldy, filled with

154

cobwebs and termites, then the other parts of the house will soon begin to rot away, too.

This house, of course, is you: your body, your mind, your feelings, and your spirit. In treatment you will be given the tools—knowledge, insight, understanding, companionship, friendship, and love—needed to build up these essential parts of you. To do the job right, you must handle these tools with skill, devotion, patience, energy, persistence, enthusiasm, and pride. Only then can you erect a structure that is solid, sound, and able to withstand both internal and external threats.

How long will it take to build your house of sobriety? The skeletal framework can be erected within a few weeks; then, over the next months, you will fortify the structure, putting on the siding, nailing down the floorboards, and insulating the walls. Within a few years your house of sobriety will be solid as a rock, sturdy, proud, and comfortable.

But the house is never, in a sense, completed. You have to work on it constantly, repair it, replace worn-out parts, get the mold out of it, clean it, dust it, scrub it, and shine it up. If you don't pay attention to this house, it will slowly fall apart, fill with cobwebs, dirt, dust, and peeling paint, and become a place you wouldn't want to live in. At that point, you are lost: you will drink again. And if you continue to drink, you will die. That is the only possibility that an active addiction offers to its victims. And that is why this house of sobriety is so crucial to your recovery.

The Blueprint

The foundation of your house is abstinence. This is the only foundation that will keep the rest of the structure from collapsing in on itself. Abstinence begins the work of walling off the addiction. When you stop drinking, you essentially starve the addiction, and as the days go by it weakens in intensity, loosening its grip on your brain and your body until eventually your mind clears and you begin to feel normal—yourself—again.

The rest of the house is built with the knowledge and understanding that the addiction is still "down there," walled

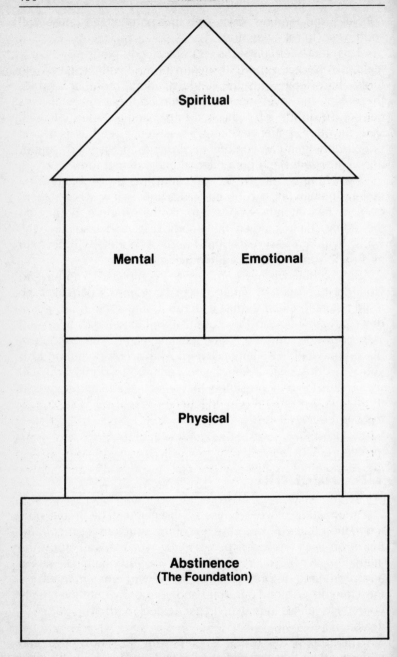

The House of Sobriety

off by the foundation. It is quiet, weak, sleeping perhaps, but still alive. If the addiction were dead or mortally weakened, there would be no need for any more work. But alcoholism is, as we've said, a *chronic* disease: the addiction will be with you—out of control or under control—for the rest of your life. Any break in the foundation will reawaken the addiction and allow it to grow stronger until it threatens to overwhelm you once again.

The foundation of abstinence is thus the most crucial and basic structure of all. But what you build on top of this foundation will protect its integrity and strength and, in the process, determine the quality and direction of the rest of your life.

The First Level: Physical

The physical "room," sitting as it does directly over the house's foundation, is vitally important. This part of your house of sobriety has to do with how you feel physically. Since alcoholism has had such a profound effect on your physical health, this room will take knowledge, patience, time, and skill to erect.

Knowledge is the key, because once you know about your disease you will understand the need for patience, persistence, and skill in combating it. In terms of your physical health, one of the first things you should know is that not all your physical problems will miraculously be healed as soon as you stop drinking. Alcohol affects every cell in the body, and healing takes time—weeks, months, sometimes years.

During this prolonged healing time, you may suffer from what are called "protracted withdrawal symptoms," which include irritability, depression, anxiety, mood swings, tension, memory loss, forgetfulness, difficulty concentrating, short attention span, insomnia, nightmares, headaches, fatigue, hunger, shakiness, excessive perspiration, and, perhaps worst of all, a recurring craving for alcohol.

While it's important that you understand that these symptoms are a lingering effect of the disease, it's also important that you understand where they come from and what you can do to alleviate them. Many recovering alcoholics are greatly disap-

pointed when they work so hard to get sober and then find out
that sobriety has significant pains of its own. They may feel as if
they have traded in one set of problems for another—only this
new set of problems comes without even taking a drink. To
many, that seems a questionable tradeoff.

But these symptoms are temporary—they will go away *if*
you take care of yourself, eat right, exercise regularly, and
avoid unnecessary stress. Understand, too, that while these
may appear to be psychological symptoms, they are actually
symptoms of physical imbalances in your body. Finally, be
assured that there is something you can do about them, and
that is what will concern you in building this first level of your
house of sobriety.

The continued suffering of the protracted withdrawal syndrome is caused by (1) lingering cell damage from the poisonous effects of alcohol; (2) malnutrition; and (3) hypoglycemia.
Alcohol has a direct, toxic effect on many organs in the body,
most notably the brain and the liver. The tenacious symptoms
of nervous irritability, moodiness, and thinking disturbances
are due in part to alcohol's damaging effects on the brain.

Alcohol has also drained away important nutrients necessary for healing and repair. Abstinence alone cannot make the
body's undernourished cells healthy again; to repair themselves
adequately, the cells need nutrients (vitamins, minerals, proteins, fats, and carbohydrates) in therapeutic amounts and pro-
portions. Thus, a balanced diet and vitamin and mineral
supplements are an essential part of both treatment and recovery. In appendix 4 you will find recommendations for taking
vitamin and mineral supplements.

In addition to malnutrition, the great majority of alcoholics
experience blood sugar problems both when they're drinking
and when they're sober. *Why* they have these problems has not
yet been proven, although alcoholism has a devastating impact
on precisely those organs (the pancreas, liver, adrenal glands,
brain, and intestinal tract) involved in blood sugar control,
and alcohol itself is a sugar-rich liquid that interrupts the
normal flow of blood sugar (glucose) to the cells. Although
the precise causes are not yet known, we do know what to
do about the symptoms of low blood sugar, which range
from "minor" symptoms such as anxiety, insomnia, and mood
swings to the more serious problems of persistent depression,

---

Diet for Sobriety

The goal of this diet is to stabilize the blood sugar by eliminating refined carbohydrates and provide a balance of proteins, natural carbohydrates, and low fat.

In addition to three meals every day (*no* skipping meals!), eat nutritious snacks (fruits, seeds, whole-grain breads or crackers, cheese, vegetables) three times every day: mid-morning, mid-afternoon, and evening.

Avoid completely: Alcohol, sweets (table sugar, candy, desserts, and sugar-sweetened drinks), and caffeine.

Add to your diet: Fresh fruits and vegetables, whole-grain foods (breads, cereals), grains, nuts, and seeds.

Cut down on: Processed meats (bacon, sausage, ham), red meats (high in saturated fats), dried fruits and fruit juices (high in sugar), white flour products, salt, and condiments (ketchup, mustard, pickles, mayonnaise, because they are high in sugar, salt and/or fat).

---

mental confusion, craving for alcohol, and even suicidal tendencies.

To counteract hypoglycemia, the recovering alcoholic must *avoid,* whenever possible, sweets, stimulants (caffeine in coffee, tea, and colas) and stress; take daily supplements; and faithfully follow a diet rich in complex carbohydrates (fruits, vegetables, and whole grains).

While comprehensive nutritional therapy is essential to your continued good health, diet and supplements are not the only elements involved in keeping your body (and mind) functioning at peak level. *Exercise* is crucial for several reasons. First, exercise will strengthen the body, promote circulation, and help ensure a steady supply of nutrients to your cells. Second, regular exercise makes you feel better, both physically and mentally. Ironically, exercise doesn't sap you of strength, but actually increases mental and physical vitality, giving you more energy and clearing up your mind so that problems seem to come into perspective.

By becoming aware of your body—how it moves and how it works—you also become aware of your power to make your body feel better. That's a good feeling. And, finally, by exercising you are developing a new way of living, in stark contrast to your alcoholic lifestyle. No matter how athletic or sports-minded an alcoholic may once have been, he eventually gave up just about everything involved with moving his body vigorously: it simply hurt too much when he had a hangover or when he was craving a drink. Besides, a drinking alcoholic always has something better to do, and we all know what that is. When you were drinking, there simply wasn't much time left for other "leisure activities."

But in sobriety you will have more time on your hands, and much of that time should be spent in making you *feel* good, making your body strong and healthy, and letting your whole self take joy in your sobriety. Taking a walk or a run outside in the fresh air, participating in a dance or aerobics class, playing softball or volleyball, working out in the weight room—any of these activities will help make you feel *alive*. Which is, thank God, exactly what you are.

Another factor crucial to your physical health is relaxation and avoidance of stress. For alcoholics, prolonged or profound stress can erode the foundation that keeps the addiction under control. Stress can, in other words, undermine sobriety and cause a relapse.

Most of us think of stress as a "mental" condition—something outside ourselves that rattles our thinking or causes worry and tension. But stress has profound effects on our inner physical health and well-being and is particularly dangerous for anyone already suffering from a chronic illness. Stress aggravates heart conditions, ulcers, even cancer. In a recent laboratory experiment two groups of rats were subjected to the stress of electric shock. One group could not escape, the other group had an escape route. The rats with no escape became listless, demonstrating a sort of "I give up" syndrome. When each group was then injected with tumor cells, every one of the rats in the no-escape group contracted cancer, while the rats who were allowed to escape were resistant. In another experiment, researchers at the Pacific Northwest Research Foundation injected two groups of mice with cancer-causing cells and placed one group in a cage that rotated in a disorienting manner.

Two-thirds of these mice died of cancer, compared to less than one-tenth from the group in undisturbed cages.

For alcoholics, stress has the same physical consequences in reactivating the disease as it has for people with cancer, heart disease, or diabetes. A man with a weak heart, for example, may suffer from irregular heart rate or even have a heart attack after hearing of his son's death. A diabetic will have difficulty regulating his blood sugar while working through the stresses of a divorce. A recovering alcoholic trying to cope with the pressures of a high-powered job may experience a change in blood pressure or pulse, disturbed sleep patterns, or general anxiety.

These are all examples of how our inner physiological workings are profoundly affected by external stresses. The alcoholic under stress is also prone to a disturbed blood sugar response due to hypoglycemia, which in itself aggravates stress. With these imbalances in inner chemistry, the alcoholic's addiction may be reactivated. The dormant addiction begins to gain strength not because the alcoholic succumbs mentally to stress and simply can't cope with it, but because his body is weakened physiologically by stress.

While stress prompts a response in many areas of the body, one set of biochemical chain reactions is particularly important for understanding the alcoholic's sensitivity to stress. Under stress, the body releases adrenaline, a hormone designed to help the body "gear up" to meet the demands of an urgent situation. Adrenaline then triggers the release of glucose, which stimulates the release of insulin, which allows the energy-rich glucose into the cells. Severe or prolonged stress can chronically upset the body's glucose-regulating mechanisms. Alcoholics, because of their hypoglycemic tendencies, are particularly sensitive to these changes. Chronic drinking also tends to damage the adrenal glands, which control the body's reactions to stress.

People with chronic, "incurable" illnesses should avoid unnecessary stress because their bodies are more vulnerable and less able to withstand the physical shocks associated with stress. Unfortunately, human beings simply cannot avoid all stress, and alcoholics in the first year or two of recovery have to put up with some extraordinarily stressful situations. The disease has impacted virtually every part of the alcoholic's life, including his family, career, finances, reputation, self-image, and confidence. While a heart attack or cancer victim emerges from treatment to sympathetic, caring, helping family and friends, an alcoholic frequently faces anger, resentment, misunderstanding, and distrust from both friends and family. Even if his family is intact and his job is waiting for him, he still must deal with the shame and disgrace of all those years of drinking, the blackouts, drunken brawls, neglect of family and friends, belligerent words, and physical and verbal abuse. Even early- and middle-stage alcoholics face severe stress in trying to pull their lives together and mop up after the insanity of their addiction.

Knowledge of the disease will help protect you against much of this stress—knowing that you were not responsible, that your behavior and even your thoughts and emotions were manipulated by your addiction. But you will find that knowledge outside of the treatment setting is imperfect, that many people will be wary of you and unsure, that others will find it difficult to forgive, and that some will never be able to think of you as anything but a drunk and a bum. You must do what you can and learn that it is not within your power to do everything.

You must, in other words, learn your limitations and grow within them. During the first year of sobriety, it's particularly important to protect yourself from stress. Don't move out of your house, if you can avoid it; don't even move your furniture around. Don't change jobs, don't make any major purchases, don't attempt to "fix" everything that was devastated by your addiction.

Be patient, take it slow, and know that time will heal much. And don't expect life to be perfect; it never is, not for anyone, and at times it is very far from perfect. But believe in change, believe in time, believe in yourself, and believe, most of all, in your sobriety.

It will help you immeasurably to develop meaningful and trusting relationships where your problems and concerns can be heard and understood. This is where the AA program comes to mean so much to so many recovering alcoholics. In dealing with your family, friends, and business relationships, it's important that you learn how to communicate your thoughts and feelings, instead of repressing them. Learning how to listen is also an important art that will help to open up the lines of communication with the people around you.

Above all, don't settle for a perpetually stressful relationship or environment: your body, like all bodies, cannot handle stress forever. You may have to ease out of a high-stress, demanding job or seek counseling for a troubled relationship. But you should also protect yourself from the "little" stresses in life. If you find yourself in situations that make you anxious or afraid—*leave.* You do not have to go to parties, you do not have to cook fancy dinners, you do not have to prove yourself to anyone. All you have to do is stay sober; and if you stay sober and take care of yourself, soon enough everything else will fall into place.

Insulate yourself from stress, recognize the signs, learn to relax, treat yourself as if you were a small, fragile child taking baby steps. They may seem like tiny, insignificant steps forward, but they are all giant steps because they are all going in the right direction—away from the power of the addiction.

The Second Level: Mental

In the physical plane of your house of sobriety, you *do*; in the mental plane, you *think.* What you think, of course, affects what you do; all these levels are interconnected and interdependent. Thus, you will have to become aware of how your thinking affects your health, your life, and your sobriety. You have to be willing to take your thoughts apart, dissect them, and then rearrange them in healthy ways. This requires knowing what sorts of thoughts are dangerous to your sobriety, and it also requires knowing how to go about changing them.

"I am an alcoholic." Whenever you begin to doubt that statement, you are in trouble. Suppose you're walking down the street and you see a smelly old drunk (that's how you view him) passed out on a park bench, using an empty bottle for a pillow. You sniff a few times, make a face, and think, *I was never that bad.* This happened to alcoholic and syndicated *Chicago Sun* columnist Paul Molloy, who describes the experience in his book *Where Did Everybody Go?*

> . . . near where the skid-row pavement starts, a vagrant
> accosted me as I looked for a taxi. He had bloodshot eyes

and dirty clothes, gave off an odor of whisky and vomit, and looked as if he had slept in a doorway that night. All he wanted was change for a drink.

Once in the cab, I put a few drops of Murine into my eyes and a couple of mints into my mouth. I thought of the plight of the poor devil I had left on the street. How could a man let himself go to waste like that? How could he abuse his body and mind and live in degradation? Then it hit me like a thwack in the ribs:

MY GOD, I'M IN WORSE SHAPE THAN HE IS.

I looked on him as a shiftless moocher with a filthy coat, three-day whiskers and a monumental hangover. A lowlife. A derelict. I saw myself as a regular citizen, bathed and shaved, with a nice suit, shirt and tie, doing what all decent men must do to feed their kids and keep them in college. I was respectable; he was a bum. A parallel came to mind; I tried to shrug it off but it persisted. And I winced when I reflected that the good-for-nothing out there and I were really fellow travelers; the difference was that he had reached his destination before I had.

Molloy credits this incident with cutting through his rationalizations and denials and helping him to realize that he couldn't handle his drinking alone. This was the beginning of his "surrender" to his disease and thus the beginning of his recovery. But what if he had used the incident instead as an excuse to continue drinking, with rationalizations like "If he's an alcoholic, then I'm certainly something different," or "I've got a problem, maybe, but I can handle it," or "I'll never let myself get like *that*." These are thoughts that occur to both drinking and recovering alcoholics, and they indicate that the alcoholic has not accepted or surrendered to his disease. He may be sober now, but his mind is preparing his body to take a drink.

Thoughts like "I wasn't that bad," or "I never really was addicted to the stuff," or "Now that guy, he's what I'd call a *real* alcoholic," are extremely dangerous because they show a mind setting the stage for the physical act of taking a drink. If you ask an alcoholic who relapsed what he was thinking about when he took that first drink, and whether he struggled with it, the answer is often, "I just did it; I didn't really think about it. It wasn't a struggle at all." Why? Because his mind had already struggled with the idea and fought out the battle in the mental arena. It was all decided before the alcoholic physically lifted the drink to his mouth.

"Stinking thinking" is what AA members call these kinds of thoughts, and for a good reason: when you think these thoughts yourself or hear someone express them, you can almost smell the growing and increasingly powerful addiction. "Stinking thinking" is absolute evidence that the addiction is attempting to take over once again and establish control. All the hallmark symptoms of the addiction—rationalization, denial, minimizing, projection—can be found in the spoken or unspoken thoughts of an alcoholic on the verge of a relapse. Listen:

"My wife is really the cause of all my problems; how can I live with this woman and expect to stay sober?"

"The psychiatrist told me my real problem was with my mother, and now that she and I are on good terms, I don't see how a drink every now and then would hurt."

"My kids are coming home for the holidays. What possible damage could it do to have a drink or two with them?"

"Why do I have to be an alcoholic? Why can't I drink like everyone else? It isn't fair."

"I'm not sure I ever really was an alcoholic; I never drank in the morning, and I never had a blackout."

"I've been sober for three years, and I feel great; how could one drink hurt me?"

Chances are you won't express these thoughts to others because you know (actually, your addiction knows) what their reactions will be. So you must learn to identify these warning signs as the whisperings of the addiction and take immediate steps to protect yourself. You must understand that this is not the logical *you* talking, but that these thoughts are the addiction's way of trying to call you back and reestablish its power over you.

What reactivates your addiction? Your body's stability can be undone by stress, illness, mounting frustrations, grief, or guilt. Perhaps you neglected your diet and drank too much coffee or loaded up on sweets. Perhaps you just became complacent—everything was going along so well that you became lazy and stopped going to AA meetings or decided to take that high-pressure job with the long hours spent traveling and the dinner parties to entertain clients. Maybe you figured you could do without your supplements, or you began working so hard that you just couldn't find time for breakfast and often skipped lunch, too.

When you don't hurt anymore, when the memories are dim and unreal and seem strangely out of touch with your life as it is now, then you can get sloppy and give up on the disciplines necessary to stay healthy and sober. This is the nature of all human beings, not just alcoholics. Heart attack victims who figure that surgery fixed them as good as new and who slip back into eating fatty foods or neglecting their exercise program; diabetics who sneak sweets; cancer victims who skip their routine checkups; high blood pressure victims who work in high-stress jobs—these are all victims of chronic diseases who "forget" how sick they once were and who become lazy now that the trauma and horror of their disease are no longer fresh in their minds. And these people, because they suffer from a chronic and incurable disease, risk a dangerous and potentially fatal relapse.

For the alcoholic, AA is one of the best ways to keep in touch with his disease and to maintain his discipline. AA helps the recovering alcoholic develop and grow as a human being by keeping him in constant touch with his disease and with others who suffer from it. Every time you introduce yourself at an AA meeting by saying, "I'm George [or Georgia or John or Joan] and I'm an alcoholic," you are reaffirming the fact that you have a chronic disease. When you hear other people's stories you remember your own, and you know that you are not alone. When you meet new AA members who are struggling to get sober, you are reminded of what it was like for you. You can unwind at AA meetings, speak all your secrets, and nobody will recoil, nobody will put you down. Instead, you'll feel caring, friendship, allegiance, even love.

Many alcoholics give up on AA, reasoning that they don't need it anymore or that they are too busy and don't have time for it. Many others argue that AA is not for them, that they are too shy or the program is for religious fanatics, or that the meetings are too smoky or too crowded or too loud. Surely, many alcoholics have been able to stay sober without AA, but that is not to say that they couldn't have used AA and benefited from it in their sobriety.

If you have difficulty with AA for any reason, try to think out the roots of this difficulty. Is it because you are, truly, shy? If so, there's no rule that says you have to speak at AA meetings; just sit and listen. Is it because the smoking or the back-slapping or the coffee drinking offends you? You can find AA groups that consist primarily of lumberjacks, or meetings made up of demure wealthy women, gay groups, black groups, physician groups, all-men or all-women groups—within this great variety you can find a group that fits your needs and your personality. Is your reluctance due to what you perceive as the religious aspect of AA? Then remember that the "higher power" AA members talk about is whatever you want it to be—it is

---

The Twelve Steps of AA

1. We admitted we were powerless over alcohol—that our lives had become unmanageable.

2. We came to believe that a Power greater than ourselves could restore us to sanity.

3. We made a decision to turn our will and our lives over to the care of God as we understood Him.

4. We made a searching and fearless moral inventory of ourselves.

5. We admitted to God, to ourselves, and to another human being, the exact nature of our wrongs.

6. We were entirely ready to have God remove all these defects of character.

7. We humbly asked Him to remove our shortcomings.

8. We made a list of all persons we had harmed, and became willing to make amends to them all.

9. We made direct amends to such people wherever possible, except when to do so would injure others.

10. We continued to take personal inventory and, when we were wrong, promptly admitted it.

11. We sought through prayer and meditation to improve our conscious contact with God as we understood Him, praying only for knowledge of His will for us and the power to carry that out.

12. Having had a spiritual awakening as the result of these steps, we tried to carry this message to alcoholics, and to practice these principles in all our affairs.

God to some, love to others, the laws of nature to others.
Again, some groups are more classically religious than others,
and by attending various meetings you will be able to find a
group of people who share your philosophies and concerns.

It's essential in your present and future life that you do not
allow yourself to become isolated or to forget what your life
was like as an alcoholic. AA will keep you in touch with your
disease, your past, and yourself; and in the process it will help
you to live happily sober for all the natural years remaining to
you.

The Third Level: Emotional

Just as what you *think* affects your sobriety, so does what you
feel. And what you feel has been mucked up by years of living
with alcohol. Many alcoholics label their drinking years as
"emotionally anesthetized." Everything may have seemed normal on the outside, but within the family unit all the feelings of
love, affection, trust, and caring were bottled up. Here's how
one recovering alcoholic describes her life as it used to be:

> I call my disease "slow burn alcoholism." I can't
> describe how damaging that type of alcoholism is. No one
> in my family ever appeared drunk or out of control and
> yet everyone drank daily and in large amounts. The major
> symptom was the absolutely inability to feel. Generation
> after generation of my family stood physically sound, yet
> emotionally empty. My dad, who drank a fifth a day,
> never took the time to be involved in anything I did. He
> never saw me ski, and I was on the national ski team two
> years in a row. The word *love* was never spoken at our
> house. The price for me, in the end, was total emotional
> isolation.

Total emotional isolation—what you feel is never commu-
nicated to anyone. It all stays inside, turning rancid, changing
to bitterness and loneliness and hatred, until inevitably all
feeling withers, and you are drained, empty, dry. Most of you
spent your adult years—those years that for most people are
spent growing up, getting to know yourself, and learning to

communicate with others—with alcohol. You grew up, essentially, with alcohol as your best friend, and your allegiance to alcohol turned everyone away until it was eventually just you and alcohol in a hostile world.

Now that you are sober and cut off from alcohol, what are you left with? Fear, loneliness, immaturity, resentments, guilt, and shattered relationships. You don't know how to communicate with others, you don't even know yourself, and you probably don't like yourself. Who are you? How do you learn how to feel and communicate again? How do you forgive yourself and begin the process of liking yourself?

In the final weeks of treatment you will learn some basic information and skills designed to help you begin to answer these questions. In sobriety you will have to learn to feel emotions once again and to let them out, communicating them to others so that the feelings can grow and flower and be felt outside yourself. Not all these emotions will be happy ones, of course, but the point of living is not just to be happy, but to feel, to experience, to live life with all its joys and sorrows. If you anesthetize yourself to pain and sorrow, you are also numbing yourself to happiness and joy.

You will also learn in treatment that you are not an alcoholic because you are immature—you are immature because you are an alcoholic. Your long association with alcohol stopped, cold, the maturing process that leads to self-identity, self-determination, and self-liking. You will learn, too, that your reactions to people and to events may be slightly askew in the first weeks or months of sobriety. You may be touchy, tender, temperamental, and thin-skinned. Everything you feel may seem enlarged, intensified. All your nerves feel exposed. These feelings, of course, are compounded and exaggerated by the physical changes going on inside you.

What can you do about your raging, sometimes uncontrollable emotions? First, learn to give yourself *time*. You suffer from a disease so powerful that it threatened your life. You need to heal, and sometimes the healing goes slowly. Be patient. Pace yourself. Don't expect too much too soon. Keep a journal so that you can track your emotional progress; be sure, however, to measure this progress in weeks and months, not hours or days. Be proud of yourself for the strides you do take, and don't despair when things seem to slide backward and you feel out of control and incapable.

Learn to accept the fact that you cannot handle by yourself all the early stresses of this new life. Whenever you feel the need, use the support system that has been built up through treatment—out-patient counseling, aftercare programs, lectures, and AA. Don't be afraid to admit to any problems you have and to share your fears and anxieties with your counselor, family, friends, or AA members.

Reaching out to others is not easy for many people, and alcoholics have a particularly tough time because they have had so little practice. But you will learn, once you admit your need for help, that it is not difficult at all to reach out, and that you are not less of a person for admitting to someone else that you are troubled or afraid. All human beings are periodically troubled or afraid; all human beings need help and support throughout their lives. Being able to admit that you are in need is actually a sign of internal strength and growth, and it begins the "connectiveness" that binds you to others, initiating friendship, affection, and love.

Learning to communicate with others is actually like learning a new language. Think of it this way: you've moved into this house of sobriety, you're living in a new and foreign place, and you will have to learn some strange rules, different codes of behavior, and innovative ways of communicating with others. All this may seem utterly strange and unusual, but with practice, and with time, you'll begin to feel at home.

There are many types of therapies designed to help people communicate effectively, and one very useful therapy used in alcoholism treatment is *rational emotive therapy* (RET). Basically, RET is aimed at turning around the observation made by the philosopher Epictetus in the first century A.D., that "men are disturbed not by things, but by the views which they take of them." An event outside ourselves (rain, for example) causes us to think certain thoughts (*I hate rainy days*), which then create specific feelings or emotions (anger, sadness, depression). Most of us think that the event itself causes the feelings. But the feelings come from the way we *think* about the event ("Stinking thinking" again!), not from the event itself.

Using RET, alcoholics are taught to identify their ideas or beliefs, challenge what is irrational about them ("Why should rain make me feel sad?") and create a new, more realistic appraisal of the event ("Since it's raining, I'll stay inside and read a book"). The point is to take responsibility for your own emotions, realizing that you actually created them inside yourself, and understanding that putting the responsibility on other people or outside events is both unrealistic and self-defeating. You must learn to act, not just to react.

One final note on emotions: You will have to learn to let go of your guilt and deal with your grief. When you were drinking, you said and did a lot of things that you may be ashamed of now, or that you agonize over, wishing you could go back and change the past. You may have been verbally or physically abusive to your spouse and your children; your drinking may have destroyed your family, your finances, your career. You feel responsible, now, and at times feel overwhelmed with guilt and grief.

But realize this: what you did and what you said back then were part of your disease. Your behavior was manipulated by your addiction, and you had no more control over your actions than a heart attack victim has over the abnormal beating of his heart. Give up your guilt, realize that you were not responsible for your behavior, reconcile what you can, and go on with the art of living. As you learn to deal with your grief over your personal losses, you must also learn not to agonize over the past; you have too much to think about in putting this new life together.

The Serenity Prayer has special meaning to alcoholics and works as both a reminder to let go of the past and a challenge to work toward improving the future: *God grant me the serenity to accept the things I cannot change, the courage to change the things I can, and the wisdom to know the difference.*

Your responsibility begins *now*—now that you are sober and understand what your disease is and what you must do to keep it under control. Once you understand this disease, knowing it from the inside out, you will have to take responsibility for your actions, committing yourself, body and soul, to the recovery tools that will build your house of sobriety. Without this commitment, you leave yourself vulnerable to your addiction and thus to the ultimate destruction of your life and the lives of everyone you care about.

Sobriety is your first and foremost priority, for without it, you will lose everything. Always remember the catechism: If you don't give your sobriety number-one priority, you will drink again. And if you drink, you will die. Death is the end point of all lives, but it is every alcoholic's responsibility to make sure that it does, indeed, come at the end and not somewhere in the middle.

Having been through treatment and learned about your disease, you now have the knowledge and the power to live, or to die. Using that knowledge and learning how to wield that power will take commitment, patience, and persistence. As AA members say, "Recovery is simple, but it is not easy."

Level Four: Spiritual

Alcoholics can be sober, physically, mentally, and emotionally healthy, and still be the most wretched, desolate people on earth. What's missing? In this prolonged metaphor of the house of sobriety, many recovering alcoholics neglect or disregard the final addition: the roof. This is the "spiritual" part of the house, and without it the entire structure is dangerously vulnerable to erosion and decay.

The word *spiritual* involves two essential components: the spirit and spiritual values. The spirit is something inside each of us, a sort of personal essence that is ethereal and invisible. Yet it is of us, a vital, animating force that is the heart of who we are, the very core and center of our being. Some people think of this spirit as "God." Other people add an *o* and think of it as all that is "good" within us and within the world we inhabit. For others, the spirit is love, peace, joy, and happiness. You will come to understand the "spirit" in your own individual way, but you must also accept the power of whatever it is you believe in and your relative powerlessness before it.

Take love, for example. You feel and respond to love, but

you did not make it or manufacture it. Feeling love for someone else is part of you and yet is much, much bigger than you. Whatever this essence of love is, whatever the presence of God or good is, it is stronger than you and larger than you. Its power encompasses the world, and it cannot be manipulated, sabotaged, or destroyed by any one person. It grows within you and is part of you, but it existed before you and it will exist after you.

The building blocks of this essence called the spirit are "spiritual values," and they include trust, caring, love, courage, honesty, humility, and forgiveness. Every one of these values has been taken over and crushed by the disease of alcoholism. Every one must be built back up again to ensure the fullness of life and sobriety. For these are values that every human being on this earth can connect to. They are, in fact, the values that bind us all together, and they are as vital to healthy life as air, food, and water. As an alcoholic, these spiritual values are the final timbers that will solidify and secure your house of sobriety.

The rebuilding of the spirit begins with a process called "surrender"—a surrender to a strength and power beyond yourself, an admission that comes from the very core of your being that you cannot control this disease, that it is not the power of your will and strength than can fight the addiction. This surrender is not a giving up in defeat—it is, in fact, the very root of your future strength. By surrendering to your powerlessness, you are opening the door to receiving help outside yourself. By humbling yourself, you actually enlarge yourself and begin the process of becoming involved in lives outside your own.

It might be difficult to understand how such ethereal concepts as "spirit" and "surrender" can have much significance for alcoholics grappling with the very real and visible problems of trying to live sober in a complicated world. How can you be concerned with humility when you've got to worry about legal fees stemming from a drunk-driving charge when you were drinking? How dare anyone speak to you about courage when you're trying to patch together a shattered marriage and make peace with your children, who have only to look at you to show their pain and distrust? And you've had it up to your ears with words like *honesty, trust,* and *forgiveness.* Let someone else work on those while you try to find a job and piece together some semblance of self-respect and self-confidence from the fragments that were your life. Just living this new life takes everything you've got—how can you be expected to reach deeper still? And, really, what good could it do?

These are the questions that trouble many recovering alcoholics, and they are not easily answered. The only honest answer is that by rebuilding the spiritual part of you, everything else will seem less difficult. You will have something within you that cannot be destroyed by pain, grief, or suffering. This dynamic of life—the spirit—will make it easier for you to smile at strangers, to laugh at yourself, to give up your resentments and hostilities, and to come out of yourself and reach out to others.

Rebuilding the spirit is not a selfless process, for in reaching out, much is returned: self-knowledge, self-confidence, and self-liking. What's amazing is that once you have these qualities, you then have the ability to be selfless. The spirit is dynamic; by growing spiritually, you grow both inward and outward, and your concerns embrace the world.

But how do you go about the job? Every alcoholic will have a different answer to this question, depending on his own personal definition of the word *spirit*. Some alcoholics find much of what they need in AA, or in church, or in the Bible. Some seek it within themselves and spend time every day meditating and reflecting. Others need to escape every once in a while to a remote cabin in the woods, to listen, read, and think. And still others become involved in caring for the poor, the sick, or the elderly—or other alcoholics struggling to get well.

Your house of sobriety will not look like anyone else's; it is yours, you alone can live in it, and it should reflect your individuality. Use the tools that you are given in treatment; build it strong, construct it with patience and persistence. Make it comfortable. Make it sturdy. Make it a place that you will want to live for the rest of your life. And then keep working on it, patching the holes, fixing the leaks, painting the walls. Care for it, protect it, take pride in it. It is, after all, more than a house: it is your life.

CHAPTER 13

Special People, Special Problems

Alcoholics are a microcosm of the entire world out there; and just as you'll find minorities—the elderly, teenagers, drug addicts, psychotics, and law breakers—in the "real" world, so will you find these same people in the real, but smaller, world of alcoholism. In this chapter we'll discuss the problems of certain subpopulations within the treatment setting and suggest methods of understanding and dealing with the special people who suffer these problems.

All these special people are victims of the very same disease that afflicts all alcoholics. What distinguishes them and makes their treatment slightly different or more intensive is the addition of other diseases or problems that complicate their addiction to alcohol. It is *not* true, for example, that women alcoholics need treatment different from that given to men; that polydrug addicts are more successful when treated separately;

that skid row alcoholics must be institutionalized for life; or
that teenagers suffer from a different type of alcoholism than
adults.

It *is* true, however, that more women than men are addicted to tranquilizers and sedatives; that a person addicted to
more than one drug has a longer and more unpredictable
withdrawal course than normal; that the elderly have additional medical complications and more severe organ damage;
that teenagers have higher relapse rates than adults; and that
skid row alcoholics are more vulnerable to seizures and delirium tremens.

In this chapter, we'll explain why these differences occur,
how they should be handled, and what impact these special
people and special problems have on other patients, the treatment staff, and the overall progression of treatment.

Women

It used to be said that women didn't get drunk; they got tipsy,
or tight, or woozy. If they got too tipsy or too tight (if, in other
words, they got drunk), they were quietly led away and never
invited back. Getting drunk has always been considered unla-
dylike. Getting drunk, for a woman, is degrading. Getting
drunk, for a woman, is disgusting. A drunken woman is, in
simple terms, an embarrassment.

Here's how Jan Clayton, the mother in the Lassie movies
and television series, described society's view of the woman
alcoholic in a speech to the national convention of the Association of Labor and Management Administrators and Consultants
on Alcoholism in San Diego, 1976:

> If a man ties one on, so to speak, at a party, "Wasn't he a
> caution? Wasn't he a card? And didn't that lampshade
> look adorable on him? But did you see his wife? Wasn't
> she disgusting?" Because that is the word society most
> often tacks on to a drinking woman—"disgusting." The
> hand that rocks the cradle is not supposed to hold a drink
> on the rocks. It's that damn pedestal, not of our making,
> not of our wanting. It places us beyond hearing or calling
> for help, way out of reach, and so the woman stays

hidden, shamed and shamefully, in that "closet in the sky," too often until everything is lost—her job, her family, and finally her life.

Things have changed quickly and dramatically in the decade since Jan Clayton made that speech, and one person has led the way: Betty Ford. When Betty Ford announced that she was addicted to both alcohol and prescription pills, she knocked the "damn pedestal" on its ear. Betty Ford is beautiful, talented, articulate, a loving mother, a devoted wife—she is, in every respect, the model woman (who happens to be married to a past President of the United States). She is also an alcoholic. And when she admitted herself into treatment for her addictions to alcohol and pills, the stigma and the stereotype of the woman alcoholic were dealt a fatal blow. Betty Ford got the message across to millions of people all over the world that ladies do become alcoholics and that having the disease is no reflection whatsoever on a woman's femininity, charm, or dignity.

Betty Ford's case highlights another problem facing the growing majority of women alcoholics: polydrug addiction. Betty Ford was addicted to alcohol, painkillers, and tranquilizers: *an estimated 70 to 80 percent of women alcoholics are addicted to other drugs.* Like Betty Ford, most of these women are normal, healthy, vibrant human beings before they become addicted. But taking pills and drinking alcohol is a dangerous and potentially deadly combination. The risks of addiction are greatly increased, as is the risk of a fatal overdose. Dorothy Kilgallen died after taking moderate doses of alcohol and barbiturates; Karen Ann Quinlan slipped into a coma after swallowing a Quaalude with a few gin and tonics. One-fifth of the lethal dose of alcohol combined with one-twentieth the lethal dose of a barbiturate can equal a lethal dose. In terms of simple arithmetic, 1 drink plus 1 pill does not equal 2 but 4, 5, 6, or more.

For anyone addicted to alcohol, pills are particularly dangerous because the pathway of central nervous system addiction is, in a sense, already paved. Any drug that causes a physical reaction similar to that of alcohol—and that includes sedatives, tranquilizers, sleeping pills, painkillers, and the opiates (heroin and morphine)—will slip right into that pathway and the user will quickly become addicted to it.

Why are women more likely to become addicted to pre-scription pills? The most obvious explanation is that women see doctors more often than men. More than 60 percent of all visits to physicians are made by women, according to the National Center for Health Statistics. Furthermore, women are more likely to report symptoms of an emotional nature—frustration, inadequacy, guilt, tension, anxiety, fear, anger, resentments—and these complaints often put the physician in an awkward position, as described by authors Richard Hughes and Robert Brewin in *The Tranquilizing of America*:

> Hearing [the] expression of emotional feelings from a male view that accepts physical symptoms as real but emotional symptoms as unreal, the doctor reacts negatively toward his female patients. He is uncomfortable, unwilling to understand, unable to communicate in a like language, frustrated by his inability to provide a cure, discouraged in his desire for a favorable outcome, impatient to end the interview, and angry that his time is being wasted. To bring a quick end to the consultation and at the same time to fulfill his expectation of providing treatment and the woman's expectation of receiving it, the doctor writes a prescription for Valium, assures his patient the pills will help, and sends her on her way with the parting informa-tion that the prescription is refillable and can be renewed with a telephone call to the office. (p. 81)

In addition to these two major problems—the stigma of being both a woman and an alcoholic with polydrug addiction—women alcoholics face a number of other troublesome compli-cations. Their disease progresses more rapidly; they are more susceptible to alcoholic hepatitis and advanced chronic liver disease; and they are more prone to depression. Hormonal fluctuations, childbearing, child rearing, and menopause can all contribute to physical changes leading to stress, tension, and anxiety. Because the woman is characteristically the child raiser, she is also the one most likely to abuse her children: a drinking or drunken mother and a crying, frustrated child make for an explosive situation.

Women suffer greater guilt and shame over their drinking (and their drunken behavior) than men do and have greater difficulty dealing with feelings of inadequacy and self-worth. Women in the past have been more sheltered than men and have fewer opportunities to get out and meet people. Because of their financial and emotional dependence, they often feel "locked in" to unhealthy or destructive relationships.

Finally, while the great majority of nonalcoholics tough it out with alcoholic spouses, husbands of women alcoholics are much more likely to end the marriage. While most men are not emotionally or psychologically prepared for taking care of a sick wife, women more naturally adopt the caretaker role. But perhaps more significant is the fact that society is much more accepting of a drunken husband than of a drunken wife.

The alcoholism treatment center staff should be aware of and sensitive to the special problems confronting women alcoholics, particularly low self-esteem, lack of assertiveness and decision-making skills, guilt and shame, financial dependence, and isolation. These special problems must not, however, be misconstrued as *causes* for alcoholic drinking. The problems unique to women are unique to every woman, alcoholic or not. In working out a recovery plan, it's important to remember that the woman alcoholic has the same basic disease as the male alcoholic, but that women are physically and emotionally different from men and that these inherent differences may require special understanding, support, and reassurance.

Teenagers

Teenage alcoholics, by definition, start taking alcohol and/or drugs at the time they're supposed to start growing up. It necessarily happens that the drugs inhibit the maturing process. This happens to adult alcoholics, too, but someone who becomes addicted to alcohol at the age of 25, 30, 35, or 40 has at least had several years to get to know himself, to work at the process of learning to like himself, and has some understanding about how to communicate and interact with others.

Teenagers, alcoholic and nonalcoholic alike, are typically self-centered: their world consists of their desires, their needs, their interests, and their friends. Alcohol and drugs serve to narrow this focus even further, lessening the teenager's interaction with others, reducing his interest in the outside world, and interfering with the normal development of social skills. Teens are often rebellious, confused, and anti-authority; regular, continued use of alcohol only intensifies the normal turmoil of adolescence.

To make things even more difficult, teenagers are much more likely to use other drugs in addition to alcohol, and many are regular users of a "garbage can" of drugs, including marijuana, cocaine, "uppers," "downers," hallucinogens, and prescription drugs they find in their parents' medicine cabinets. Convincing a teenager that his drug use is serious and potentially deadly may seem as productive as hitting your head against a brick wall. Teenagers have a firm belief in their invincibility—it simply doesn't occur to them that they might get addicted, that they might overdose, that they might need treatment, or that without treatment they might die. Death and disability are for old people; teenagers "can handle it."

Peer pressure for teens is very intense, and one of the most common fears that teenage alcoholics express is, "How am I going to live without booze? What will I do? Who will be my friend?" As one recovering teenage alcoholic put it, in the October 2, 1984, issue of Family Circle: "To me, stopping [drinking] represented an end to laughter, to joy, and to partying. How could I go to a party and not drink? I didn't know how to do that. That's what frightened me more than anything else. What do you do when you don't drink? Who do you hang out with?"

When asked to describe the reasons why they drink or use drugs, teenagers are much more likely to say, "to be sociable," "to get drunk," "to celebrate occasions," or "to escape problems," while adult alcoholics are more likely to answer "to forget," "to relax," and "to reduce pain."

These unique aspects of teenage alcoholism—peer pressure, a delayed maturing process, challenging of authority, self-centeredness, use of both illicit and prescription drugs, and fear of life without drugs—make their treatment slightly more challenging. Many treatment centers have separate, specialized adolescent units with specially trained staff and in-patient treatment lasting up to three months. Other treatment centers mix their teenage patients with the adult alcoholic population, operating on the basic philosophy that the teenagers benefit from close contact with older, wiser, "parenting" adults.

Whether teens are treated in separate units or with the adult patients, special handling and understanding are absolutely essential. Within the treatment situation, teenagers often flagrantly challenge the authority of the staff. They can be ill mannered, undisciplined, and unkempt. It's crucial that the staff understand that this is more than typical adolescent behavior—the addiction is working inside a tender and vulnerable mind and body that has few defenses against it.

The mood swings and general irritability that signal the addiction's effect on the central nervous system are exaggerated in teenagers, because their bodies are also being subjected to the rapid and profound chemical changes associated with adolescence. The usual hallmarks of addiction—denial, defensiveness, rationalization, and irritability—are often expressed in teenagers as cockiness, arrogance, aloofness, and cynicism. Teens in treatment are more likely to challenge the staff's authority, break the rules, stomp out of meetings, and blow up at staff members or other patients.

While the adolescent alcoholic's problems require special understanding and attention, it's crucial that teenagers not be allowed to overwhelm the other patients and create an atmosphere of tension and constant struggle. Keeping the census of teenagers down (perhaps one or two teens in a group of ten adults) will help to keep things in control, and firm and consistent handling by the staff is essential. It's also crucial that staff members keep their eyes and ears open—mixing with the teenage patients, sitting with them at meals, listening carefully to their comments or complaints about specific patients—in order to detect any potential troublemakers and deal with them before they create problems for the other patients.

Finally, teenagers are infamous for bringing contraband—alcohol, marijuana, cocaine, prescription pills—into treatment or having their friends deliver drugs to them on visiting days. When confronted with this serious infraction of the treatment center rules, they may become hostile, defensive, and abusive. It is not uncommon to hear a teenager defend such behavior with a statement like, "Look, I'm off booze now, and marijuana isn't going to kill me, so stop bugging me." Again, the staff and the other patients can have a profound influence on such a patient, and direct confrontation may be particularly effective. (For further discussion on the issue of contraband and dealing with it within the treatment situation, see p. 199.)

The relapse rate for teenagers is generally higher than for the adult alcoholic population. Again, the teenager often lacks the social skills, maturity, and sense of identity and self-worth to deal with the conflicts and pressures of adolescent life and can be easily distracted from a solid, disciplined commitment to long-term recovery. However, with a staff trained to understand the special problems of teenage alcoholism, longer treatment time, family involvement in treatment, and attendance at Alateen, AA, and NA (Narcotics Anonymous) meetings, the great majority of teenagers in treatment can be helped to a permanent recovery.

The Elderly

Elderly alcoholics present a special challenge in that their disease is generally more advanced, they use more prescription and over-the-counter drugs, they often live alone and have no one to care for or support them, and their lives may be characterized by loneliness, isolation, depression, and boredom.

The pill-taking is especially ominous. People 65 and older make up approximately 10 percent of the U.S. population but consume more than 25 percent of all prescription drugs and an even higher percentage of over-the-counter drugs. A 1977 study conducted by the National Institute of Drug Abuse showed that two-thirds of all people over 65 reported using drugs, and, after cardiovascular drugs, sedatives and tranquilizers were the most commonly used. Fifty percent of those interviewed said they used alcohol in combination with prescription and over-the-counter drugs (from aspirin to cold tablets to laxatives) and nearly 20 percent claimed to be frequent users of alcohol. The regular use of drugs by older people is complicated by the fact that, due to the aging process, they are less able to metabolize, absorb, and eliminate chemicals; thus, a combination of small amounts of alcohol and drugs can be life-threatening.

Most alcoholics, of course, do not reach old age: either they get treatment and permanently stop drinking, or they die early, of accidents, heart attacks, liver disease, cancer, or any number of the other medical complications of alcoholism. Those alcoholics who do make it into their 60s or 70s generally have progressed into the later stages of alcoholism and experience a greater incidence of malnutrition, withdrawal complications, seizures, DTs, and heart, liver, and lung ailments. Severe organ damage, including brain damage, can easily be confused with senility. Furthermore, the elderly patient is more physiologically resistant to treatment, with slower healing processes and less physical ability to "bounce back" after treatment. As is true for any elderly patient with a chronic disease, relapse is more likely.

In treating the elderly, patience and persistence are crucial to success. In the early weeks of treatment, medical management may need to be more aggressive, with heftier doses of vitamins and minerals for longer periods of time and special attention to nutritional problems aggravated by poor eating patterns. In terms of long-term recovery, the staff should concentrate on the specific problems of loneliness, isolation, grief, inactivity, and the use of other drugs for conditions associated with advancing age.

The Skid Row Alcoholic

Just 3 percent of alcoholics can be labeled "skid row." This statistic, of course, is in direct conflict with the stereotypical view of alcoholics: that they are smelly old bums passed out on park benches. Most alcoholics have money in their leather wallets, clean clothes on their showered backs, a roof over their well-groomed heads, and a loving family adept at picking up after them. Nevertheless, there are between 300,000 and 600,000 "skid rowers" in the United States—and not one of them is a "hopeless cause."

Skid row alcoholics are, generally, those men and women who have little or no financial resources, no family to care for them, no job, no home, and no hope for the future. They sleep outside or in shelters provided by charitable agencies like The Salvation Army. They beg, borrow, or steal cheap wine, beer, or hard liquor. They sometimes resort to drinking vinegar, mouthwash, cough syrup, or Sterno. Their disease is advanced into its late stages, they are typically severely malnourished, and they have numerous other complicating diseases such as pneumonia, infections, frostbite, etc.

Tragically, these people cannot afford private, in-patient treatment, and they have been viewed as hopeless, incorrigible, and unsalvageable by our fellow citizens and government officials. Treatment for the skid row alcoholic has traditionally consisted of a few nights in the county jail or a day or two in the county detox ward, after which they are returned to the streets and, once again, beg, borrow, or steal to feed their addiction. With such "treatment," the skid row alcoholic will eventually die of exposure, advanced liver disease, a heart attack, stroke, malnutrition, or a knife in the back.

No alcoholic, no matter how advanced his disease, should be considered hopeless, and the late-stage skid row alcoholic, like all other alcoholics, can be helped to live a happy, fulfilled, and sober life. Federal, state, and local governments could only profit by operating and financing treatment centers, based on the principles outlined in this book, for indigent alcoholics. For those who would complain about "yet another government handout," look at it this way: it is at least as financially prudent and efficient to successfully treat 40 to 60 percent of these alcoholics than to continually recycle them through detox wards, jails, public assistance programs, welfare, and emergency rooms, with a "success rate" bordering on zero. And certainly it would be kinder, saner, and more sensible.

Treatment for the skid row alcoholic should mirror the treatment of any other alcoholic, but with specific attention to medical problems associated with the late stage of the disease (liver disease, chronic brain damage, heart problems) and to the special problems of people living on the street (malnutrition, exposure, infections, etc.). Detoxification may take as long as two weeks, and the intensive recovery period may extend to two or three months, with some patients requiring up to six months or more of in-patient treatment and protection. Halfway houses (see p. 91) are an ideal resource for indigent alcoholics. Special emphasis should be placed on helping them to become employable, find a job and a place to live, and gradually piece together a new life.

The Psychotic Alcoholic

The percentage of psychotic alcoholics is the same as the percentage in the normal population; alcoholics are no more likely to suffer from severe, permanent psychological problems than, say, someone with diabetes or cancer. By "psychotic" we mean a major emotional disorder with derangement of personality and loss of contact with reality, where the person sees, hears, or perceives voices, images, or ideas that aren't real. Types of psychoses include paranoia, schizophrenia, depression, and manic-depressive illness.

Alcoholism and drug addiction do induce a sort of temporary psychosis or mental insanity involving depression, anxiety, paranoia, and nervousness. During withdrawal, for example, the alcoholic's psychological state can be profoundly disrupted. Alcoholics used to be given psychological tests either immediately upon admission to treatment or within a few days of admission, and these tests often revealed serious psychological disturbances. When testing is delayed until ten days to two weeks after admission, however, the great majority of these tests normalize.

A careful medical examination is essential in evaluating mentally and emotionally disturbed patients. The physician or nurse should be alert for (1) any previous history of psychotic episodes; (2) previous hospitalization for "mental" illness; (3) suicide attempts or preoccupation with suicide; and (4) prolonged or profound depression. In taking this history, it's important to remember three crucial factors: (1) many psychologically "normal" alcoholics become belligerent, violent, depressed, even paranoid during the withdrawal period, and these symptoms may take a week to ten days to disappear; (2) because of the numerous misunderstandings surrounding alcoholism and its victims, physicians traditionally have treated the symptoms of the disease as a psychiatric disorder; therefore, diagnosis of psychosis should not be based solely on past treatment or medical opinion; and (3) alcoholics who are also addicted to prescription or illicit drugs such as heroin, morphine, or cocaine are particularly prone to "crazy" behavior that may last as long as several weeks; their craziness is, in fact, drug-induced.

A patient who appears behaviorally disturbed should be kept under close and continual observation, and special efforts must be made to remove any objects that might be used in a suicide attempt. One-on-one monitoring may be necessary, or the staff may decide to request evaluation by a mental health professional and potential transfer to a lock-up ward for protection and control. While depression and suicidal thoughts are not uncommon in "normal" sick alcoholics during the detoxification period, they will lessen and eventually resolve after a few weeks of treatment. In attempting to determine the seriousness of a suicide threat, the staff should be on the lookout for *concrete* and *specific* ideas or fears, such as a patient's fear that if he is left alone in his sixth-floor room, he'll jump out the window, or a specific threat such as drinking cleaning fluid, hanging himself by his belt, or cutting his wrists with a razor.

The psychiatric patient poses a problem in that the medications used to control the psychosis (generally a major tranquilizer such as Mellaril, Thorazine, or Prolixin) tend to antagonize the addiction to alcohol. Thus, if a psychotic alcoholic patient regularly takes mood elevators, antidepressants, or tranquilizers, the chances are good that he will at some point begin to drink again because the addictive pathways are being fueled by the medication. In general, the best plan of action with psychotic patients is to get them sober, reduce their antipsychotic medication as much as possible, and, if possible, eliminate the medication entirely. It's important to find a physician or mental health professional willing to cooperate and monitor the patient with minimal or no drug use. (Some medications appear less offensive to the addiction than others. Haldol, for example, appears to be better than Thorazine, as it is able to correct sensory distortions while not overtranquilizing or sedating the patient.)

The Polydrug Addict

Poly means "many"; *drug* refers to any mind- or mood-altering chemical; and *addict* refers to physical dependence. Many people think of "addicts" as street people shooting up heroin or free-basing cocaine. But many thousands of people in this country are addicted to legal drugs that were originally prescribed to treat depression, pain, anxiety, tension, or sleep disorders. Thus, the words *polydrug addict* refer to anyone who is addicted to more than one drug—legal or illegal.

The Legal Drugs

Maggie has been taking Valium (and drinking gin) for almost twenty years. She started taking Valium for stress due to her divorce, but new stresses piled up through the years until she seemed to be in a constant state of anxiety and depression. She tried to quit the pills, once, but her anxiety exploded into panic, and she began to hear "voices" and tinny, terrifying, trumpetlike noises in her head. Her doctor quickly switched her to an antidepressant, but it didn't work as well as the Valium. Maggie tried to hold her Valium dosage to 10 mg four times a day, but as her anxiety increased, so did her Valium use. She was brought into treatment after attempting suicide with an overdose of Valium and gin.

Fifty-four-year-old Maggie is typical of many patients admitted into alcoholism treatment centers: she's addicted to both alcohol and pills; the pill is Valium, the most common relaxant/tranquilizer prescribed by physicians; she tried to keep to the prescribed dose but eventually had to increase it to receive any relief; and she is profoundly depressed, even suicidal.

In one sense, however, Maggie is lucky: she's addicted only to two drugs. Take the case of Mary Ann Crenshaw, author and former *New York Times* fashion reporter, who came into treatment with a suitcase full of different drugs: Navane, a tranquilizer used to treat emotional and mental illness; Eskalith (Lithium), a mood stabilizer; Placidyl, a sedative and hypnotic drug used primarily to help people fall asleep; Valium, a tension reliever and muscle relaxant; Percodan, a narcotic painreliever; tetracycline, for an infected thyroid gland; papase, a papaya enzyme used for bloat; Kanulase and Librax (pancreatic enzymes and bowel relaxers containing Librium) for pancreatitis; and aspirin, antihistamines, sinus decongestants, nasal sprays, vitamins, and minerals. Crenshaw's withdrawal from these drugs was slow and agonizing. As she wrote in her book *The End of the Rainbow*, "I felt like the ball in some wild pinball machine, flipped about on little swingarms by an unseen, sadistic player."

Maggie and Mary Ann Crenshaw are no longer the exceptions at alcoholism treatment centers: many centers, like the well-known alcoholism service at Long Beach General Hospital, report that as much as 45 percent of their patients (and sometimes more) are polydrug addicted. The percentage is higher for women than men—at the Betty Ford Center, for example, 50 percent of the beds are filled by women and 90 percent of these women are cross-addicted to both alcohol and drugs. Eighty to 90 percent of teenagers admitted to alcoholism treatment centers are regular users of prescription and/or illicit drugs. The elderly are at obvious risk for polydrug addiction because of the drugs they take for medical and psychological problems.

The polydrug addict presents a number of special challenges to the treatment staff. They are, in general, sicker than patients addicted only to alcohol; they experience a more prolonged and uncontrollable urge to drink or take drugs again; they are more likely to experience seizures and hallucinations if treatment is delayed; and their withdrawal course is longer and more unpredictable.

Furthermore, unless the staff members are specifically trained in understanding and dealing with polydrug addiction, they will typically misinterpret the symptoms of withdrawal as evidence that these patients are emotionally sick, and will either overmedicate them or suggest transferring them to a psychiatric ward. Untrained and inexperienced staff members tend to be uncomfortable with polydrug patients, impatient with their seemingly hysterical behavior, and often harbor the belief that these patients are "too sick for the program," or perhaps even "hopeless." The patients themselves are extremely sensitive to the staff's insecurity and anxiety and, combined with their own drug-induced fears and anxieties, are very likely to bolt from treatment.

Special training and insight will, on the other hand, help the staff to be more sensitive to the problems of polydrug addiction and withdrawal and will significantly increase the success rate of treatment for these patients. In general, it's essential that the staff understand the following unique aspects of polydrug addiction:

1. The withdrawal course from prescription drugs is very different from that for alcohol alone (see appendix 5). Alcohol

withdrawal, for example, typically begins on the first or second day after the patient stops drinking or cuts down significantly, and the withdrawal symptoms usually resolve within four to five days. Withdrawal from barbiturates and other intermediate-acting sedatives typically begins four to five days after the patient stops using the drug, reaches its greatest intensity by the sixth or seventh day, and subsides within eight to ten days. Long-acting drugs such as Valium cause an escalating withdrawal, with signs and symptoms (increased blood pressure and pulse, profuse sweating, tremors) for up to ten days and then fluctuating in intensity for a period of two to four weeks. In Valium withdrawal, the symptoms also come in *waves* of varying intensity, rather than the classical pattern of rapid onset, peak, and then gradual decline.

2. The delayed (protracted) withdrawal from Valium causes more symptoms than signs, meaning that the patient is extremely anxious, depressed, agitated, and, in general, miserable, but in the extended (latter) phase often does not have significant tremors, sweating, nausea, or vomiting. Thus, it's more difficult for the staff to recognize the withdrawal syndrome for what it is, and untrained staff members are more likely to misinterpret the patient's complaints as hysterical, psychosomatic, or simply the ramblings of a difficult and uncooperative patient.

3. The typical withdrawal symptoms for sedative addicts include extreme anxiety, nervousness, insomnia, a feeling of pounding inside caused by rapid heartbeat, and an overwhelming sense of helplessness and hopelessness. Some patients report sensory distortions (one woman, for example, thought the grain of wood in her door was forming ugly faces and making fun of her), and frank distortions of reality such as auditory or, less likely, visual hallucinations.

4. Because of the intensity and unpredictability of the withdrawal, these patients are often obsessed with leaving treatment and may attempt to manipulate the staff and other patients in an effort to be released.

In treating the polydrug addict, it's important, first of all, to give constant encouragement and support. The staff should continually reassure the patient that he is not crazy but, instead, is experiencing the symptoms of withdrawal. The alcohol/drug addict should be helped to understand that these symptoms can last for weeks, even months, and that peaceful times may be followed by waves of panic or emotional disruption. Understanding the nature of the withdrawal syndrome will help the patient to weather through it, and he will be able to separate his own personality and behavior from those behaviors initiated and governed by the addiction.

On admission, the physician or nurse should take a very careful alcohol and drug history, in an attempt to get the full picture of length and dosage of drug use. The severity and length of the Valium withdrawal syndrome, for example, depends as much on how long the patient has been taking the drug as on how much he has been taking every day. However, polydrug patients are notorious for hiding or minimizing their drug use for a number of reasons: they fear censure or rejection; they have convinced themselves that because the drugs are prescribed by a physician (and marked refillable) they cannot be harmful or addictive; and they firmly believe they have a medical need for these drugs. The right attitude—understanding, support, lack of judgment or censure—can go a long way in helping the staff to get an accurate and complete picture of drug and alcohol use.

While using a substitute tranquilizer or sedative drug is often not necessary for alcohol withdrawal, it is essential for anyone with a history of prolonged sedative or tranquilizer use, in order to maintain control of the patient and prevent seizures and drug-withdrawal psychoses. Substitute drug therapy should begin as soon as possible and, for Valium users, long before withdrawal begins. Otherwise, the withdrawal symptoms are likely to be more severe, and the patient is more likely to leave treatment in order to medicate himself.

How much medication to give these patients is a complex question: the trick is to give a sufficient amount to control the extreme agitation and anxiety of the withdrawal syndrome but not to give so much or to continue the medication for so long that it prolongs the addiction.

Alternatives and adjuncts to sedatives and tranquilizers are available and have been effective in treating the symptoms of polydrug withdrawal. Inderal and other beta blocker drugs block certain chemical reactions in the nervous system, helping the patient to feel calm, slow down the racing, pounding sensations, and stabilize blood pressure and pulse. Tryptophan, an amino acid and natural mood elevator, helps relieve insomnia and depression in some patients. Avoiding both sugar and caffeine is absolutely essential for both alcoholics and polydrug addicts, and a healthy diet (see page 159) will go a long way toward reducing feelings of stress, tension, and anxiety and alleviating depression, mood swings, panic reactions, and irritability.

Illicit Drugs

In addition to the "legal" prescription drugs, illegal or illicit drugs are increasingly a problem for many alcoholics, particularly teenagers. The illicit drugs most commonly used by alcoholics include marijuana, cocaine, hallucinogens (LSD, PCP), amphetamines, and, less often, opiates and heroin.

A major problem facing the users of these drugs is the social stereotype that anyone who uses illegal drugs is somehow inherently deviant and belongs to a lower class of people—the so-called street people. Even alcoholics, who have for centuries been the object of similar scorn and moral condescension, tend not to accept drug addicts and to exclude them from friendships and discussions, reasoning that they are altogether a "different sort of people."

Staff members tend to share this attitude and orientation toward these patients, viewing them as unmanageable, undependable, threatening, and out of control. A fearful, intimidated, and biased staff will not stand much chance against an addiction to both alcohol and drugs such as cocaine, speed, or heroin, and many of these patients either leave treatment AMA ("against medical advice"; see p. 193) or quickly relapse after treatment.

The opiate- or cocaine-dependent person seems to be "driven" by an exceedingly strong addiction and generally requires a longer time in treatment. The acute detoxification period lasts about the same amount of time as that for the alcohol-only addict, but the *protracted withdrawal* period can last for weeks or even months, with the addict experiencing a penetrating and persistent drive to use the drug he's addicted to.

Cocaine is a particularly troublesome addiction. In the past, it was believed that cocaine was not physically addictive at all, but only psychologically habituating. Yet, cocaine addicts show all the signs of addiction—compulsion to use the drug, loss of control, increased tolerance, and continued use despite adverse effects—and their addiction is extremely difficult to control, even after months of abstinence. One man, a lawyer, went through an in-patient treatment program and had been "clean" for several months when a client paid him with a gram of cocaine. The lawyer, sweating and tremulous, had to call a friend to come into his office and flush the white powder down the toilet—he simply couldn't do it himself. It is characteristic of cocaine addicts to hate what cocaine has done to their lives but to retain a fierce obsession, almost a love, for the drug.

Cocaine, like heroin, stimulates the part of the brain that is responsible for producing the pleasurable sensations of reward. Laboratory animals with unlimited access to cocaine lose up to 40 percent of their body weight within a few weeks, have difficulty sleeping, neglect grooming activities, and typically die from drug-induced convulsions or viral infections within two to three weeks. In other studies, laboratory animals with access to cocaine by pressing a bar would continue to press the bar to the point of exhaustion or death, even after the cocaine was no longer being delivered.

Another major problem for cocaine addicts is the use of other drugs—alcohol, tranquilizers, sedatives, sleeping pills, or, most effective of all, heroin—to ease the unpleasant symptoms of a cocaine "run." A recent survey of five hundred callers to the national helpline (1-800-COCAINE, established in May 1983) reported that 68 percent of the callers were using tranquilizers, marijuana, alcohol, or heroin to relieve jitteriness, restlessness, sleeplessness, and paranoia. Seventy-five percent of these callers admitted that they had lost control over their cocaine use, and 67 percent said that despite repeated attempts, they were unable to stop using the drug. Ten percent of the callers had lost their jobs, 25 percent their spouses, 44 percent their friends, and 35 percent all their monetary resources.

While the actual *physical* withdrawal from cocaine is not particularly troublesome or distressing for the patient, the cocaine hunger of these addicts is intense and can be ignited by the slightest memory or stimulus. One patient, attending a lecture in treatment, sat down next to a woman who wore the same perfume as his former cocaine-user girlfriend wore; he was instantly overwhelmed by an urge to use the drug and had to leave the lecture to get himself under control. Many cocaine addicts report that they simply can't participate in the "drunkalogues" so commonly heard in group and individual counseling sessions, in which the alcoholic recounts the events of his drinking days: just talking about cocaine revives the cocaine addict's intense hunger for the drug.

While addiction to cocaine and the opiate drugs is powerful and perhaps more penetrating than addiction to alcohol alone, these addicts are no different, psychologically, emotionally, or morally, from alcoholics or sedative/tranquilizer addicts. They are addicted to a central nervous system drug, and while the withdrawal symptoms and course vary, the *process* of addiction is similar in all cases. While the *force* of addiction to cocaine, heroin, or Valium may be stronger and take longer to control, the addiction management itself is the same and requires the same control and understanding from the staff.

The cocaine or opiate addict must be helped to understand and come to grips with the nature of his addiction, the need for abstinence from *all* drugs, and the necessary commitment to the tools of addiction management. With firm control from the staff and with the understanding that the addiction will, over time, lessen in intensity, these addicts have an excellent chance for successful recovery.

Special Problems

Against Medical Advice (AMA)

AMA—or leaving treatment "against medical advice"—is the medical equivalent of the military AWOL. The key to keeping the AMA rate as low as possible—from 5 to 10 percent—rests in the staff's ability to work as a tightly knit team, to recognize the signs indicating that a patient is considering leaving treatment, and to work fast to redirect the patient back toward treatment and recovery.

The staff must not be distracted by the patient's behavior or line of talk but must focus instead on the addiction process at work, which often reveals itself in subtle ways. Talk of leaving treatment, for example, is in the nature of the addiction and is to be expected, just as it is to be expected that a person with a broken leg will complain of pain and urge the doctor to remove his cast. Without this understanding of the addiction, the staff can get confused by the patient's behavior, misconstrue his complaints as evidence of stubbornness or belligerence, and neglect the basic problem, which is a struggling addiction seeking to get its needs met.

A struggling addiction shows itself in a number of ways (see chapter 10), and the staff must be trained to recognize and confront the addiction before the patient is overwhelmed by it. Sometimes it's necessary to stage an intervention, calling in a family member, boss, friend, or lover to help convince the alcoholic of the need to stay in treatment and the serious consequences that will ensue if he decides to leave AMA.

Leaving AMA can often be aborted simply by anticipating the needs of the patient. Rather than ignoring the complaints or labeling the complainer "difficult," it's important to treat the problem, make the alcoholic feel that he is being cared for, and assure him that the staff members will do everything they can to help him. If, for example, a patient complains of a recurring headache, a nurse or physician should be consulted. If a patient is worried about his bills being paid, a member of the staff should check things out with a phone call to the spouse or the patient's bank. If a patient complains about an ingrown toenail, frequent soakings and periodic checks can allay fears and potential agitation.

In responding to a patient's complaints in simple, basic ways, the staff conveys the message that they are in charge, everything is under control, and the patient's needs will be taken care of. If, on the other hand, the staff ignores minor complaints, the patient is likely to feel neglected, become worried and agitated, and, perhaps, decide that since he's not getting the care he needs and feels he deserves, he'll leave and get it elsewhere.

Keeping the AMA rate low can take a good deal of time, effort, and detective work. In nonspecialty settings, such as a general hospital ward, the staff is not trained specifically to understand and deal with the different behaviors of addiction, and patients on such wards are notorious for manipulating one staff member against another and weaseling their way out of the hospital before anyone even examines them. The addiction is actually aided and abetted by the staff's organization and lack of training and experience in dealing with addictions. The nurses on a general hospital ward typically care for a number of doctors' patients, and thus do not work as a close-knit team focusing on the single problem of addiction. As a result, the alcoholic's addiction can gain the upper hand, while the nurses, doctors, and orderlies become upset, angry, and frustrated because the patient refuses to follow directions. Other hospital patients may be confused and frightened, and pandemonium reigns.

Many doctors and nurses who work in general hospitals will roll their eyes and moan when you mention the word *alcoholic*—they have come to believe that alcoholics in general are difficult, manipulative, and untreatable patients, and they want as little to do with them as possible. The AMA rate on such nonspecialized wards may be as high as 70 to 80 percent.

Alcoholics have a disease that requires specialized knowledge and training (not to mention an open mind, patience, and a gentle spirit). They deserve the very best care they can get, because the quality of that care will directly affect their chances for recovery. It's hardly fair to blame a patient for the failure of his treatment when the treatment itself is inadequate, ill conceived, and improperly executed.

Seizures

Alcoholics with a history of drinking daily and in large quantities (a pint or more a day) and who have marked tremors (jerking and twitching movements of the body) are prone to having seizures during withdrawal, particularly if they have a history of previous alcohol withdrawal seizures. These "rum fits" are major motor seizures occurring in withdrawal in a patient with no previous history of other seizure disorders and with normal EEGs (brain wave tests). Patients withdrawing from addiction to Valium or barbiturates are also more likely to experience a seizure in withdrawal, particularly if they quit "cold turkey" or come off the drug too quickly. In these cases, the seizure is generally a late manifestation of withdrawal, occurring around the tenth day of treatment.

A careful alcohol and drug history will help target those patients most vulnerable to seizures; proper sedation, vitamins and mineral supplements, and close medical supervision will avert seizures in the great majority of patients. (With comprehensive care, less than 1 percent of patients will have seizures.) The staff should be on the alert for increased irritability in a patient, both in the way he acts and in central nervous system signs such as hyperreflexia (exaggerated deep tendon reflexes like the knee jerk), increased startle reflex (jumping or startling at the slightest noise or movement), heightened restlessness, worsened insomnia, etc.

It's particularly important that the staff resist labeling such patients as difficult or stubborn and instead recognize the signs and symptoms as evidence of withdrawal and central nervous system instability. One woman, for example, was in her second week of treatment and had been tapered off detox medications when she had two episodes of going weak in the knees and dropping to the floor. Because she stayed conscious, the staff believed she was faking a seizure in an effort to be put back on drugs. The next day she suffered a grand mal seizure.

Seizures are dangerous because they may cause a patient to fall and injure himself; they may follow one after another (called "status epilepticus") and be life-threatening; and they may be caused by some other serious, potentially life-threatening problem, such as a tumor, brain hemorrhage, or infection, and be misdiagnosed as alcohol/drug withdrawal. Status epilepticus is not common with alcohol withdrawal seizures but is more likely to occur in barbiturate withdrawal seizures.

Withdrawal seizures are more frightening in appearance than they are in fact, and unless they are caused by another medical problem or accompanied by injury to the patient, they do not indicate any serious or long-term recovery problem.

Delirium Tremens (DTs)

Of all the physical manifestations of withdrawal, the DTs are the most horrifying of all. While DTs can, in almost all cases, be prevented with adequate medical treatment (sedation, nutritional supplements, and close supervision) during withdrawal, once an alcoholic is "into" them, the mortality rate is 10 to 20 percent—thirty to forty times the withdrawal fatality rate for heroin addicts.

Delirium tremens provides a stunningly visual picture of the profound disturbance in the central nervous system caused by the withdrawal of alcohol from a body that literally needs it to function and may, in fact, die without it. The victim is mentally disoriented and hallucinating. He may claw at giant bugs or take a broom and try to fend off rabid rats. His hands shake uncontrollably and his legs are unsteady.

Left untreated, the tremors will take over the victim's entire body. He sweats profusely, soaking his bedclothes and sheets every hour or two. His bed shakes and trembles as if in an earthquake. He will ramble on senselessly, unaware of the time of day, where he is, or who is in the room with him. He may mistake the staff as family members and hold an involved conversation with Aunt Kathryn, who is long since deceased. He may jump out of bed and aimlessly wander around as if in search of something (but he couldn't tell you what).

The victim of DTs is often combative, agitated, and unable to respond to reason. He may misconstrue help as harm, misinterpreting the nurse's injection of medicine as poison and, in a panic, accusing her of trying to kill him. Eating utensils may be perceived as swords or sharp knives. His face is a mask of terror and fear.

The "horrors," as some sufferers call the DTs, typically begin three to four days after the alcoholic stops drinking and can last anywhere from three to seven terrifying days. Once begun, there's no way to stop them—the staff can only keep the patient as calm as possible through constant attention, proper sedation, and continual reassurance (see pages 127–129 for more information about treating DTs).

Hypoglycemia*

Hypoglycemia, or low blood sugar, is a chronic condition that can cause a number of unpleasant symptoms including nervousness, sweating, nausea, confusion, irritability, depression, and mood swings. Alcoholics are particularly susceptible

*For a complete discussion of hypoglycemia, read chapter 4 of *Eating Right to Live Sober,* by Ketcham and Mueller.

to abnormal fluctuations in their blood sugar (glucose) levels, and this is true both when they're drinking *and* when they're sober. Alcohol itself disrupts the blood sugar level because it is so rich in sugar, and regular, heavy drinking sets up a sort of rollercoaster effect in which the blood sugar level first spikes and then, as alcohol is metabolized and eliminated, drops like a rock. Furthermore, years of heavy drinking will weaken and, in some cases, damage those organs—the pancreas, liver, intestinal tract, brain, and adrenal glands—responsible for keeping the blood sugar at normal levels and can contribute to acute and long-term blood sugar problems. Finally, alcoholics tend to eat poorly and irregularly, further complicating their blood sugar problems.

Common Symptoms of Hypoglycemia

Anxiety
Craving for sweets
Crying spells
Depression
Difficulty concentrating
Exhaustion
Forgetfulness
Headaches
Heart palpitations
Irritability
Indecisiveness
Insomnia
Lack of appetite
Mental confusion
Mood swings
Muscle pain and backaches
Nervousness
Sweating
Trembling
Vertigo

Because hypoglycemia is such a common problem for alcoholics* and the symptoms mimic psychological or behavioral

*A 1981 survey by L. Ann Mueller, M.D., reported problems in blood sugar regulation in 93 percent of alcoholics who had been sober for at least two weeks, with two-thirds of the patients demonstrating active symptoms.

problems, it is important to properly diagnose this disorder. One method used is a six-hour glucose tolerance test. This test tells how well the body can tolerate concentrated sweets and provides a sort of mirror to see what happens in real-life situations when the hypoglycemic eats sugar or sweets. The patient is given a concentrated dose of sugar (usually in a liquid form), blood samples are drawn regularly over the next six hours, and the blood sugar curve is then charted on a graph. The patient's subjective experience during the test must also be recorded, and the symptoms can then be correlated with the rise and fall in blood sugar. For example, a patient might report feeling queasy, shaky, and anxious when her blood sugar drops; another might experience a panic reaction, like the adrenaline rush that occurs in a terrifying situation; still others will report headaches, mental confusion, irritability, and drowsiness, or become belligerent or even violent; in rare cases, a patient may faint or have a seizure during the test.

Treatment of hypoglycemia includes avoiding, whenever possible, the "Three Unhealthy S's"—sweets, stimulants (caffeine, nicotine), and stress—and replacing them with the "Three Healthy S's"—suitable diet, snacks, and supplements (vitamins and minerals taken daily). The diet recommended for controlling blood sugar problems is high in complex carbohydrates (fruits, vegetables, and whole grains), fiber, and protein, with three nutritious snacks daily (mid-morning, afternoon, and evening).

With guidance in understanding the need for nutritional therapy and help in meal planning, recipe selection, and choosing a supplement, the alcoholic will be well prepared to follow the diet and in doing so will find relief from the distressing symptoms associated with hypoglycemia.

Contraband

Contraband is the word used for items smuggled into treatment; it usually refers to drugs or alcohol. Obviously it's crucial to keep the alcoholic treatment ward free of all alcohol and drugs. But on an open ward where patients are free to see visitors, stroll the grounds, and even leave the premises, problems occasionally arise with contraband. Generally, alcoholics with a history of heavy drug use (prescription or illicit), teenagers,

and late-stage alcoholics are the most likely to sneak in drugs
or alcohol, usually in the first week or two of their treatment.

The first thing the staff can do is make sure that patients do
not bring contraband with them when they come into treatment. Searching through his personal belongings can make a
patient feel that he's not trusted or even that he is, in a sense,
being violated, so it's important to explain exactly why the
search is being conducted: aftershave and perfumes, for example, contain alcohol and might be grabbed up by one of the
sicker patients; razor blades can be used in suicide attempts;
all medications, including aspirin or cold tablets, must be kept
at the nurses' station.

A full body search may be necessary for patients with a
history of hard and heavy drug use, even to the point of
searching body cavities that might be used to temporarily store
drugs. Again, it's crucial that the patient is helped to understand that it's the addiction that is considered devious and
untrustworthy, not the individual himself.

Someone who brings drugs into treatment can create a
good deal of anger and resentment among the other patients.
It's the staff's duty to use this anger to turn the situation around
and get the offending person straightened out. It is unfortunately true in the dynamics of treatment that one bad apple can
spoil the whole barrel, and the staff must work quickly and
definitively to cut through to the danger before it spreads. The
offender should be confronted immediately and told that bringing alcohol and/or drugs into treatment represents a serious
breach of the rules. If the patient admits that he used drugs and
sincerely seems to regret it, he can be allowed to continue
treatment and may be required to begin all over again, at Day
1. If the patient denies the charge or tries to bluff his way out of
it, the other patients can be called together to verbalize their
thoughts and feelings. As one man said to a teenager who was
caught smoking marijuana: "I came here to get well, and when
I heard that there was marijuana on the ward, I was scared—I
didn't feel safe anymore. I felt as if my treatment was being
invaded and undermined."

The purpose of such a group meeting is not to humiliate the
offender but to help him understand the seriousness and reality
of his out-of-control addiction and what his actions mean to the
group as a whole. If a patient continues to deny that he brought

contraband into treatment, remains hostile and arrogant, and expresses the desire to leave treatment, he should be discharged.

All the special people and special problems described in this chapter can be dealt with in the normal treatment situation. As we've discussed, patience and persistence are often essential, as is the understanding that despite their unique problems, all these people suffer from the same basic disease and require the same basic treatment. With special handling and understanding, problems can be surmounted, patients will feel comforted and assured, and the process of recovery is allowed to progress unimpeded.

CHAPTER 14

The Diary of Jennifer Chase

Jennifer Chase is a pseudonym, but this is her story just as she wrote it. Names, exact dates, places, and other distinguishing facts have been changed to protect Jennifer's privacy. Minor editing changes have been made for the purposes of clarity.

Jennifer is 32 years old and a freelance graphic artist. She had been drinking a half-gallon of wine daily for the year prior to her treatment. The treatment staff diagnosed her as a middle-late-stage alcoholic.

Jennifer was separated from her husband, Tim, who was in the process of filing for divorce. She entered treatment "voluntarily" to avoid involuntary-commitment procedures initiated by her husband and a close friend. In his affidavit filed with the superior court, Jennifer's husband cited frequent episodes of verbal and physical abuse when Jennifer was drinking, driving while drunk, poor hygiene, loss of jobs due to drinking, accidents, and suicidal threats. Jennifer had been in treatment at another center three months before the treatment she describes in this diary, but relapsed shortly after discharge.

In her diary Jennifer discusses many of the problem areas common to recovering alcoholics: guilt, fear, anger, resentment, ultrasensitivity, inability to identify and deal with feelings, financial worries, sleep difficulties, estrangement from family, loss of self-esteem, and career problems. As you read her words, you will live through the four weeks of treatment with her and experience her personal growth as she progresses from the confusion and toxicity of early recovery, to a period of vacillating between keeping control in her own hands and surrendering to the program, and, finally, her struggle to internalize what she has learned in treatment and commit herself, heart and soul, to recovery.

Day One

Last night, at about 8:15, I arrived at the treatment center— frightened, anxious, and knowing that treatment was necessary as I could no longer control my drinking. My mother and Tim checked me in. I could hardly sign my own name due to the shakes. It was a sad departure for Mom and Tim, but a relief to all of us. The usual nurse examination[1] was performed, and I was introduced to my roommate. We talked until 1:30 A.M. —that helped my anxiety.

I slept sporadically through the night because of withdrawals, anxiety, and outside noise. In the morning, I felt somewhat frightened and shaky—I'm still taking medication for withdrawals. I read the introduction package to the treatment center; the other patients were at a lecture on nutrition or in feedback groups.[2] My anxiety began to substantially subside as the patients were very friendly and I became more "at home." I had a physical exam and received my clothes and went to lunch. Now I was a part of the family and was feeling the love of people who care, as we are all in this together. Went to a lecture on RET,[3] a new concept for me which I find fascinating. I was assigned to a group and we met—what a closeness among these people—I belong!

Dinner and fellowship[4] was wonderful. The movie after it (If You Loved Me, which I had seen before) brought back feelings of remorse and guilt—that's what happened to my marriage. How sad and how I hurt.

We went upstairs and played cards. What fun, and I am starting to feel physically better. The patients are bringing back my self-esteem and are we laughing!

[1]The initial assessment, conducted in this case by a nurse, consisted of taking drinking and medical histories and recording vital signs (blood pressure, pulse, and temperature).

[2]In feedback groups, the patients discuss their problems and adjustments in treatment, and the staff gives them "feedback" on their progress (or lack of it).

[3]See pp. 170–171 for a description of rational emotive therapy (RET).

[4]"Fellowship" is an AA meeting.

Day Two

Had a nonrestful night—slept but had bad dreams. I finally got to sleep around 4:00 A.M. Woke up tired but my energy level picked up after breakfast. I've accepted being here now and am enjoying the patients—in fact, we're having fun talking about why we are here and what happens when we are released. The lecture on "denial" was superb! I learned so much—new material that I hadn't learned at the Center.[1] Karen, my counselor, pointed out the one big mistake I made after release from the Center—I went back to an alcoholic boyfriend and boss. I feel guilty about not having any control, since I had the tools; but now I understand that relapse is common. Six patients in my same class have relapsed.[2]

Our group session[3] emphasized the points brought out in the lecture which we generally discussed. I was able to open up somewhat with my experiences with denial and relapse. Guilt is subsiding slowly, but anxiety over loss of my marriage bothers me the most—I'm still blaming myself.

The patients are definitely helping now—talking seems to be the best therapy. I don't get so irritated anymore now that I'm detoxicated.[4] The Week Wind-down Group[5] brought out sev-

eral good points. I believe the staff here really tries to help and cooperate with the patients.

The film we saw by Father Martin brought back some anxiety. I felt so guilty about destroying our marriage with alcohol and wish Tim was back. The pain is bad and the patients (some of them) knew something was wrong. I cried for a while and awaited the AA meeting. What a miracle that was! Wish there was another one tomorrow. I was temporarily released of my blame, guilt, and anxiety. Everyone was high that night. I was disappointed that my Mom and my husband didn't come tonight and won't come tomorrow. I need support and feel some loneliness. Despite this, I feel peaceful. I shared some of my feelings with Paul, my nurse. He further said to release my guilt, it's a disease. I'll get more tools here. My confidence in me is returning.

[1]The Center is a pseudonym for the rehabilitation program where Jennifer had been treated three months earlier.

[2]Approximately one-third of patients admitted to in-patient treatment have had some type of previous treatment—out-patient counseling, psychotherapy, two- to three-day detoxification, etc. Given effective, in-patient treatment, the relapse rate is around 15 to 20 percent.

[3]In this particular treatment center, six to ten patients are assigned to a specific counselor and this group meets together twice each day throughout the treatment sequence.

[4]The grammatically correct word is *detoxified*.

[5]Once a week, each group has a wind-down session in which patients air their complaints, irritations, observations, worries, problems, etc. This isn't a therapy session per se, but a forum in which general nuisance items are addressed, such as feelings about the treatment rules and regulations, food, staff members, inner conflicts, etc.

Day Three

Last night was another restless night. After breakfast I took a nap and didn't go to the 9:30 family discussion[1] as none of my family came. That disappointed me, and I got on the "pity pot"—if they want me to get help, why don't they take an interest? So, I decided to pray about it and then read Under the

Influence.[2] *I've read it before, but it never hurts to read it again.*

The lecture was fascinating! I've always heard "an alcoholic can't be helped." Dr. Jones says the reverse—Hallelujah!! Hope I can convince my family and husband of this. They can be a big help.

Tim visited me during visiting hours. We talked about the Center, us, posttreatment, and alcoholism in general. I still love him and feel threatened by his girlfriend, but I refuse to let that dominate my treatment. I'm here for me this time—no matter what happens to us. Besides, there's hope!

Open house[3] was a blast! Seeing all those recovered alcoholics brought tears to my eyes. They were so happy and really convinced me that it's worth it. Tim was there—I think he has a better understanding of AA. He'll be at the Tuesday night meeting.

The film today was directed at women—The Last to Know. I sure could identify with that.

The AA meeting was good but much too large. I'm finding that AA meeting secretaries tend to call on the "old timers" and leave the new guys out. Guess that's okay—they speak from experience. I'm no chicken to speak—have never been too shy!

After the meeting we talked about it and played cards. Sure am liking the patients here—we all talk freely—well, almost all—some stick to themselves. Too bad, talking is half the therapy.

[1]The family discussion is a time for family members to learn about the disease and participate in the treatment program.

[2]*Under the Influence: A Guide to the Myths and Realities of Alcoholism,* by James R. Milam, Ph.D. and Katherine Ketcham (Madrona Publishers, 1981; Bantam paperback edition, 1983).

[3]Open house is not a regularly scheduled function but at this particular time was a special reunion of "graduates" to which the current patients were invited.

Day Four

I had a great sleep! My new roommate is a sweetie from Alaska. She got into drugs—sure glad I never did.

Am getting my energy back, maybe too much! Am getting testy with the staff but not in an obnoxious way. I like to tease and they like it. They are really great people and can take a joke. All say I'm looking great! I tried convincing one of them that I needed a "pizza pass," but they wouldn't go for it. Darn!

Since we had nothing scheduled until noon, some of us went to an AA meeting. It was a predominantly gay meeting, which I am used to, having worked with several gay people. It was a very good meeting—gays tend to be very honest, no bullshit.

I visited with my Mom after lunch. It was a comfortable visit, and we got several financial matters straightened out. Tim stopped by. For a while it was a good visit—we talked about treatment again and what he's been doing at work. Then the tune changed when he said, "Things are more complicated for us, as there's someone else in the picture." I knew he was seeing someone else, but hadn't been dwelling on it. Jealousy always hurts. He told me about her high-flying job—BIG DEAL—he got a sugar momma! Then he started talking about old times, my demandingness, lack of judgment, and inability to make rational decisions. This upset me! He left and then I thought all this through—this is not going to affect my being here—I'm here for treatment, not to worry about us. I talked to my Higher Power "God" and really felt serene and peaceful. At times through the night, I had moments of anxiety and remorse, but it subsided when I reminded myself that I'm here to get well, and besides, maybe I won't want him!

The AA meeting was awful. Tomorrow will be better.

Day Five

Didn't sleep well but feel okay this morning. Have dreams about being at home and at work. Nothing about my husband. I'm concerned about legal fees, if necessary, but that's future tripping—who knows what will happen.

The relapse lecture was similar to one I'd heard at the Center, but refreshing. I learned some new material—now I have some more insight as to my own relapse.

At group we talked about relapse and heard some firsthand experience. Doesn't bother me to share my story if I can help someone else. It helps me, too.

Our afternoon lecture was on "Alternatives to Drinking." The options were AA and "get a sponsor," although I believe it should have been more thorough, i.e., exercise, music, reading, visit a friend, take a walk, etc.

After the lecture I returned to my room and then was called to the front desk to receive one dozen balloons with the card "Get Well, Love, Tim." This rather confused me due to yesterday's conversation. I couldn't get to the phone before 5:55 as it was busy. When I called to thank him, he was gone and had his answering machine on. Guess I'll have to wait until tomorrow to "dialogue" with him.

We went to the Longshoreman AA meeting. This is one I will pursue upon discharge—there's good sobriety, clean language, and good fellowship. I'm getting much more at ease speaking out—but then again, I've never been shy!

Have been thinking more about what kind of job to look for upon discharge and have decided to try for a job with an advertising firm. Tomorrow I am going to make some contacts.

Day Seven

Forgot to write in my diary last night. It was a good day—can't remember anything significant.

Had a good night's sleep. Woke up feeling chipper and ready for a good day.

The first lecture was on nutrition, the presentation was very precise and thorough. It was interesting to hear again how we have hurt our bodies through using chemicals and how we need to repair them through nutrition.

We studied Step Six—removing defects of character.[1] It was like an AA meeting, with good insight from all.

We all took a walk today—refreshing! Much needed. The rest of the afternoon we had time for reading.

The lecture on marijuana was informative, but my mind wasn't on it. I've never used drugs.

We went to a Speaker's Meeting.[2] It's the largest meeting I've been to. The people are strange, but I understand the group has great sobriety. The two speakers were women who have been through pure hell! I am thankful I never got that far, yet, and have a chance to rebound now.

I had my interview with Karen, my counselor. I felt pretty good about it on the whole. Since I just finished at the Center in November, it is difficult for me not to compare it with my treatment now. I have seen several strengths and weaknesses in both programs so far and don't think it's possible to discount the Center. Apparently, I also "stick up for patients." If I am asked my opinion, I honestly give it—sure, I have a habit of protecting others—I've always been that way—but I will work on it.

Several patients had a "rap" session after our meetings to compare notes. I sensed some unrest due to the large number of new patients coming into treatment. The overall impression is that there is not enough individual attention and that the center is understaffed. I tried to calm them down, as I've seen it before—things will be better tomorrow. Hope I didn't overstep my boundaries by "taking care of the patients," but I felt this was appropriate.

[1]AA Step Six: "We were entirely ready to have God remove all these defects of character"; for a complete listing of the Twelve Steps, see p. 167.

[2]AA meeting featuring one or two guest speakers.

Day Eight

Had the best night sleep yet—guess I'm finally settling down.

The head counselor gave a speech on communication. We covered areas in verbal and body communication. Am concerned somewhat with my listening power, but will work on that.

Our growth group[1] was healthy for all—I learned a lot about prejudice and racism as we have three minorities in our group. Think perhaps we all have been prejudiced against because of our drinking. Think I may have cut off some good relationships or potential relationships unknowingly. Will have to be more sensitive.

In our group session, we finished up what we began in growth group plus a First Step from one of our members.[2] Think I won't have any problems with my First Step—at least I'm hopefully past denial.

The afternoon lecture on grief surprised me since I couldn't figure out how grief related to alcohol. Now I see how the steps work—denial, depression, guilt, anger, acceptance, and reconstruction. Think I'm past denial now and am fluctuating among the others on a regular basis in various areas: i.e., job, finances, family relations, etc. At least now I know these feelings are normal and acceptable and, most of all, expected.

The lecture was likewise informative, precise, and very true to point. It's refreshing to know what to expect and what tools we will need in these encounters.

AA was good, but I didn't speak—maybe tomorrow.

[1]A growth group is a study group held after certain lectures to discuss the materials presented in the lecture and apply them personally.

[2]The First AA Step ("We admitted we were powerless over alcohol—that our lives had become unmanageable") is a particularly important step to emphasize in treatment, since both treatment and recovery are impossible unless the patient accepts the seriousness and devastating impact of his disease. In a "First Step" the patient makes lists of destructive behaviors caused by powerlessness over alcohol and examples of how life has become unmanageable and then discusses these lists with the staff and other patients.

Day Nine

This morning's lecture was on medical aspects of alcoholism—the effects of alcohol on our bodies. Heard a lot about stress and the alcoholic, which was easy for me to relate to. Hopefully, RET will aid in dealing with stressful situations. Would like to take a look inside me to see how much damage has been done to my various systems. One system I'm concerned with is my reproductive system, as my periods haven't been very regular since I've misused alcohol. I have already noticed a difference in my digestive system since I'm eating regularly now. My memory has markedly improved as well as my irritability. Things don't bug me as much.

In group we discussed communication and also had feedback. I don't mind criticism, but certain allegations were made that were totally unfounded and not true. I am discounting all as hearsay and will drop it. Before, I would have fought this kind of crap, but now I don't have time to waste—mental or physical. Group brings people closer together as one entity, but it's amazing how the members discuss the day's topic outside of group and the contrast of opinions expressed in group vs. outside of group. I have seen a lot of "lip service" during treatment both with counselors and health staff. Patients are anxious to "get out" so they sometimes fake it.

The unit is filling up far too fast for the staff to handle adequately. There's a buzz of unhappiness in the air due to the insufficient personal attention the patients are receiving and the inconsistency of rules and policies. I'm a sounding board for lots of this. It doesn't bother me too much. It seems to bother the staff a bit—they think I have a lot of anger. Perhaps so. I'll review this.

Group was a continuation of group in the morning. Communication was the topic. I sense a real disinterest in our group. No one wants to express his or her opinion. Karen asks for participation, no one volunteers, and then she is forced to throw out her opinion and ask if we agree or disagree or for comments. That works for a while, and then we are back to Step 1. Oh well, she needs more experience. Some members of our group feel she would be better for aftercare—perhaps this should be considered.

The evening lecture was on AA, NA,[1] Al-Anon, etc. There was nothing new to me, but Tim came, and he found it interesting.

We went to Seaside again for AA. I think I may find myself hanging out there a lot since it's so close to my home. The people are fun to watch and have great stories—convincing to say the least.

After AA, of course, there was another patient bitch session. I just sit back and listen. "Who gives a rat's ass?" is my idea. I'm here for treatment, not to be a social butterfly. Could go to a charm school for that!

---

[1]Narcotics Anonymous follows the same general principles as AA and is geared to people with a drug or alcohol/drug addiction.

Day Ten

Morning lecture: dry vs. clean and sober, quality recovery. The main gist I got out of this is that you can be dry and/or clean, but doing "stinkin' thinkin'." Quality "clean/sober" recovery requires RATIONAL RET.

Our regular group met to discuss the remainder of a First Step and say goodbye to two people. There were some heated discussions regarding denial, rationalization, and minimizing. I don't believe anything was resolved but I picked up on several thoughts and will analyze them as they pertain to me.

Our afternoon wind-down was reasonably peaceful. Rules were announced and verified. There was some dissatisfaction, but so what! At least there will hopefully be some consistency.

I'm noticing that my hair is getting back its sheen—doesn't feel like straw—and my nails are getting longer.

Day Eleven

Energy is incredible! Tim came for the family discussion group. Am able to sort out feelings now. Don't know if I want him back so am being cautious. Mom came for the lecture, which was very interesting and informative. The rest of the day was spent reading and B.S.ing with patients. Went to in-house NA meeting for curiosity. Now am trying to figure out the "now-whats" since I'm sober. There's a lot of anger and discontent among patients and I'm still the sounding board. Think I'll find a job where I have more contact with people.

Day Twelve

Spent most of the day visiting with family and B.S.ing with patients. Went to two AA meetings—still am not sharing. Did First Step for group—now it will be easier. Decided I like general discussion meetings although I need to voice First Step at AA meetings. Maybe this week. Tim stopped by as a surprise at noon—still can't figure relationship out. I'm thankful this time sobriety is #1.

Day Thirteen

Am sleeping regularly now. Anxiety is rare but still present.

A guest lecturer spoke about: Step 1. He's an interesting and perceptive person with the ability to elicit information and feelings from people.

In group, we discussed the First Step again. Looks as if I'm in the early-middle stage of alcoholism.[1]

The afternoon lecture was on over-the-counter drugs. I'm thankful we were given a list of those prescription drugs which contain chemicals that would threaten our sobriety.[2]

Our evening film was Father Martin's Guidelines. Mom and Tim came to watch the film and for the family meeting. I didn't get a chance to have an extended conversation with either of them and quite frankly don't like to be in the same room with both of them. I feel "ganged up on" and can feel tension in the room. If I leave, they talk and immediately stop when I return. I don't trust them as a result of intervention, and it has really affected my trust in anyone. I'm being very cautious now with anything I say. I read my First Step at group today. Karen thinks I'm angry—very angry—especially because of this intervention. I am not angry because I have worked that through in the past three weeks. However, my self-esteem due to this action is minimal, and I feel defeated. I feel much better when I'm earning a living so I'm anxious to market myself again. Think that will make a big difference in my self-esteem. I feel now when I get a job, I'm going to tell these people to get the hell out of my life—i.e., mind your own business. Guess this is where my anger (what's left of it) is still harboring. I want to stay sober now and I don't need spies—it breeds paranoia and I'm sick of it. Now that I'm able to reason, I feel Mom and Tim—especially Tim—are going through the motions of Al-Anon because "it's the thing to do," but I don't believe they're sincere. Think I'll have to work on trust. Karen and others in group don't think I'm opening up to everyone enough, but I *told them I'm selective about whom I open up to and spill my guts—before I would have to anyone—now that trust is gone. I'm glad I'm strong enough to fight total defeat—I like me!* ⋅

[1]Jennifer's counselor diagnosed her as late-middle stage.

[2]See appendix 7, p. 272 for such a list.

Day Fourteen

Woke up feeling anxious about divorce. Started thinking about attorney's fees and "What if we get divorced? How am I going to pay for it?" I don't want to get back together for financial purposes only—can't be dependent on anyone else anymore. I feel a need to run my own life alone for a while. Otherwise, the significant other may enable me to drink again—I need time.

The lecture was on nutrition. Looks as if vitamin C is a very worthwhile supplement. Hope I can carry out my nutrition program after discharge—I'm not good at cooking for one.

After lunch we had a meal-planning session, but it turned into a fiasco due to a disagreement between two patients. The tension seems to be getting thicker daily among those patients who will soon be discharged. They are testing the others' knowledge, and patients—I'm staying clear of all this—need to concentrate on sobriety, not seniority!

Also had a lecture on drugs. I'm still shutting off all references to drugs, as I have never used them. They don't interest me, and I block out all reference to them. I'm sure many people I know use drugs, but they've never exposed that part of their lives to me.

Had a conference with Karen. I opened up more to her than I do at group—still am having problems trusting people after this intervention, as I feel anything I say will be held against me. We decided to have a conference with Mom and Tim before discharge so I can tell them how I feel. Karen will be a great help as I'll need to be monitored. It's stressful thinking about moving home to my house with my spying mother—I don't want to accept a job to "get away from it all."

Sure like AA—that will be my saving grace this time.

Day Fifteen

The morning lecture was on attitudes toward self and others and sobriety. I can definitely see a change in my attitude toward myself—especially with regard to the guilt I harbored. My self-esteem is improving, but I think it will keep rising after discharge and getting a job. The humility I have because I don't have a job is playing on my conscience. It's time Jennifer covers her own ass and makes her own decisions. Having my mother living with me is a continuous problem. She always voices her opinion or suggests ways I should be spending my time, and I feel obligated sometimes to do it her way to keep her happy. I'm sick of having others pull my strings. This could be dangerous in my recovery, as it could breed isolation—a good set-up to drinking. Looks like I'll be spending more time at AA meetings than I ever guessed—good thing I like them. Actually, they are the answer to my successful recovery. Hopefully, my conference with Tim and Mom will alleviate some of this tension.

In group we further discussed attitudes. Our group has two "old-timers"—me and one other person. I'm enjoying watching the new people grow.

Our group after lunch centered around two patients' First Steps. Next week, I'm sure one will finally admit he's addicted to all chemicals and realize there's no such thing as a "substitution" for any drug.

Our afternoon lecture was on relapse—especially important to me as that's where I messed up before. It's very clear where I missed the boat—didn't follow through with my plan. I keep reading my first day entry and am reminded of the PAIN—that convinces me to stay sober.

The lecture on the spiritual aspect of AA was well done. I believe in God and am an active member in my church, so turning my will and life over to Him is easy. I did before, but drinking prevented me from clearly and honestly practicing my faith. For those people who don't have a defined faith, the lecturer gave some good alternatives. Otherwise, many people will be stuck at Steps 3 and 4.[1] I'm

*still working Steps 1–4, as I don't want to forget any faults—
I'd rather make a clean sweep all at once than in bits and
pieces.*

[1]Step 3: "We made a decision to turn our will and our lives over to the care of
God as we understood Him."
Step 4: "We made a searching and fearless moral inventory of ourselves."

Day Sixteen

*Our morning lecture was on RET. I need more information on
this—I RET after the fact.*[1]

In group we had two coin ceremonies.[2] *I found it difficult
to say nice things about one person as we had had a tiff earlier
in the morning. Wish I would have told Karen some "behind
the scenes" conversations I had with this person—there was a
lot of "lip service" given in group by her.*

*Wind-down was peaceful. We said lots of goodbyes. Have
a whole new "crop" of people now.*

Karen had the intervention team[3] *talk to me. I'm very angry
at my Mom re: being here and her influence on me while living
with me over the last six years. It's obviously apparent that she
will have to leave.*

*Saw a film on alcohol—physical effects of drinking on the
body. No one should drink alcohol!*

*The evening women's stag AA meeting was O.K. I still
prefer outside AA meetings.*

[1]Rational Emotive Therapy helps people learn the appropriate emotional reaction to people or situations. Jennifer is saying that she reacts to an insult or
criticism in her old ways and thinks through the RET steps "after the fact."

[2]The coin ceremony is a type of graduation ceremony in which patients
finishing their treatment are given a coin engraved with the treatment center's
name and sometimes the patient's name and graduation date. The coin is
passed around the group and as they receive the coin, each group member
talks to the "graduate," wishing him luck, giving encouragement, offering
words of wisdom, and saying goodbye.

[3]The intervention team consists of those significant others who are trying to be
of help and taking an active interest in the patient's treatment. In Jennifer's
case, this team included her counselor, mother, and husband.

Day Seventeen

Woke up anxious again. Should I stay another week or not?[1] *Had a big fight with my Mom last night regarding her invasion of my privacy and how the hell I'm going to pay for treatment if I stay another week—especially since I've arranged for three job interviews this week. Wish I had been more in control. Now I know what mood swings are.*

Tim got depressed at family group. He does this often—it affects me. I feel he picked what he wants to hear. The lecture on augmentation[2] *was the best. I sure have done that—when will this crap leave my system? I'm sick of being out of control—it makes me feel hopeless and desperate. I feel like I'm losing it—especially with everyone pounding at me! Now I know why people make geographic cures.*[3]

I think everyone should see the series of films called I'll Quit Tomorrow. *They are an excellent portrayal of the progression of the disease.*

We went to the Blue Ridge AA meeting. Nothing exceptional, but it kept me sober.

[1]This particular treatment center is set up with three weeks as the minimum stay; some patients, especially those with previous treatment failures, are encouraged to stay an extra week.

[2]Because of alcohol's direct, toxic effects on the brain, the brain is hypersensitive and overresponsive. Thus, the recovering alcoholic, particularly in the first weeks of treatment, will "make mountains out of molehills" and generally overreact to stressful or upsetting incidents. As the brain heals, augmentation gradually lessens and the alcoholic experiences more "normal" reactions.

[3]In an attempt to stop or cut down on drinking, many alcoholics try moving to a different location—the geographic cure.

Day Eighteen

I went home on a pass. Tim picked me up for church—we went to a new church. I didn't want to go to my own as I'm not ready to admit to everyone I failed at controlling my alcoholism.

After church, we went to his apartment. There was obvious

evidence of his and his girlfriend's sexual encounters. He doesn't
know I know—it really hurt—why is he still interested in me—
what is he thinking of? Should I drop him? Should I find a new
attorney? Our divorce trial is set for November. Why am I
jealous? I had an affair last fall. How the hell do you RET this
one?

Went to my house with Tim. Mom was cooking dinner for
all—next-door neighbor was there—he had just put his wife in
a rest home and had made funeral arrangements. She is dying
from alcoholism. I asked Mom why she asked him over (she
told me the Friday evening before that she had asked him), and
she said she felt that we should really have him over since
Sharon was so ill. Great! Just what I need—a depressing dinner
conversation my first Sunday home. "Oh, he'll just talk about
his garden and dog and won't even bring it up," Mom said.
Bullshit! The first thing he said when I asked him how he was
is, "Not very good—I just made funeral arrangements for Sharon.
That's something you should see; it's definitely due to her
drinking." What a happy thought! I went into the kitchen,
thanked Mom for making the afternoon so pleasant, cooled off
for five minutes, and then offered to go to the store for some
milk. It was nice to be alone. I spent thirty minutes at the store,
came home, ate, and then Tim and I went for a walk on the
beach. My stomach felt like hell—I wanted to run away from it
all. Mom took me back to the Recovery Center, and I went to
an AA meeting. Started feeling physically ill as I came down
with a cold.

Went to bed at 11:00 P.M. It was hard to get to sleep—kept
calling on my Higher Power but my mind kept drifting to the
problems of the day. Damn! Thought I was doing good—now I
feel like I'm going backwards.

Day Nineteen

Woke up sick—physically and emotionally. Think I'll stay another week—I can't fathom going home tomorrow feeling this
way.

The lecture on psychological problems hit home especially
since I'm at the height of all feelings. Am anxious for group. I

feel guilt, remorse, insecure, desperate, hopeless, shame, worth-
less, fearful, ugly, and defeated. Not much left is there? Haven't
felt suicidal—yet.

Guess who was the "victim" at group? Yup—me. I'm not
being honest—am putting up shields. I still don't trust anyone
since the intervention—"anything you say may be held against
you" keeps going through my mind. Am still future tripping—am
fearful of unknown. Sometimes I'm afraid of losing everything—
the next I'm excited about sobriety and what's in store for me.
Now I feel schizophrenic. Hope it's not true. Karen is frustrated
with me, and I with her. I don't want to tell her what she wants
to hear, and besides, I don't know what she's driving at. Maybe
things will clear up soon. They sure are foggy now.

Afternoon group consisted of two First Steps and discussion
of the morning lecture. I just sat and listened—felt defeated
anyways.

Our afternoon lecture was on sequence of events—i.e.,
admit, educate, compliance, acceptance, surrender, aftercare.
At this point, I'm caught between acceptance and surrender—
total surrender that is.

I have a virus that's going around, and I'd love to have a
pill for this cold—this is the first time I've used nonaddictive
drugs for a cold.

The AA meeting was great. We went to Broadway. At this
point, I think I'll try a Big Book or Step Meeting[1]—just for a
change.

[1]A Big Book meeting focuses on *Alcoholics Anonymous*, "the big book,"
which consists of essays by Bill W., the founder of AA, and personal stories by
alcoholics. A Step Meeting concentrates on one of the twelve AA steps.

Day Twenty

Woke up feeling very sick—physically. Also, had some anxiety
over 8:00 A.M. meeting with my mother and Tim.

The meeting was good and bad. Of course I felt ganged up
on, but that subsided now and then. It was enlightening with
respect to Tim's viewpoint—he's still the same. Had a some-

what haughty attitude as if he said "I told you so." If it made him feel better, fine. It made me sick and brought back old uneasy feelings—the ones I felt when I was drinking. Now that I'm sober, I am going to examine those feelings. I'm also examining feelings regarding my mother living with me—it will help financially for a while. However, I think she'll have to go come this fall.

Our lecture was on nutrition. The lectures are starting to repeat themselves now—this repeat cleared up the balance of my questions on nutrition and alcohol. I think the B vitamins are helping me to think more clearly, although it's tough to say with this darn cold—feels like someone insulated my mind.

We reviewed Step 8.[1] Think I'll wait to make a list of those I've hurt. I've made amends to some people already, but I think I'll need to make amendments to those amends.

Learned more about cocaine and am thankful I never tried it.

AA, again, was great—another First Step.

[1]Step 8: "We made a list of all persons we had harmed, and became willing to make amends to them all."

Day Twenty-one

Am still very anxious. Am feeling sick to my stomach over possible loss of marriage. Guilt is overwhelming. Why can't I forgive myself and blame this disease? Do I want us to make it because I'm insecure? If so, what a way to start or restart a relationship. In my mind's eye, I know what I want but am wondering if the disease is causing me to fantasize—so much has changed with regard to sharing. The biggest is our Christian faith. I'm still a Christian, whereas Tim left and wrote a letter to our church renouncing his faith—he said he wrote it to hurt me. I don't need this now!

Our lecture was on spirituality—Step 3. I can't imagine practicing this program without a Higher Power. Sometimes I'm impatient for answers and get angry. I feel, for example, God brought us together so why is this happening? Past experience should tell me the answer to this—trust Him. He knows.

In group we discussed spirituality and how we view our Higher Power. Karen was ill so we ad libbed it. I feel this should be a regular feature of the week—there's a lot more openness without a head figure. In our afternoon group, we discussed "the last straw"—what is the most terrible incident that would cause you to drink. It was generally loss of family. However, two people said "friends." The younger patients are concerned about peer pressure and doing old things without booze. Health is another—if I found out I had a terminal disease, would I drink? Depends on how much sobriety I had—who knows.

The head counselor lectured on progression. It was a reminder to all how serious this disease is. We don't heal—we maintain sobriety.

Day Twenty-two

Slept the best ever last night. It must have been the Vicks Vapo Rub! Felt like jogging, but the staff wouldn't let me out—rats!

There are nineteen people leaving between today (Thursday) and Sunday—that's incredible! Most came here after I did—now I'm the senior patient so am pulling rank. We walk where I want to go and go to AA meetings where I want to—just kidding.

In group we said good-byes to two members—they're so much more with it. Hope they stay that way.

Our lecture was a repeat of RET three weeks ago. Am now able to understand the concept better. Tim brought me a book on RET to help clarify some questions I had.

Day Twenty-three

In group we did role playing with a student from the university. Wish they would incorporate that on a regular basis. Communication of sober feelings is entirely new to us. I'm used to irrationally reacting to confrontations or dealing with problems in a drug-affected way. It's exciting having a chance to make a fresh start. I feel as if I'm graduating from college and looking for a new job. Think I need to do more homework.

We saw my favorite Father Martin film—Chalk Talk. Wish my whole family could see it—it's definitely the "meat" of understanding alcoholism.

There were some patients who didn't have rides to NA or AA so we held our own meetings, and I chaired. It's amazing how we absorb the structure of AA through going to AA meetings. Think someday I'll be a secretary[1] when my sobriety is more secure. We talked about our first drink and about spouses with drinking problems. It went for the entire one and one-half hours. Then we had to stop as the other patients came back and wanted coffee. This really comforted the new patients. There were enough "educated" patients to help them through the initial fears and apprehensions.

[1]The AA secretary is a voluntary position which lasts for six to twelve months. Duties include keeping track of donations (there are no membership dues or fees in AA), setting up the literature (all AA pamphlets and materials are free), arranging for the meeting room (usually in churches, where the rental is free or minimal), and general "housekeeping" (making coffee, setting up chairs, cleaning up after the meeting, etc.).

Day Twenty-four

Felt pretty good this morning. Am looking forward to the weekend.

Our morning lecture was on games that alcoholics play. I could identify with all of them. Basically, lying to protect my addiction—yuck! Who wants to protect that? Sometimes I feel defeated, but I don't want to play "kick me." Instead, I want revenge—on my addiction. Think this is taking the form of anger.

We discussed games in group. We all play the same games. I'm glad that's over with.

Wind-down was tame—no gripes at all.

I'm starting to "future trip" now as my discharge date draws nearer. Am thinking of sobriety, job, social life, family, husband, and a myriad of other areas. Will definitely concentrate on sobriety and a job for the time being. The others will have to take their course.

Day Twenty-five

The lecture was on alcoholism and heredity. I wish my Dad could have heard it—he can't figure out why I'm an alcoholic even though he is, too, and he lost a brother to alcoholism. I haven't seen him for four months so don't know if he's drinking now.

Saturday was long and lonely—I had no visitors but kept busy at cards. This is the worst day for everyone as there are few organized activities. To stir up trouble, some patients decided to draw up a petition regarding the food.

Day Twenty-six

Sunday was a good day. Spent five and one-half hours with Tim—it was well spent. I'm ready to leave. Have got to plan AA meetings and life after treatment. Liquor is not in my vocabulary anymore. Living is. Exercise, nutrition, and quality life are in my cards now—no more Jokers!

Day Twenty-seven

Had another good sleep last night. I'm now getting anxious about discharge—reality is hitting home. I'm going to be on my own soon—me and my sobriety.

Our lecture this morning was on finding an AA sponsor. Think I better find a more reliable sponsor as mine is dependent on me for rides to AA meetings. I have five people to call so I'll make contact immediately.

In group we had First Steps. Sure brought home memories of my first week.

We studied Step 4—think I better wait a couple weeks before taking my inventory. It will take me that long to remember half of what needs to be inventoried.

Went to Mill Creek for AA—I'm sure that will be a regular meeting for me—especially in the next few months.

Day Twenty-eight

Today is the day—I'm out. Have a lot of fear—what if I drink? I don't want to—is my intelligence sufficient to combat my addiction? I have the tools and support but now it's up to me.

My coin ceremony was subdued. Read my "Hello-Good-bye"[1] letters plus my Aftercare Plan.[2] Then I spoke with Karen. It was a good session, and I feel more confident. I have one week of AA meetings planned so need to carry that plan out. This week will set my pace. I pray my emotions will keep their place—behind my intellect—this time I HAVE to make it.

HELLO SOBRIETY

HELLO JENNIFER

[1]In the "good-bye" letter the patient writes good-bye to his old lifestyle, detailing what it was, how it affected him, and why he is terminating it. Then he writes a "hello" letter to what he hopes his new lifestyle will be.

[2]The Aftercare Plan is a specific plan the patient agrees to follow after discharge. It includes specific information on attending AA meetings, counseling sessions, and follow-up groups, and details any special areas of direction or counsel a particular patient may need.

PART THREE

Staying Sober

Going Home

You're facing that treatment-center door again, only now you're looking out instead of in. You've been sober for several weeks. You've said your good-byes. You've graduated. But what's this? Your heart is pounding, your palms are sweaty, your voice is shaky, and your legs are trembling. What's happening?

You're going home. And going home after being sheltered and protected, understood and loved can be terrifying. What will it be like "out there"? Will your family be able to forgive you? Will your friends welcome you? Will you fit in? How will you cope with all the hundreds of little details that have been neglected these last few weeks? Should you take time off or go straight back to work? What if you don't have a job—can you get one, will someone hire you? What if you feel the urge to drink again—what do you do? Will all those years of drinking catch up to you so that you'll have permanent brain damage or liver disease or heart problems? Can the knowledge and tools you gained in treatment really carry you over into this new life? What if life is no better sober than when you were drinking?

These questions disturb the inner peace of many recovering alcoholics. When you face that door, suitcase in hand, you may feel overwhelmed with fear, sadness, anxiety, even hope-

227

lessness. Recovery may seem such an elusive goal: the harder you work, the more work there is to be done. How long will it take before you are truly well, your physical health stabilized, your emotions in check, your mental powers at top form? How long will it be before things are smoothed over in your life and you can begin to work on the future instead of always having to mop up the past?

Most experts agree that recovery takes two years to become firmly established and that the recovering alcoholic will progress through three stages: early-stage recovery (one to six months), middle-stage recovery (six to twelve months), and late-stage recovery (one to two years). Each of these stages has its own particular difficulties to work through, but as you progress through the stages you will feel stronger and more capable. You will begin to feel confident about where you are going, and you will learn to trust in your ability to get there, despite occasional setbacks.

The Recovery Curve shows that after one month in treatment you have worked through only a small part of your total recovery. Despite an upsurge of improvement, you have barely begun your journey toward your maximum potential recovery. The next five months are considered the most difficult and demanding, with the highest risk of relapse. With continued hard work, however, you will be well on your way, and sometime between your first and second year of recovery you will rise above your predrinking level of happiness and well-being.

Rather than feeling overwhelmed by all that lies before you, it may help to think of recovery as climbing a challenging but extraordinarily beautiful mountain. The going is tough at times—you will stumble on rocks, feel lonely and tired, and at times wonder if the climb is worth it. But the views are spectacular, the air is fresh and clean, and, despite occasional bouts with pain and fear, you feel truly alive. When the climbing is particularly tough, try to concentrate on putting one foot in front of the other, breathe deeply, watch the trees thinning, and look out at the scenery.

Take your time—don't push too hard. This is not a race, you're not competing against anyone, you don't have to prove anything to anybody. Feel confident that you will get to the top

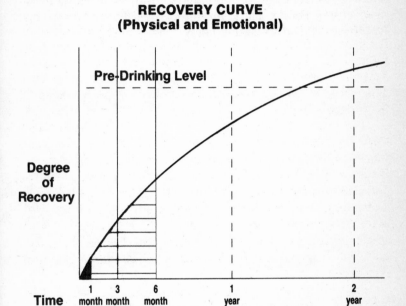

RECOVERY CURVE
(Physical and Emotional)

Pre-Drinking Level

Degree
of
Recovery

Time
1   3   6   1   2
month   month   month   year   year

Early   Middle   Late
Recovery   Recovery   Recovery

if you follow the trail, refuse to take shortcuts, and give yourself time to rest and reflect.

As the climb continues, you will learn to enjoy your increasing physical strength and mental sharpness. With each step upward you are stronger; with each step you have performed a small miracle: you are sober, today. As you continue climbing, that miracle will become less miraculous and more an accepted and essential part of your daily life. When you've reached the mountaintop, you will have gained a deep and abiding respect both for the climb and for yourself. And that respect will help to carry you through all the tomorrows that you have worked so hard to enjoy.

CHAPTER 15

Early Recovery
(1–6 months)

Most alcoholics who are going to relapse do so within the first six months after they leave treatment. This is a physically demanding, mentally draining, and emotionally exhausting period of reentry, when you must make numerous complicated adjustments in your life and establish a new pattern of daily living. You are vulnerable because you are so freshly sober and so inexperienced at living life without alcohol.

Returning to your old life as a new, sober person can be a profound shock. You are extremely sensitive to your surroundings. You have difficulty watching television because every fifteen minutes there's another beer commercial. Reading gives you a headache because every other page of your favorite magazine advertises how sexy and pleasurable it is to drink alcohol. At restaurants you are suddenly keenly aware how much everyone drinks. Social functions are deadly boring or excruciatingly nerve-racking, now that your head is clear and you can see the world as it really is.

In treatment, everyone understood about alcoholism. On the "outside," you encounter a lot of ignorance, and thus you experience a lot of pain and rejection. Comments like "Are you really serious about this sober stuff, Jack?" or "Come on, you weren't that bad," cut deep, leaving an empty, hollow feeling whistling through you. Encouragements to "Go ahead, have just one," make you furious. The look on your husband's face when he finds you sitting at the sewing machine, your former favorite hiding place for vodka bottles, makes you redden with shame and fury.

These first six months of sobriety can be rough going. One of your first steps should be to strengthen your new support network. Find your sponsor* in AA and call him whenever you feel lonely, afraid, sad, or depressed. Go to AA meetings several times a week; if you can work it out, go every night and perhaps attend some meetings during the day. Call your friends from treatment; keep in touch with your counselors. Encourage your family and friends to attend Al-Anon and Alateen.

Most in-patient alcoholism treatment centers offer an *aftercare* program, with a typical minimum of ten to twelve weekly sessions conducted at the treatment center by staff counselors. Aftercare is a crucial part of your treatment; although no one can force you to attend these sessions, the motivation should be strong within you. Aftercare provides the bridge between treatment and your new life, helping you to take the tools you've acquired in treatment and apply them to the practical aspects of daily living.

Aftercare is ongoing counseling, guidance, and treatment, and the weekly sessions are intended to help you survive, sober, the rough transitions that must be made in the first few months of sobriety. In these first months you are inexperienced. You haven't had enough practice living sober in the world "outside" treatment. You haven't had the time, yet, to fit into

---

*A "sponsor" is a dedicated member of AA, with a well-established sobriety, who acts as friend, guide, and counselor to a newcomer to AA. In the past, the sponsor acted as a sort of "big brother watching you" but the role has developed into a true friend who is always there when you need him and who, in truth, needs your friendship, support, encouragement, and counsel as much as you need his.

your AA group or to feel the strength of your friendship and connection with your AA sponsor. You may have difficulty acting assertively,* making decisions, or reaching out to friends. You're new, fragile, vulnerable. You need help working through all the myriad big and small problems that can occur in the first months of recovery.

What are these problems? How many recovering alcoholics suffer from them? How long do they last? What do they indicate about your potential for permanent recovery? And what, specifically, can you do about them?

Social attitudes. Alcoholism is still considered, by most people, an emotional weakness, a symptom of a character disorder, an unacceptable form of behavior, a weakness of the will. It's a disease, sure—but what caused this disease in the first place? You drank too much. And why did you drink too much? Because you were lonely, sad, depressed, screwed up, angry, or resentful . . . or all of the above. And, meanwhile, you didn't care about anybody but yourself. You kept drinking, letting the rest of your world fall apart, and then you thumbed your nose at it. Why couldn't you drink in moderation? Why did you have to drink so much that you ruined everything? Yeah, you got a disease. But in more ways than one, you deserve it.

Get used to these sentiments, because you're going to run into them, in one way or another, throughout your recovery. They may not be spoken out loud, but you can "hear" them in the way someone shakes your hand, observes you at a party, or steers the subject away from anything to do with alcohol, as if just the word will make you start to drink again. Or the words may be hidden in innocent-sounding sentences like, "Can't you just have one drink to celebrate?" or "Moderation, I always say, everything in moderation," or "I never knew you had a, well, a problem," or "Alcoholism may be a disease for some people, but let me tell you about my Aunt Charlotte. . . ."

As much as you know now about alcoholism and the many

*Assertive is not the same as aggressive. Assertive behavior communicates your thoughts and feelings while respecting the rights of others to have their own, sometimes conflicting, thoughts and feelings. Aggressive behavior communicates your thoughts or feelings, but does not respect the right of others to do the same.

misconceptions surrounding it, it still hurts to hear these words, particularly when they come from people you love and respect. Recognize the hurt (it won't do you any good to ignore it), understand that the words come from ignorance and not from any meanness of spirit, and then leave the words behind you and go on with living your life.

The next decade will see an enormous push in the direction of knowledge and truth about alcoholism. But just as it took many years for the shame and stigma of tuberculosis to die out (just seventy to eighty years ago TB victims were shunned by the rest of society and typically lost their jobs, their self-respect, and often their families), so will it take time to combat the ignorance surrounding alcoholism. Be patient, then, and firm of purpose, understanding that you are one of a steadily growing vanguard of people "in the know." With time and the continuing spread of knowledge, the stigma of alcoholism, like the stigma of tuberculosis, will become a thing of the past.

Social interactions. Now that you're sober you can see how drinking changes people, raising their voices, lending bravado, destroying tact, and diminishing reason. You never noticed all that when you were drinking, too, but now you can think of several thousand things you'd rather do than watch other people drink. As Lewis Meyer moans in his book *Off the Sauce,* "My idea of hell is of a place where there is an endless series of dinner parties preceded by cocktails."

Since this is a drinking society, however, can you realistically expect to avoid all social functions that involve alcohol? Probably not. Weddings, Christmas parties, reunions, birthdays, anniversaries, and retirement celebrations can't always easily be avoided. And if your husband or wife is a senator, an ambassador, or the president of a company, you will probably have to endure more than your fair share of parties with open (and freely flowing) bars.

But—if such commitments threaten your sobriety in any way—if you become exceedingly agitated, anxious, nervous, or upset, and particularly if you start craving "just one" to help you through, or find yourself thinking that if you do get through, then you deserve "just one"—*don't go.* It's as simple as that.

And don't feel guilty about it, either. Cocktail parties and other social occasions where alcohol is the main focus are generally noisy and stressful—that's the primary reason why people drink so much. And drinking people get obnoxious, spill drinks, stub cigarettes out on the floor, ask dumb questions, drone on about boring subjects—this isn't real life! This isn't fun! So leave if you want to, without feeling that you owe anyone an explanation or an excuse.

What do you say at one of these functions when you're offered a drink? There's really no best answer as long as the gist of it is clear—"No, thanks." (Then you can cross your fingers and hope that the host has something more to offer you than water with ice cubes.) It helps some people to drink something that looks like alcohol (tonic or cola with lime, sparkling cider, apple juice in a wineglass) because they feel less conspicuous and less likely to be accosted by nosy people.* Or you can be completely straightforward and say, "No thanks, I'm an alcoholic."

What response will you get? Some people will clam up, some will turn bright red, others will walk away, sipping furiously at their drinks. There will also be those who say, "Really? Good for you!" or "You seem to be adjusting beautifully," or "Great! How long have you been sober?" Bringing your disease out into the open can help you adjust to it and expose other people to the fact that alcoholics are normal people who do recover and who can say "no" to alcohol—all good and important lessons.

If someone reacts negatively ("That's too bad," or "Oh, my, you *look* perfectly normal"), you can call on your sense of humor and goodwill and either try to explain that you *are* normal and sobriety is heaven compared to the hell of drinking, or walk away and look for someone more interesting to talk to.

Expectations and doubts. It's the nature of human beings to expect too much too soon. With alcoholism, the problem is that after several weeks in treatment you look great, you can not only walk a straight line but run one for several miles, you read the newspaper and remember what you read, you understand the punchlines in jokes . . . you seem, in other words,

---

*Alcoholics with a good, solid orientation about their disease and recovery usually won't need this kind of "cover."

perfectly healthy, and there's absolutely no physical evidence that says you're still "sick." So, you and everyone around you assume you're in tip-top shape, good as new, strong as ever.

Then, when you get grouchy or lose your temper, or become depressed or filled with fear, you and everyone else automatically think, *Uh-oh*. You haven't had a drink in six weeks, but here you are experiencing the same old feelings of hopelessness and despair. You begin to doubt yourself and to doubt the things you learned in treatment about the nature of alcoholism. You doubt your ability to get well and even doubt that you are "normal" like everyone else. Your family is afraid to trust you, and each time you lose your temper, everyone retreats in fear.

This fear is misguided. Suppose you'd just been treated for a broken leg. You emerge from the hospital, expecting a long recovery period. You understand that you'll be laid up with a cast for six to eight weeks, then you'll limp around on crutches, and finally you'll use some physical therapy techniques to progressively strengthen your weak leg. During this recovery period, people will pamper you, bathe you, open doors for you, and cook for you. If you fall, someone will help you up (they certainly won't think that the fall is your fault or that it was caused by a lack of willpower). You'll take it easy, be careful not to push yourself, and your family will help you out, encourage you, and not be discouraged themselves when you are frustrated or in pain.

What alcoholism does to your body takes at least as long as a broken leg to heal, but since there's no "cast"—no visible sign that the body is still fragile—the expectation exists that all is well and back to normal. You must, therefore, learn to think in terms of *inner* healing and recognize the symptoms of a healing brain and body for what they are instead of misreading them as evidence that you are somehow abnormal. To feel depressed, sad, anxious, lonely, and afraid *is* normal in the beginning of your recovery. Expect these emotions, and they won't frighten you when you feel them. Help your family and friends understand that this healing process takes time, and occasional setbacks are to be expected. Without this understanding, you and your loved ones will feel guilt, confusion, and fear, which will only deepen your anxiety and make this early recovery period more difficult.

Depression. More than 50 percent of alcoholics in treatment report symptoms of depression. (In some studies, the
reported percentage has been as high as 90 percent.) The
symptoms include:
* feelings of hopelessness
* frustration
* feelings of being trapped
* low energy
* low motivation
* dislike of yourself or others
* bleak outlook on the world
* inability to concentrate
* inability to make decisions
* decreased sex drive
* frequent headaches
* insomnia, nightmares, restless sleep

There are basically two kinds of depression: *exogenous,*
which is caused by external circumstances like loss of a job,
financial difficulties, divorce, or death of a loved one; and
endogenous, which is caused by internal, metabolic upsets
such as biochemical changes in the brain, hormonal imbalances, and blood sugar abnormalities.

Most alcoholic depression has been labeled "exogenous"
and there are always, with every alcoholic, numerous outward
circumstances that seemingly support this label. However, the
real cause of depression for most alcoholics is endogenous.
Alcoholics with depression show certain inner biochemical
abnormalities—hormonal and nutritional—that are not seen in
alcoholics with no depression. Studies show that depressed
alcoholics have imbalances in their nerve-hormonal responses
from the brain to the adrenal glands, which can disrupt the
body's response to stress. Another area of hormonal imbalance
in recovering alcoholics is the *thyroid* gland, and problems
there can contribute to fatigue and depression.

Nutritional imbalances that can cause depression include
B-vitamin deficiencies, calcium or magnesium deficiencies, hypoglycemia, and disturbances in the neurotransmitters, the chemical messengers in the brain. Studies of depressed patients reveal
common deficiencies in vitamin B_6 and tryptophan, a protein
component and forerunner in the manufacturing of the neurotransmitter serotonin, which is a mood elevator. Estrogen, in-

terestingly, can block the activity of vitamin B_6 and speed up the use of tryptophan, making it less available to form serotonin; this may help to explain why more women suffer from depression than men. Low levels of tyrosine, a precursor to the neurotransmitter norepinephrine, have also been linked to depression.

For alcoholics who experience persistent depression, mood swings, and/or sleep disturbances, a reasonable supplement plan, in addition to a good, sound diet and general maintenance vitamins, would include a month's trial of:

tryptophan:	1 gram, three times daily
niacin:	500 mg, twice daily
B_6:	50–100 mg, twice daily

Before attempting self-therapy, however, the reader is strongly urged to consult a nutritionally oriented physician.* Amino acids such as tyrosine and tryptophan are available without a prescription, but large doses or long-term use can produce chemical changes in the body that require medical supervision.

Sleep disturbances. Like depression, sleep problems can easily be misinterpreted as evidence of problems in the alcoholic's emotional life. But again, there's plenty of evidence to show that the real cause is physiological.

It may surprise you to hear that the first months of abstinence are often more disturbing to peaceful sleep than all those years of heavy drinking. In the first weeks of sobriety, sleep rhythms show dramatic alterations, causing restlessness, fragmented sleep, multiple awakenings, and nightmares; for some alcoholics, years may go by before sleep patterns fully stabilize. You can't take a sleeping pill, but there's plenty you can do to get a better night's rest:

• *Stabilize your diet,* which will stabilize your brain and body chemistry. Hypoglycemia is a common malady for recovering alcoholics; a stabilizing diet, with three nutritious snacks, will control the symptoms. Some alcoholics report waking up

*The International College of Applied Nutrition is a society of physicians who have developed an interest and specialty in applied nutrition and preventive medicine. For a listing of health professionals in your area, send a letter explaining what you want, along with a self-addressed stamped envelope, to the college at P.O. Box 386, La Habra, CA 90631.

soaked with perspiration or with a pounding heart. This may be caused by a drop in blood sugar and can be controlled by having a snack (cheese and crackers, fruit, glass of milk) before bed. *Milk* is a particularly good addition to your bedtime snack (if you don't have a milk allergy) because it contains tryptophan, which helps induce sleep.

• *Take vitamin and mineral supplements.* Vitamins and minerals aid the healing process in the central nervous system; a shaky, unstable nervous system is directly related to sleep disturbances.

• *Take a hot bath* to relax and calm your nerves.

• *Practice relaxation techniques* before bedtime (see Reading List).

• *Work out problems before you go to bed.* Remember the AA slogan: "Turn your problems over." Realize what you can and can't do, solve what you can, and learn to let go of those problems you can't change or solve.

• *Don't worry.* You won't die because of a lack of sleep; your body will sleep when it must.

• *Trust in time.* As your body gradually adjusts to life without alcohol and the healing process continues, you'll begin to sleep longer and more peacefully.

• *And remember:* **never** *take sleeping pills, tranquilizers, or sedatives.*

Stress. In our modern world, there's no way to avoid all stress. What you can do and, as a recovering alcoholic, what you must do, is avoid all unnecessary stress, learn to identify when you feel stress, and deal with it before it affects your physical and psychological well-being.

There are little stresses and big stresses; both can be bad for you. The little stresses—traffic jams, boring parties, insensitive questions, prying neighbors, yapping dogs, crying babies, smelly garbage, broken toys, no milk in the refrigerator—can cause your muscles to bunch up, your temper to flare, and your sense of humor to shrivel and dry up. These are the stresses that, in your former life, raised that little red flag in your brain, the one that said, "Boy, could I use a drink." In the early days of your recovery that flag will continue to pop up during these little stresses. After a good stretch of stress, you may find yourself really wanting, maybe even craving, a drink.

Deal with these little stresses as best you can and learn to recognize when you are feeling unusual stress. For example, a traffic light that turns red when you get to it might ordinarily cause you to feel a stress level of 2 or 3 on a scale of 10, accompanied by a few gentle swear words and a deep sigh. Pounding your hand on the steering wheel, holding your head in exasperation, and spewing out a venomous attack on the city planners and all the other idiots who put this particular light in this particular place to bother *you*, rates a stress level of 7 or 8, which is a bit much for a mere traffic light. Something else is going on here, and to calm yourself down and get those muscles unbunched, you'll have to recognize that fact and deal with it promptly.

When you feel stressed, exercise, relaxation techniques, deep breathing, and taking time out to think and reflect will all help you calm yourself down. Longer-term solutions include regular attendance at AA meetings, slowing down at work, getting enough sleep, eating properly, taking regular vacations, involving yourself in community or volunteer work, taking stress management classes, etc.

If *too much time* is part of your problem, get involved, make lists of all the things you always wanted to do, and then do them. If *too little time* is your problem, you will have to learn to slow down and cut out unnecessary commitments.

The big stresses don't occur so frequently, but are not so easily avoided, either. You can walk instead of driving a car, or choose a route with fewer traffic lights, but you can't avoid sickness or death, and many of us must learn to live through divorce, separation, career changes, geographic moves, childbirth, thefts, fires, etc. What do you do in these situations? You realize first of all that you are human, and human beings must live with pain and loss; and second, remind yourself that you are an alcoholic and thus you must protect yourself against your body's inherent addiction. You will have to work through these stresses "naturally"—without chemical relief. Stay armed against your addiction by reaching out to others, attending more AA meetings, keeping on track with healthy eating patterns, exercising more, and taking time to rest and relax.

With the big stresses, time is the best healer of all. But you must use your time productively, investing in it and giving to it, instead of passively waiting for it to heal you. Just as your

garden will choke up with weeds if you neglect it, so will your
emotional health become choked off if you don't actively work
on removing the "weeds" of past hurts and pain and, at the
same time, planting new seeds of love, friendship, and caring.
Those seeds will take time and nurturing to germinate, but with
your active help they will grow and flower.

The big stresses in life are never simple to deal with, and if
they occur in early recovery, they can knock the wind out of
you. Many recovering alcoholics relapse when their spouses
sue for divorce or custody of the children, when a loved one is
in an auto accident or suffers from a stroke, when the company
transfers the family from California to Kansas, when the house
burns down, the dog dies, or the bank forecloses.

Every recovering alcoholic, in fact, will drink again if he is
not centered in and committed to a program of sobriety maintenance. That is why you must keep your "house of sobriety"
strong, and continually fortify it against stress and strain. Once
you understand your disease and are free of the addiction's
manipulations and controls, you have a moral obligation to
assemble and use the tools of protection that you were given in
treatment, regardless of any external turbulence in your life.

Morality comes into play now because you understand the
disease and its fatal consequences, and you know the ways and
means of protecting yourself against your addiction. You have
the choice, now, to live without alcohol or to risk your life and
the lives of everyone you love by drinking again. Within that
choice lies your moral obligation.

In recovery, you must learn to use the help that is offered to
you through AA, family, friends, counselors, or other support
systems. Do not allow your recovery to be eroded by pain,
hurt, loneliness, or loss. Dealing with the pain—confronting it,
trying to understand its causes, working for solutions—won't
make it hurt any less, but it will stop the hurt from festering
inside you, sapping your energy, diverting your attention, and,
eventually, strengthening your addiction.

CHAPTER 16

The Middle Stage of Recovery

(6 months–1 year)

While the early stage of recovery is concerned primarily with physical and early psychological adjustments to sobriety, the middle stage is generally a time of active emotional growth. During this stage, many of the alcoholic's relationships will change, often with a good deal of struggle and anguish. The process of recovery is, again, an evolution, and if the alcoholic is actively working on this process, which he must do if he is to progress in recovery, he will change and grow. Seeing these changes and having to adapt their own lives to accommodate them can be extremely difficult for family members and friends who may feel threatened and unnerved by the rapid alteration in the alcoholic's personality and behavior.

The recovering alcoholic, after all, is becoming someone

new and unfamiliar—and the unfamiliar can be terrifying. *Who is this person who has come out of treatment?* the family may wonder. *Is this the real Frank, or is the real Frank just waiting to jump out at us again? Why does he spend so much time at AA? Why, when he needs help, does he turn to his alcoholic friends rather than to us? When he's grouchy or tired, does that mean he might drink again?*

The alcoholic, too, is walking on eggshells. He's changed dramatically, yet everyone else acts the same. He looks at the faces of his family and sees fear, resentment, and distrust. Here, he thinks, are the living reminders of his past, and he knows that they have terrible weapons they can use against him—weapons learned from the past that shoot straight at the heart. All these people still have their guard up, their protective armor on. *How,* the alcoholic wonders, *can I take the fear out of their eyes, the distrust out of their hearts?*

The recovering alcoholic may feel that the gulf separating him from his family is deep and wide, perhaps even unbridgeable. He feels that they cannot possibly understand what it was like to be a drunk, to suffer through a living hell, and then to emerge, transformed. They say they understand, but how can they really understand, at the bottom of their souls, what it means to be an alcoholic? They can't know, either, what it is like to start from scratch, to let go of the past, to stop worrying about the future, to live each day as it comes. The recovering alcoholic may feel as if he is constantly trying to prove himself; he feels a tremendous pressure to do everything right, and when he makes even a small mistake or misstep, he tends to experience an overwhelming sense of failure and hopelessness.

To understand the alcoholic's rapidly changing emotions during early recovery, the family must become actively involved in the recovery process. If they simply sit back, hold their breath, and wait for the alcoholic to get himself "fixed," the gulf between them will widen until they have little to say to each other. As the alcoholic changes during recovery, the family needs to understand why the changes are taking place, what they signify about the nature of recovery, and, most significantly, how their own behavior has been controlled and manipulated by the addiction. The family members must change and grow along with the alcoholic, recognizing their own involvement in the disease and committing themselves to the progressive stages of healing and repair.

Active participation in the treatment program begins this process. Regular attendance at Al-Anon and Alateen meetings keeps the momentum going, giving the spouse and children the help, support, and encouragement they need to see and work on their own problems. Years of living with the addiction have taught the family members to think, respond, and relate in unhealthy, destructive ways; Al-Anon and Alateen help them "unlearn" these behaviors and emotions to forge a new, healing method of relating to themselves and to their loved ones. In these groups, family and friends learn the 3 C's: "I can't cure it, I can't control it, and I didn't cause it." And they learn how to "let go"—to stop fighting, to stop trying to control their lives and the lives of others, and to accept people as they are and not as they might want them to be.

When a recovering alcoholic comes home from treatment, the roles within the family often change, creating resentments and hostilities. The daughter who in the old days cooked and cleaned for the family, put the kids to bed, and "mothered" her mother now faces an abrupt and rather humbling return to mere "daughter." The son who is smoking pot and drinking with his friends deeply resents his recovering alcoholic parent's concern and may insist that any protestations are the height of hypocrisy. The sexually frigid wife who used her husband's alcoholism as an excuse to refuse sex now faces a willing and needy male. The man who had an affair with his secretary while his wife was having an affair with her bourbon now has a sharp-witted, observant woman waiting for him to come home every night for dinner.

These role upheavals can be jarring and unsettling, but with time, patience, and understanding, most families are able to settle into a much more balanced and normal relationship. There is one relationship, however, that cannot work: it's impossible for a recovering alcoholic to have a normal relationship with a drinking alcoholic spouse or lover. The drinking spouse will resent his recovering partner because recovery threatens his own continued drinking. He will do anything he can to undermine this recovery, from pleas ("Come on, have a drink, it's my birthday!") to taunts ("Couldn't handle it, could you?") to verbal abuse ("You're so high and mighty, you always think you know what's right"). Living with a drinking alcoholic spouse while you're trying to recover is like running on the proverbial treadmill: you're just not going to get anywhere, and it's more than likely that you'll wear yourself out trying.

In such a situation, you have several choices: get help for the drinking spouse or, if that fails, separate temporarily to give yourself a respite and get your recovery started on solid ground. A separation will also give a strong and clear message to your partner that you mean business and are dead serious about staying sober. Either the drinking partner will agree to treatment or he will continue to drink, in which case your path of health and his of sickness will gradually grow further and further apart until the relationship is inevitably severed.

While some relationship problems are seemingly unsolvable, for most families the problems and fears are short-lived and solutions are available. Again, however, the family must become an active part of the recovery process, learning about the disease, finding help for their own problems resulting from living with an alcoholic, and becoming involved in support groups like Al-Anon or Alateen. The fear, distrust, anger, and resentment must be worked out on a continuing basis or they will come back to haunt the family.

These "hauntings" may seem totally unrelated to the disease, but with understanding and insight, the connection becomes clear and the problems are more easily worked out. Mary, for example, lived with her alcoholic mother for years, even giving up an offer of marriage from the man she loved because she was afraid that if she moved, her mother would start drinking again. Jonathan always felt terrible resentment and loneliness whenever he visited his wife's family; he eventually realized that watching the loving, open relationship between his wife and her parents made him feel the lack of love he had experienced with his alcoholic parents. Beth's husband died of cirrhosis of the liver, and when her son began to show the symptoms of alcoholism, she withdrew to the point where she would hang up whenever he called her.

As these examples illustrate, everyone who lives with an alcoholic is deeply affected by the disease; getting the alcoholic sober won't solve all the other family members' problems. Everyone involved in this disease, however peripherally, needs help, understanding, and guidance. Again, one of the very best sources of help is Al-Anon. People whose loved ones have been sober for years continue to go to meetings because they continue to grow and learn. Many recovering alcoholics regularly alternate AA meetings with Al-Anon meetings in a continuing attempt to understand the feelings, fears, and experiences of nonalcoholic friends and family.

Recovery is a process that goes on and on and on; there's no end to it. It's a process of growth and discovery, being and becoming. And, because it is a process of living and of life, your recovery will continually bring forth new awarenesses, insights, and challenges.

Sexual problems. Sexual problems, fears, and insecurities often need to be dealt with in the middle phase of recovery. Such problems as impotence, frigidity, and even lack of interest in sex are fairly common among nonalcoholics, and alcohol certainly doesn't help anything. Contrary to popular opinion, alcohol isn't an aphrodisiac. It may decrease inhibitions and cause the appearance of improving sexual function, but it is, in fact, a physiological suppressant to sexual function. Which is a clinical way of saying that the equipment doesn't work so well with booze.

In one study, college males were given alcohol and then shown sexually stimulating pictures and evaluated for the response and degree of erection. The sexual response decreased at all blood levels. Male alcoholics frequently complain of impotence. Female alcoholics have a decreased sex drive (sometimes to the point of frigidity), in addition to menstrual irregularity and even a cessation of menstruation in some.

Despite these days of so-called liberation and sexual freedom, alcoholics and counselors often feel considerable discomfort when discussing sexual issues. The alcoholic typically believes that he is the only one troubled with sexual problems. Over the years he's heard, hundreds of times, that he is psychologically messed up, and he just assumes that his sexual difficulties are related to these psychological problems.

As if to overcompensate for the lack of attention sexual problems have received in the past, some treatment programs begin sexual counseling in the first month of treatment. In *A Private Practice*, by Patrick Reilly, M.D., a true story about a physician treated for alcoholism and drug addiction, the author tells of the therapist who lent him the keys to her private office and encouraged him to lock the door behind him and look at the sexually revealing photographs under the convenient bed. Such a heavy emphasis on sex may be too much too soon, since alcoholics in the first weeks of recovery are hardly out of the fog enough to know who they are, let alone to handle the complexities of their sexuality.

Early in treatment the emphasis should be on the healing processes of the body and relationships, both of which are essential for satisfactory sexual performance. It's difficult if not impossible for a couple to successfully relate sexually when there is so much lingering resentment, anger, mistrust, blame, and guilt to be confronted and worked out first.

It helps, too, to know that more than one-half of middle- and late-stage alcoholics experience sexual dysfunction related to the physical effects—hormonal, neurologic, and/or toxic effects on the testes—of the disease. In one study, 50 percent of male alcoholics reported impotence for as long as six months of abstinence. In the absence of anatomic abnormalities, these effects typically clear up within the first year of recovery; if problems persist, the patient can be referred for hormonal assessment and potential treatment.

"No alcoholic can know the whole wonder, excitement, and completeness of the sex act until he has been off the sauce *for at least a year!*" claims recovering alcoholic Lewis Meyer in his book *Off the Sauce*. It may not take that long for you, or it may take a bit longer, but with that old triumvirate—time, patience, and understanding—the sexual problems of most alcoholics will eventually work themselves out.

Grief work. The major push of recovery is to create a new life without alcohol, but before you can be wholly successful, you must look back and finish working out some of the unresolved pain and sadness of your past. Grief may be directly related to your alcoholism—a friend killed in the car you were driving when drunk, loss of custody of your children, a divorce due to your drinking, a son or daughter who refuses to talk to you. Or your grief may be seemingly unrelated to your disease—your mother dying from cancer, a son killed in Vietnam, a brother killed in a hunting accident, an abortion you had at the age of 15.

Even if some trauma in your past has nothing to do with your alcoholism, it will have an effect on your recovery unless you deal with the feelings, bring the hurt and anger out in the open, and begin to seek acceptance and peace. To work through the stages of the grief process—shock, denial, depression, anger, guilt, and acceptance*—you will undoubtedly benefit from help and support. Most alcoholics believe that they are, in one way or another, responsible for the loss of or separation from their loved ones; they need to be allowed to express their grief—most haven't discussed it with anyone—and then grieve without being overwhelmed by shame and guilt.

Alcoholism itself interferes with and stifles the grief process, deadening emotions, isolating its victims, changing brain function, and creating abnormal responses. Due to alcohol's numbing effects on the emotions, a loss that you experienced ten or even twenty or thirty years ago may still be unresolved. In treatment, you will be encouraged to identify your losses, no matter how long ago they occurred, accept the feelings associated with the loss, work through your depression and anger, and resolve your guilt.

The final step of the grief process involves accepting the reality of the loss, learning to detach yourself from it, and becoming actively involved in current relationships and objectives. Working through the grief process is, in reality, the act of learning how to live fully and completely in the present, rather than being consumed by emotions and behaviors that belong to your past.

---

*Elisabeth Kubler-Ross's work revealed five stages of the grief process—denial, anger, bargaining, depression, and acceptance. The six stages discussed here are more typical of the grief process experienced by alcoholics and other chemically impaired people. These stages are outlined in "Grief Work with Substance Abusers," by Gail Denny and Laura Lee, *Journal of Substance Abuse Treatment,* vol. 1, 1984, pp. 249–254.

CHAPTER 17

The Late Stage of Recovery

(1 year–the rest of your life)

For most recovering alcoholics the late stage of recovery is a time of smooth sailing, interrupted by a few minor squalls. You've navigated through some rough weather and choppy seas, but the major disturbances are behind you. Furthermore, you're experienced now: you've made it through some difficult times, you have confidence in yourself and faith in your problem-solving tools, and your "crew"—your family and friends—trusts and believes in you.

The big danger now is that you will become lazy, overconfident, perhaps even sloppy. You may be so proud of yourself for the accomplishments of the last year that you loosen up a bit, figuring that you'll give yourself a break. After all, going to an AA meeting twice a week *does* cut into your schedule, and it *would* be nice to have some extra time at home with the kids. Or perhaps you decide that decaffeinated coffee just doesn't do it for you, and gradually you work into a habit of four or five cups of strong coffee every morning. Sweets are awfully tempting, and, really, what possible harm could a daily doughnut do? You're trying to be better about a budget, so maybe you should cut out those costly vitamin and mineral supplements. Now that you're well and healthy again, the boss is piling up the work. You just don't seem to have the time to take those long walks anymore, and your exercise class is way the heck downtown anyway. The relaxation techniques were great when you had the time, but your life is so full that you've forgotten all about them.

All of these behaviors and thoughts fit into a category called *complacency*. Complacency is a very dangerous state of mind for recovering alcoholics, just as it is for anyone else with a chronic disease. When diabetics become complacent, they ease up on their diets, sneak sweets, and skip meals. It may take a month or more but eventually this "cheating" could cause insulin shock, diabetic coma, even death. Recovering cancer patients become complacent when they figure that two checkups a year is at least one too many and cancel their appointments. High blood pressure victims who gradually ease into their former high-stress lifestyles are letting complacency jeopardize their health.

Relapse is always a possibility with chronic diseases, even after years of good health. Alcoholics are not safe from relapse even after ten, fifteen, or twenty years of sobriety, *unless* they continue to use the tools they acquired in treatment. The most basic of these tools, as we've said, is knowledge of the disease. Keep *Recovery, Under the Influence,* and *Alcoholics Anonymous* (the "Big Book") on your bedside table, read them frequently, and refer to them whenever you find yourself confused, frustrated, angry, or upset. Any books that you find particularly helpful should also be a well-used part of your personal library.

The process of living your recovery and maturing within it will, in and of itself, protect your sobriety. As you learn to deal with your anger, moods, and feelings, you will know a greater serenity and peace of mind. You will become actively involved in living your sobriety, caring about what happens to you, and living your life as a joyful challenge.

If you think, instead, of recovery as a dreary task to finish as quickly as possible, you have some important work to do to improve your sobriety. There is a difference between being "dry" and being "sober," and the difference can be found in how much joy you take in your life.

Dry versus	**Sober/clean**
NO ALCOHOL/DRUGS	**NO ALCOHOL/DRUGS**
Don't care what happens	Cares what happens
Not drinking is a big sacrifice	Not drinking is gift to self
Miserable	Happy—peace of mind
Bored	Actively involved
Guilt—shame	FREE of guilt and shame
Aimless	Sense of direction
Unrealistic goals	Realistic goals
Eat poorly	Eat properly
Same old lifestyle	New lifestyle
Same old friends	New friends
Same old activities	New activities
Hopelessness	Hope
Victim of life (Why me?)	Life is a challenge
Pot/Valium (escape/relief)	Drug-free life
Self-centeredness	Other-centeredness
OVERCONFIDENCE	HUMILITY

Developed by Jacques Workman, Head Counselor, Comprehensive Treatment Center, Seattle, WA, 1981. Revised and adapted by Milam Recovery Centers, Inc., Bothell, WA.

In the art of learning how to live sober and truly enjoy your sobriety, the ability to "let go" is particularly important. Letting go is the process of accepting people and things as they are and not wishing they were something else or trying to change them to suit you. It is giving up on the idea that you can change the

world, that you should be perfect, or that life owes you something. It is recognizing your limitations and relinquishing problems that are unsolvable or too much for you to handle. Letting
go is the ability to differentiate between the important and the
unimportant things in life. It is the refusal to agonize over the
past or worry about the future: it is the ability to live your life
day to day.

Alcoholics Anonymous, of course, is one of the most powerful tools that you have for reinforcing and strengthening
your sobriety. You will never "outgrow" AA, for it's not
what you hear or learn there that is most crucial, but what
you feel: friendship, caring, understanding, acceptance, and
love.

The nutritional program is another tool that must become a
permanent part of your sobriety. Eating the wrong foods—sweets,
caffeine, junk foods—can make you vulnerable to depression,
fatigue, mood swings, headaches, insomnia, irritability, and
the craving to drink. Eating the right foods can protect you
against these symptoms, increase your energy and vitality, and
strengthen your commitment to sobriety. Do not underestimate
the power of good nutrition to help you live happily and
contentedly sober.

Avoidance of prescription and over-the-counter drugs is
crucial to your continuing good health. When you leave
treatment, ask your counselor, physician, or nurse for a
letter explaining that (1) you are a recovering alcoholic; (2) all
central nervous system medications have the potential to
reactivate your addiction; and (3) to maintain your sobriety
you must avoid all such drugs except, perhaps, in crisis
situations.

If you become seriously ill or require major surgery, you
will have to draw up a restabilization plan. It's important to
have this plan ready before you become ill and are exposed to
drugs, since you won't be thinking very clearly once you're
hospitalized (see appendix 6). Give a copy of this plan to your
doctor as soon as you leave treatment, another to your spouse
or children, and perhaps a copy to your boss or best friend.
And always remember that taking central nervous system
drugs, even as prescribed by a physician, is exceedingly
dangerous and must be closely supervised, with any drug use

ended as soon as possible. For a list of prescription and over-the-counter drugs that affect the central nervous system, see appendix 7.

Finally, you must understand exactly what you are trying to avoid by using these protective tools. Relapse is more than just a return to drinking: it is also a return to alcoholic thinking and feeling. In fact, alcoholic thoughts and emotions are a necessary preliminary stage for the actual event of lifting that drink to your mouth. Relapse begins with a state of mind that is exactly like your state of mind in the old drinking days. Your mood changes, suddenly; you get a tension headache or a nervous stomach; or maybe you start behaving "funny," giggling uncontrollably, or acting weary or bored. Or you may suddenly become obsessed with your health, your job, or a troubling relationship. Your behavior seems reasonable, if somewhat unusual, and neither you nor your family or friends are particularly concerned.

But you're emotionally confused. And that emotional confusion is a sign that something deeper, more insidious is at work. It's easy to lay the blame on some outward circumstance, but remember that emotions have their origins in the chemical and electrical signals in the brain. Emotions have, in other words, a physical connection, and they originate in that part of the body most traumatized by alcohol addiction—the brain. When your emotions are confused, you can be sure that the psychological events are accompanied by physiological changes taking place inside you to help create the "alcoholic state of mind." Without immediate attention, your emotional symptoms will accelerate and swell, rising to a crescendo that may sweep you headlong into a relapse.

Experts have identified a process known as "BUD," or "building up to drink," that sometimes occurs in recovery. At the beginning of the BUD, you're slightly irritated, bored, restless, or moody. These feelings increase steadily, gaining momentum until you feel as if you are losing control over your life, your feelings, and your reactions.

A return to the "alcoholic state of mind" is only the first step in the progression toward relapse. In the second step your behavior shows this subtle inward change, and you begin to withdraw from those people, places, and activities that support your sobriety, including AA, your sponsor, treatment friends and staff, sober friends or neighbors, etc. The process of denial will begin to fortify itself again, and you may find yourself resenting your family and friends and thinking back with fondness and regret to "the good old drinking days."

Sometime during this second step of the relapse process, your body may give a clear warning that all is not well: your hands tremble, you perspire profusely, your heart pounds, you feel physically wrung out, nervous, and exhausted. Eventually, these emotional and physical symptoms will "peak," and you will experience extreme discomfort, depression, unhappiness, and feelings of despair and hopelessness. You feel as if your life has been turned upside down and emptied out. At this point, if you have been carried along unknowingly by the BUD, you will drink again.

If you learn to recognize the symptoms of BUD, however, and view relapse as a process rather than the single, seemingly

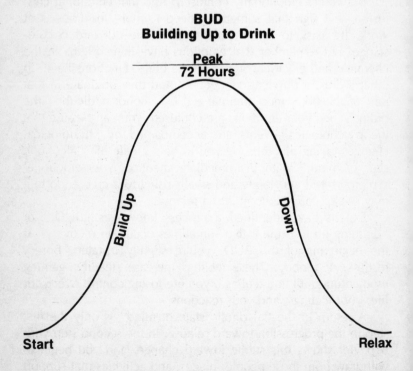

BUD
Building Up to Drink

Peak
72 Hours

Build Up

Down

Start

Relax

isolated event of drinking again, you can avoid or be helped through the peak period, experiencing a gradual decline and diminishment of symptoms until the crisis is over. As soon as you begin to feel the onset of the BUD—the anger, irritability, and mood changes—acknowledge that these may be symptoms of physiological events taking place within you and begin, immediately, to do something about them. Call up your resources, evaluate your stresses, check out your diet, get more rest, increase your supplements. Call your AA sponsor, go to an AA meeting, talk to a family member or a close, sober friend who understands alcoholism and the process of relapse. Go for a long walk, do your relaxation and breathing exercises, take a steam bath or a physical massage. Do whatever will help you over the "peak" without, of course, using alcohol or drugs.

The process of BUD has nothing to do with willpower or lack of it. You have a chronic disease, and the BUD is one of its potential flare-ups. As long as you understand that relapse is a gradual process, signaling that your addiction is gaining power and trying to take control, you can learn how to stop it in its early stages. *Always* keep your respect for this disease you have and continually protect yourself by keeping your "house of sobriety" strong and secure.

Living sober is a process of diligence, dedication, and self-scrutiny. But what gifts you receive for your labors! Joy will be yours, as will happiness. You will feel pain, too, but as the flip side of joy and not, as before, the defining emotion of your life. You will gain self-knowledge, self-liking, self-worth, and self-respect. You will learn how to reach out to others, and you will receive, in turn, the deep satisfaction of having others reach out to you. You will experience a love of life; and, most basic of all, you will have a life to love.

Life: You have reclaimed it from your disease. It is yours now, to live, to enjoy, to learn from, and to cherish as a gift from your God and from yourself.

HERE'S TO LIFE!

Michigan Alcohol Screening Test
(MAST)

Points		Questions
(0)	1.	Do you enjoy a drink now and then?
(2)	2.	Do you feel you are a normal drinker?*
(2)	3.	Have you ever awakened the morning after some drinking the night before and found that you could not remember a part of the evening before?
(1)	4.	Does your spouse (or parents) ever worry or complain about your drinking?
(2)	5.	Can you stop drinking without a struggle after one or two drinks?*
(1)	6.	Do you ever feel bad about your drinking?
(2)	7.	Do friends and relatives think you are a normal drinker?*
(0)	8.	Do you ever try to limit your drinking to certain times of the day or to certain places?

(2)   9. Are you always able to stop drinking when you want to?*

X(4) 10. Have you ever attended a meeting of Alcoholics Anonymous (AA)?

(1)   11. Have you gotten into fights when drinking?

(2)   12. Has drinking ever created problems with you and your spouse?

(2)   13. Has your spouse (or other family member) ever gone to anyone for help about your drinking?

(2)   14. Have you ever lost friends or girl/boy friends because of drinking?

(2)   15. Have you ever gotten into trouble at work because of drinking?

(2)   16. Have you ever lost a job because of drinking?

(2)   17. Have you ever neglected your obligations, your family, or your work for 2 or more days because you were drinking?

(1)   18. Do you ever drink before noon?

(2)   19. Have you ever been told you have liver trouble? Cirrhosis?

(2)   20. Have you ever had delirium tremens (DTs), severe shaking, heard voices or seen things that weren't there after heavy drinking?

(4)   21. Have you ever gone to anyone for help about your drinking?

(4)   22. Have you ever been in a hospital because of drinking?

(0)   23. (a) Have you ever been a patient in a psychiatric hospital or on a psychiatric ward of a general hospital?

X(2)   (b) Was drinking part of the problem that resulted in hospitalization?

(0)   24. (a) Have you ever been seen at a psychiatric or mental health clinic, or gone to any doctor, social worker, or clergyman for help with an emotional problem?

X(2)   (b) Was drinking part of the problem?

(2)   25. Have you ever been arrested, even for a few hours, because of drunk behavior?

(2)   26. Have you ever been arrested for drunk driving after drinking?

*Negative responses are "alcoholic" responses.

A total of 4 or more points is presumptive evidence of alcoholism, while a 5-point total would make it extremely unlikely that the individual was not alcoholic. However, a positive response to 10, 23, or 24 would be diagnostic; a positive response indicates alcoholism.

Alcoholism Lab Profile

These are common laboratory tests in which abnormalities are often found in alcoholics. The absence of abnormal functions does not, however, rule out alcoholism or indicate normal functioning. In the liver, for example, fully one-third of the cells must be damaged before the liver function tests show up as abnormal. Thus, many early- and middle-stage alcoholics will show absolutely normal values on these tests.

In addition to the tests included here, a full chemistry survey for alcoholics would include tests to measure calcium and phosphorus (both minerals); glucose (blood sugar); blood urea nitrogen (BUN) and creatinine (both kidney-screening tests); total protein, albumin, and albumin/globulin ratio (blood protein status tests and indirect measures of liver function); sodium, potassium, chloride and bicarbonate (electrolytes); and cholesterol.

Liver Tests

SGOT, SGPT, LDH, GGTP, and ALK PHOS are abbreviations for cellular enzymes (i.e., SGOT stands for serum glutamine oxaloacetic

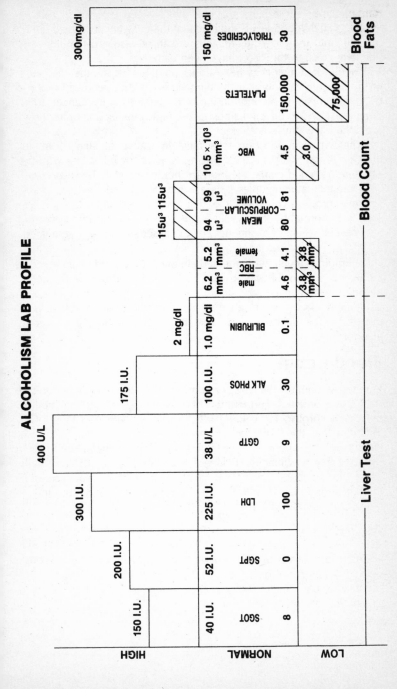

ALCOHOLISM LAB PROFILE

transaminase). These particular enzymes are concentrated in cells in the liver. High blood levels indicate that the enzyme has leaked out of the cells into the bloodstream; thus, it can be assumed that the cells (the liver cells, in this case) have been damaged.

An elevated liver enzyme test does not tell what the specific cause of the damage is, only that the damage exists. Causes might include the direct impact of alcohol on the cells, hepatitis virus, cancer, toxic chemicals, and/or infectious abscesses. In a drinking alcoholic, however, the likely cause is alcohol.

The two liver function tests most indicative of alcoholism are the GGTP and SGOT. If these two tests are elevated, along with the MCV in the blood count, alcoholism should definitely be suspected.

During treatment, liver tests are monitored and, in most cases, improve progressively over the first few weeks of abstinence, resolving to normal by four weeks. If the tests continue to be abnormal after several weeks of abstinence, other causes should be investigated.

Bilirubin is a yellow-pigmented chemical processed by the liver. If the liver is malfunctioning, it will "back up" the bilirubin in the body, turning the skin yellow and causing jaundice. Again, the presence of jaundice doesn't pinpoint a cause, but only shows that the liver is in distress. In the alcoholic, however, this distress is most likely due to alcohol.

Blood Count

In many alcoholics, the RBC, or number of red blood cells per unit of measure, is reduced. Furthermore, the size of the cell, as indicated by the mean corpuscular volume (MCV), is frequently too large. This indicates that the blood cell manufacturing system is faulty and is producing large, immature red blood cells that are inefficient in their oxygen-carrying capacity. Enlarged red blood cells are commonly caused by alcohol's direct toxic effect on the bone marrow (the RBC manufacturing plant) and/or decreased folic acid (a B vitamin that is needed for normal RBC manufacturing).

Blood Fats

Triglycerides (blood fats) are frequently elevated in active drinking, not because alcohol has a lot of fat in it (actually, it has none), but because alcohol interferes with the normal processing of fats and sugars in the liver.

COA Quiz*

People who grow up with an alcoholic adult in the family often have predictable personality characteristics. Some develop because no adult showed the child how feelings are expressed appropriately, or how to be close to another person. Others can emerge as self-protective reactions to a chaotic or frightening home life. Still other traits can be the result of birth order in the family. Research demonstrates that all these factors affect the adult personality of the child raised in an alcoholic home: poor adult role modeling, the necessity for defenses to survive, and whether the person is the oldest or the youngest of the children.

If you are the child of an alcoholic, see how often you agree with the following statements, which are typical for people who are reared with an alcoholic parent. They are also common to people raised by parents who don't drink much, but who were themselves raised by an alcoholic. This is because parents tend to reflect their own home environment in the way they raise their children. Alcoholism has been called "the three generational family disease."

Give yourself ten points for each of the following statements if it is often true of you or sounds like you as a child.

☐ 1. I take care of other people, but no one takes care of me.

☐ 2. No matter what happens, I feel I get blamed for it.

☐ 3. Usually it's best when no one notices me.

☐ 4. I'll do almost anything to get a laugh.

☐ 5. It's really hard for me to figure out what I want in relationships.

☐ 6. People praise me for all I've done but I never feel I've done enough.

☐ 7. I think I'm just no good.

☐ 8. I'm more comfortable with computers than people.

☐ 9. I usually change the subject when people get excited about something.

☐ 10. I'm not sure what people want me to say when they ask about my feelings.

☐ 11. It's hard for me to be close to people.

☐ 12. It's probably my fault my family has so many problems.

☐ 13. People say I could achieve more, but I don't have the self-confidence.

☐ 14. Sometimes I wish someone would just tell me what to do.

☐ 15. I work hard at getting approval.

☐ 16. I always try to do the correct thing.

☐ 17. Most of my friends get in trouble.

☐ 18. My animals are my best friends.

☐ 19. I'm really attracted to strong people.

☐ 20. Angry people scare me.

☐ 21. My job involves teaching or healing other people.

☐ 22. As soon as I am old enough I'm leaving home.

☐ 23. I procrastinate a lot.

☐ 24. It's hard for me to sit still. I'm usually hyper.

☐ 25. I feel different from other people.

☐ 26. People think I'm a nice person but my spouse complains I won't get close.

☐ 27. If everyone would leave me alone, I'd be O.K.

☐ 28. It's hard for me to relax with someone else around.

☐ 29. When I was a kid, I was the class clown.

☐ 30. If I don't give in to others, I feel guilty.

Scoring:

If you answered yes to 1, 6, 11, 16, 21, and 26 you are probably the oldest child, the only child, or the oldest girl or boy in your family.

If you tended to agree with 2, 7, 12, 17, 22, and 27 you are more likely to be the second child or the second sister or brother child in your family.

A predominance of *yes an-swers to 3, 8, 13, 18, 23, and 28* would indicate that you are the middle child.

Identifying with answers 4, 9, 14, 19, 24, and 29, suggests the likelihood that you were the last born.

Overall Score

An overall score of over 100 indicates a strong identification with typical traits of adult children of alcoholics, though you may find you are not in the birth order indicated. If you find you don't agree with many statements, you may still recognize the behavior of someone close to you.

The good news is that you can clarify these characteristics if you want to, and a good source of help is support groups such as Al-Anon and Children of Alcoholics.

*Reprinted with permission from *Alcoholism/The National Magazine,* November-December, 1984.

Vitamin Dosages for Alcoholics

Part 1
Recommended Dosages for
Early Stages of Recovery

Vitamin	Daily Doses
A	10,000–25,000 IU
E	300–600 IU
K	1–10 mg
C	2–10 gm
B_1	100 mg
B_2	10–50 mg
B_3	1–3 gm
B_6	10–50 mg
Folacin	1–4 mg
Pantothenic acid	50–250 mg

These are treatment dosages to be given in the first weeks or months of recovery. They should be administered only under medical supervision.

Part 2
Recommended Safe
Maintenance Dosages

Vitamin	Dosages for Alcoholics	U.S. RDA
A	5,000–10,000 IU*	3,000 IU
D	400 IU	200 IU
E	100 IU	12–16 IU
K	500 mcg	300–500 mcg
C	500 mg–2 gm	60 mg
B-1 (thiamine)	2–5 mg	1.0–1.4 mg
B-2 (riboflavin)	2–5 mg	1.2–1.6 mg
B-3 (niacin)	100–200 mg	13–18 mg
B-6 (pyridoxine)	2–5 mg	2.0–2.2 mg
B-12 (cobalamin)	3.0 mcg	3.0 mcg
Folacin	400 mcg	400 mcg
Pantothenic acid	20–50 mg	4–7 mg
Biotin	100–200 mcg	100–200 mcg**

*Alcoholics with chronic liver disease will require medical supervision for vitamin A supplements.
**No RDA has been established, but this is considered a safe and adequate dosage.

The U.S. RDAs were updated in 1980 by the Food and Nutrition Board. In some cases the units of measure used in this chart have been changed to correspond with those most commonly used in supplements. However, the dosage is the same as the 1980 RDAs. No RDA has been established for vitamin K, biotin, or pantothenic acid; the dosages given here are considered "safe and adequate amounts" by the Food and Nutrition Board.

Withdrawal Courses for Addictive Drugs

Drug	Intoxication Signs and Symptoms	Withdrawal Signs and Symptoms	Length of Acute Detoxification	Recurring Withdrawal Symptoms	Common Detoxification Agents
SEDATIVES					
Alcohol	Slurred speech, poor coordination, confusion, drowsiness, clumsiness, depressed respirations and blood pressure	Anxiety, sweats, tremors, flushed face, irritability, sleeplessness, confusion, seizures, delirium	3–5 days	Not usual	Librium, Serax, Vistaril, Valium, Alcohol[1]
Valium			Slow drug taper up to 2 weeks	Common	Librium, Valium
Phenobarbital			Slow drug taper for 2–4 weeks	Common	Librium, Phenobarbital
NARCOTICS					
Heroin	Pin-point pupils, euphoria, nodding, sleepiness, anxiety, depressed blood pressure and respiration, elevated pulse	Yawning, dilated pupils, gooseflesh, vomiting, diarrhea, runny nose and eyes, sleeplessness, anxiety, irritability, elevated blood pressure and pulse, craving for narcotics	3–5 days	Common	Methadone or other tapering opiate or non-opiate withdrawal regimens[2]
Morphine			3–5 days	Common	
Demerol			3–5 days	Common	
Methadone			2 weeks +	Common	

				Drug intervention usually not required
STIMULANTS Amphetamines	Rapid pulse, elevated blood pressure, dilated pupils, sweats, tremors, hyperactivity, loss of appetite, irritability, sleeplessness, delirium, seizures	general fatigue, apathy, depression, drowsiness, irritability, paranoia	3–5 days	Common
Cocaine			3–5 days	Common
HALLUCINOGENS Marijuana	Rapid pulse, elevated blood pressure, dilated pupils, flushed face, red conjunctivae, anxiety, hallucinations, time-space disorientation, rambling speech	Few signs of withdrawal; craving for marijuana; general anxiety and restlessness	2–3 days	Possible prolonged craving — None, usually

[1]LOW DOSE ALCOHOL WITHDRAWAL
Traditionally, alcohol was used by laymen to taper a drunk off a binge. With the advent of sedative medication, this practice was discouraged. The use of general sedatives was thought to be more "clinical," and to achieve better control with less toxicity.

In recent years, however, the alcohol withdrawal model has been revived. Leading the way in this detox method is Dr. Walter Gower, M.D., of North Central Alcoholism Research Foundation, Inc., Fort Dodge, Iowa.*

Benefits:

1. Small amounts of alcohol provide clinical control without toxicity; the body is "geared" metabolically to alcohol and using alcohol as the "drug" agent for detox makes a smoother transition to sobriety.

2. Patients show more rapid CNS clearing as compared to detoxifications with longer acting general sedatives.

3. The detox model is less expensive to effect as it can be managed by non-medical staff who have been appropriately trained. However, it can—and is—used in hospital settings, as well.

Treatment Regimen:

½ oz. vodka (80–100 proof) with ½ oz. water, administered every 1–6 hours for detox control. Indications for use are the same as for sedative intervention. This can be used alone or in combination with sedatives such as Librium. (Patients with seizure histories are better protected during withdrawal with the combined regimen.)

*Transition, "A half-ounce of Prevention for the DT's," September, 1983.
"The Relationship of Ethanol to the Occurence of Delirium Tremens with Prophylactic and Therapeutic Considerations." Presented by Dr. Gower at the National Alcoholism Forum, 1979; abstracted in *Alcoholism Update,* Vol. II, No. 3, Aug–Sept, 1979.

²OTHER–OPIATE WITHDRAWAL PROTOCOL

—Darvon N-100: 1–2 every 4–6 hours to control detox signs and symptoms; taper to discontinue in 3–4 days.
—Catapres 0.1 mg. initially; repeat in one hour if needed, then 0.1–0.2 every 6–8 hours as long as blood pressure is no lower than 90/60. This can be used for 7–14 days to control opiate withdrawal symptoms.

Taking Drugs in Crises—
Restabilization Plan

Many recovering alcoholics have needlessly relapsed and started drinking again after taking central nervous system (CNS) drugs in unavoidable situations like accidents, injuries, or surgery. The following steps will help recovering alcoholics prepare themselves and protect their sobriety when exposed to CNS medication.

1. First, it's essential that the alcoholic fully understand why major pain medications and general anesthetics are dangerous to sobriety.*

2. If you are scheduled for surgery in which CNS drugs will be used and are unavoidable, plan a course of restabilization. It's important to do this before you are exposed to the drug(s), since you won't be thinking very clearly once you're under the influence of the medication.

*Local anesthetics that simply numb the skin are safe for the alcoholic.

The best and safest plan is to return to your in-patient alcoholism treatment facility after you've been released from the hospital where you were treated for the illness, accident, or surgery. A two- to three-day stay, under the care and protection of staff who understand alcoholism and the consequences of using CNS medication, will help your body readjust and stabilize itself.

For many alcoholics, however, this may not be feasible, and here are some suggestions for such cases.

(a) Don't take prescription CNS drugs home from the hospital, if at all possible. Extend your stay in the hospital if your doctor feels that you need to continue on major pain medications, sedatives, or sleeping pills.

(b) Once released from the hospital, have someone stay with you in the first week of home recovery. This will help protect you from the power of the addiction (reawakened by exposure to the CNS drugs), which could manipulate you into getting more drugs (or alcohol) in this unstable phase.

(c) Increase your vitamin C to 2 to 4 grams a day for four or five days if there are no medical contraindications. Vitamin C will help detoxify your system naturally.

(d) Follow a good, balanced diet and don't give in to cravings for such common offending foods as sugar, caffeine, and junk foods.

3. Alert your family or a close friend to the above plan in case unexpected tragedy should occur, exposing you to CNS drugs. Then, they can take the steps necessary to protect you and your sobriety.

Drugs That "Wake Up" the Alcoholic's Addiction

Part 1: Drugs That Affect the Central Nervous System

Analgesics (pain medication)

Codeine
Codeine compounds
  Aspirin with codeine
  Empirin with codeine
  Fiorinal with codeine

Percogesic with codeine
Tylenol with codeine
Tylox
Darvon and Darvon compounds
Darvocet
Fiorinal
Midrin

Narcotics: opiate derivatives and synthetics
  Codeine and codeine compounds (above)
    Demerol
    Dilaudid
    Methadone
    Mepergan
    Meperidine
    Morphine
    Talwin
  Percocet
  Percodan

Anesthetics

All general anesthetics
Local anesthetics are safe if not otherwise contraindicated

*Anticonvulsants**

Clonopine
Mebaral
Mysoline
Tegretol
Valium

*Consult with your doctor and/or alcoholism specialist before changing anticonvulsant medications.

Antidepressants

Adapin
Amitriptyline
Asendin
Aventyl
Deprol
Elavil
Etrafon
Limbitrol
Ludiomil
Marplan
Meprobamate
Nardil
Norpramin

Parnate
Pertofrane
Sinequan
Tofranil
Triavil
Vivactil

Antidiarrhea medications

Donnagel-PG
Lomotil
Paregoric
Other opiate-derivative or opioid types

Antihistamines (decongestants)

Many over-the-counter and prescription varieties (because of their secondary effect of drowsiness, antihistamine preparations are suspected of having a low-level effect on the central nervous system)
Decongestants *preferred* for alcoholics include
Pseudoepinephrine agents
Sudafed

Antinauseants

Atarax
Compazine
Phenergan
Vesprin
Vistaril
Others with antihistamine properties (same caution as above)
Antivert
Dramamine
Merezine
Tigan

Antispasmodics

Belladenal
Bellergal
Combid
Donnatal
Librax
Pathibamate
Valpin PB
Others with antihistamine properties (same caution as above)
Bentyl

Bronchial dilators

Alcohol-based inhalators
Bronchial dilators in liquid (elixir) form
Bronchial dilators with phenobarbital or other sedative combinations
Marax
Mudrane
Quadrinal
Tedral
Theofedral
Valpin

Cough and cold medicines

All alcohol-based expectorants, cough and cold preparations
All antihistamine decongestants: use same caution as under antihistamines
Cough suppressants with narcotic compounds
A.P.C. with codeine
Actifed-C
Hydocan
Tussionex tablets
Cough suppressants with non-narcotic compounds but with C.N.S. effects:
Dextromethorphan (DM)
Formula 44 cough discs

CoTylenol tablets and capsules
Expectorants and cough medicines recommended as *safe*
Glycotuss tablets
SSKI (Potassium Iodide Drops)
Tessalon

Muscle relaxants

Dantrium
Flexeril
Norflex
Norgesic
Robaxin
Soma
Valium

Sedatives/sleeping pills

All barbiturate medication
Amytal
Butisol
Nembutal
Pentobarbital
Pentothal
Secobarbital
Seconal
Tuinal
Non-barbiturate sedatives
Ativan
Dalmane
Equanil
Hydroxyzine
Mepergan
Noludar
Phenergan

Stimulants

Amphetamines
Desoxyn
Dexedrine
Non-amphetamine diet pills
Parnate
Pertofrane

Ritalin
Tofranil

Tonics

All alcohol-based elixirs

Tranquilizers

Benzodiazepines
  Ativan
  Librium
  Limbitrol
  Serax
  Tranxene
  Valium
Hydroxyzines
  Atarax
  Hydroxyzine
  Vistaril
Meprobamate and combinations
  Deprol
  Equanil
  Milpath
  Miltown
Phenothiazines
  Chlorpromzine

Etrafon
Mellaril
Prolixin
Serentil
Stelazine
Thorazine
Triavil
Vesprin
Others
  Haldol
  Navane
  Taractan
  Loxitane
  Moban

Note: This is not a complete listing of drugs that affect the central nervous system, but includes common drugs in major categories for which alcoholics need to exercise discretion and caution. In all over-the-counter drugs, read labels carefully, and for medicines prescribed by your doctor ask for information regarding contents.

Part 2:
Medications Containing Alcohol Commonly Stocked in Hospitals and Pharmacies

Drug	Percentage of Alcohol	Drug	Percentage of Alcohol
Actol Expectorant Syrup	12.5	Belladona Tr.	67.0
Alertonic	0.45	Benadryl Elixir	14.0
Alurate Elixir	20.0	Bentyl—Pb Syrup	19.0
Ambenyl Expectorant	5.0	Benylin Expectorant	5.0
Anahist	0.5	Brondecon Elixir	20.0
Anaspaz—Pb Liquid	15.0	Bronkelixir	19.0
Aromatic Elixir	22.0	Butibel Elixir	7.0
Asbron Elixir	15.0	Calcidrine Syrup	6.0
Atarax Syrup	0.5	Carbrital Elixir	18.0
Bactrim Suspension	0.3	Cas Evac	18.0

Drug	Percentage of Alcohol	Drug	Percentage of Alcohol
Cascara Sagroda (Aromatic)	18.0	Gevrabon Liquid	18.0
Cerose & Cerose DM Expectorant	2.5	Hycotuss Expectorant & Syrup	10.0
Cheracol & Cheracol D	3.0	Hydryllin Comp	5.0
Chlor-Trimeton Syrup	7.0	Iberet Liquid	1.0
Choledyl Elixir	20.00	Ipecac Syrup	2.0
Citra Forte Syrup	2.0	Isuprel Comp. Elixir	19.0
Coldene Cough Syrup	15.0	Kaochlor	3.8
Cologel Liquid	5.0	Kaon Elixir	5.0
Conar Expectorant	5.0	Kay-Ciel Elixir	4.0
Copavin Cmpd Elixir	7.0	Lanoxin Elixir Pediatric	10.0
Coryban D	7.5	Lomotil (liquid)	15.0
Cosanyl DM & Cosanyl Syrup	6.0	Luffylin—GG Elixir	17.0
		Marax Syrup	5.0
Darvon—N Suspension	1.0	Mediatric Liquid	15.0
Decadron Elixir	5.0	Mellaril Concentrate	3.0
Demazin Syrup	7.5	Mesopin Elixir	12.5
Dexedrine Elixir	10.0	Minocin Syrup	5.0
Dilaudid Cough Syrup	5.0	Modane Liquid	5.0
Dimacol Liquid	4.75	Mol Iron Liquid	4.75
Dimetane Elixir	3.0	Nembutal Elixir	18.0
Dimetane Expectorant	3.5	Nico—Metrazol Elixir	15.0
Dimetane Expectorant— D.C.	3.5	Nicol Elixir	10.0
		Novahistine Elixir	5.00
Dimetapp Elixir	2.3	Novahistine Expectorant	5.0
Donnagel Suspension	3.8	Novahistine DH	5.0
Donnagel PG Suspension	5.0	Novahistine DMX	10.0
Donnatal Elixir	23.0	Nyquil Cough Syrup	25.0
Doxinate Liquid	5.0	Organidin Elixir	23.75
Dramamine Liquid	5.0	Ornacol Liquid	8.0
Elixir Theophylline	20.0	Paregoric Tincture	45.0
Elixophy	20.0	Parapectolin	0.69
Elixophylline—K1	10.0	Parelixir	18.0
Ephedrine Sulfate Syrup U.S.P.	3.0	P.B.Z. Expectorant with Codeine and Ephedrine	6.0
Ephedrine Sulfate Syrup— Note U.S.P.	12.0	P.B.Z. Expectorant with Ephedrine	6.0
Feosol Elixir	5.0	Periactin Syrup	5.0
Fer-In-Sol Syrup	5.0	Pertussin 8 Hour Syrup	9.5
Fer-In-Sol Drops	0.2	Phenergan Expectorant, Plain	7.0
Geriplex—FS	18.0	Phenergan Expectorant with Codeine	7.0

Drug	Percentage of Alcohol	Drug	Percentage of Alcohol
Phenergan Expectorant V.C., Plain	7.0	Tedral Elixir	15.0
		Temaril Syrup	5.7
Phenergan Expectorant V.C., with Codeine	7.0	Terpin Hydrate Elixir	42.0
Phenergan Expectorant, Pediatric	7.0	Terpin Hydrate Elixir with Codeine	42.0
		Theo Organidin Elixir	15.0
Phenergan Syrup Fortis (25 mg)	1.5	Theolixir (Elixir Theophylline)	20.0
Phenobarbital Elixir	14.0	Triaminic Expectorant	5.0
Polarmine Expectorant	7.2	Triaminic Expectorant D.H.	5.0
Potassium Chloride Sol. Standard	10.0	Tuss-Ornade Syrup	7.5
		Tussar S.F. Syrup	12.0
(a no-alcohol solution can be requested)		Tussar-2 Syrup	5.0
		Tussend Liquid	5.0
Propadrine Elixir HC1	16.0	Tussi-Organidin Expectorant	15.0
Quibron Elixir	15.0		
Robitussin Syrup	3.5	Tylenol Drops	7.0
Robitussin A.C. Syrup	3.5	Tylenol with Codeine Elixir	7.0
Robitussin PE	1.4	Tylenol Elixir	7.0
Robitussin D.M. and Robitussin C.F.	1.4	Ulo—Syrupp	6.65
		Valadol Liquid	9.0
Roniacol Elixir	8.6	Valpin—PB Elixir & Valpin	5.3
Rondec D.M. Syrup and Drops	0.6	Vicks Formula 44	10.0
		Vita Metrazol Elixir	15.0
Serpasil Elixir	12.0		

NOTES:
1. Mouthwashes—Scope, Listerine, Cepacol, Colgate 100, Micrin— all have approximately 15–25% alcohol.
2. All elixirs contain some alcohol.
3. Liquids that do not contain alcohol:

Chloraseptic mouthwash/ gargle	Kaopectate and Parget, etc.
Liquiprin (acetaminophen)	Sudafed Syrup
Dilantin Suspension	Actifed Syrup
Alupent Syrup	Triaminic Syrup
	Naldecon Syrup
	Nydrazid Syrup

Courtesy of
Milam Recovery Centers, Inc.
14500 Juanita Drive N.E.
Bothell, WA 98011

National Alcoholism Resources

Addiction Research Foundation
33 Russell Street
Toronto, Ontario M5S 2S1
CANADA
  416/595-6056

Al-Anon Family Groups
  World Services
P.O. Box 862
Midtown Station
New York, New York 10018
  212/302-7240

Alateen (same as above)

ADPA
Alcohol and Drug Problems
  Association of North America,
  Inc.
444 North Capitol Street, N.W.
Washington, D.C. 20001
  202/737-4340

A.A.
Alcoholics Anonymous
General Service Office
P.O. Box 459
Grand Central Station
New York, New York 10163
  212/686-1100

American Council on Alcohol Problems, Inc.
3426 Bridgeland Dr.
Bridgeton, Missouri 63044
314/739-5944

American Council for Drug Education
204 Monroe Street
Rockville, Maryland 20852
(formerly: American Council on Marijuana & Other Psycho-active Drugs)
301/984-5700

AMSA
American Medical Society on Alcoholism & Other Drug Dependencies
12 West 21st Street, 7th floor
New York, New York 10010
212/206-6770

AHHAP
Association of Halfway House Alcoholism Programs of North America
786 East 7th Street
St. Paul, Minnesota 55106
612/771-0933

ALMACA
Association of Labor-Management Administrators and Consultants on Alcoholism, Inc.
1800 N. Kent Street, Suite 907
Arlington, Virginia 22209
703/522-6272

CSPI
Center for Science in the Public Interest
1501 16th Street, N.W.
Washington, D.C. 20036
202/332-9110

COAF
Children of Alcoholics Foundation, Inc.
200 Park Avenue, 31st floor
New York, New York 10166
212/351-2680

Hazelden Foundation
Box 11
Center City, Minnesota 55012
800/328-9000

ICAA/American
International Council on Alcohol and Addiction/American Foundation
P.O. Box 489
Locust Valley, New York 11560
516/676-1802

ICAA
International Council on Alcohol and Addiction
Case Postale 189
1001 Lausanne
SWITZERLAND

The Johnson Institute
7151 Metro Blvd.
Minneapolis, Minnesota 55403
612/341-0435

MADD
Mothers Against Drunk Driving
669 Airport Freeway, Suite 310
Hurst, Texas 76053-3944
817/268-6233

Multi-Cultural Prevention Resource Center
c/o Annette Green
1540 Market Street, Suite 320
San Francisco, California 94102
(substance abuse among Native Americans, other minorities)
412/355-4291

NADAC
National Association of Alcoholism
   and Drug Abuse Counselors
3717 Columbia Pike, Suite 300
Arlington, Virginia 22204
   703/920-4644

NAATP
National Association of Addiction
   Treatment Providers, Inc.
2082 Michelson Drive
Irvine, California 92715
   714/476-8204

NACOA
National Association for Children
   of Alcoholics, Inc.
31706 Coast Highway, Suite 201
So. Laguna, California 92677
   714/499-3889

NALGAP
National Association of Lesbian
   and Gay Alcoholism
   Professionals, Inc.
1208 E. State Boulevard
Fort Wayne, Indiana 46805
   219/483-8280

NASADAD
National Association of State Alcohol and Drug Abuse Directors,
   Inc.
444 North Capitol Street, N.W.
Washington, D.C. 20001
   202/783-6868

NBAC
National Black Alcoholism
   Council
417 South Dearborn Avenue,
   Suite 700
Chicago, Illinois 60605

NCALI
National Clearinghouse for
   Alcohol and Drug Information
P.O. Box 2345
Rockville, Maryland 20852
   301/468-2600

NCA
National Council on Alcoholism,
   Inc.
12 West 21st Street, 7th floor
New York, New York 10010
   212/206-6770

NCA/Washington Office
National Council on Alcoholism,
   Inc.
1511 K Street, N.W., Suite 320
Washington, D.C. 20005
   202/737-8122

NIAAA
National Institute on Alcohol
   Abuse and Alcoholism
Parklawn Building
5600 Fishers Lane
Rockville, Maryland 20857
   301/443-3885

NIDA
National Institute on Drug Abuse
Parklawn Building
5600 Fishers Lane
Rockville, Maryland 20857
   301/443-4577

NNSA
National Nurses Society on
   Addiction
2506 Gross Point Road
Evanston, Illinois 60201
   312/475-7300

National Safety Council
444 North Michigan Avenue
Chicago, Illinois 60611
   312/527-4800

National Self-Help Clearinghouse
Graduate School & University
Center
City University of New York
33 West 42nd Street, Room 1222
New York, New York 10036
212/840-1259

RID
Remove Intoxicated Drivers
P.O. Box 520
Schenectady, New York 12301
518/372-0034

RSA
Research Society on Alcoholism
4314 Medical Parkway
Suite 300
Austin, Texas 78756
512/454-0022

Rutgers University
Center of Alcohol Studies Library
New Brunswick, New Jersey 08903
201/932-4442

SADD
Students Against Driving Drunk
P.O. Box 800
Marlboro, Massachusetts 01752
617/481-3568

The Christopher D. Smithers
Foundation, Inc.
P.O. Box 67
Mill Neck, New York 11765
516/676-0067

DOT
U.S. Department of Transportation
National Highway Traffic Safety
Administration
Office of Alcohol
Countermeasures
NTS-21
400 Seventh Street, S.W.,
Room 5130
Washington, D.C. 20590
202/366-9581

Women for Sobriety, Inc.
P.O. Box 618
Quakertown, Pennsylvania 18951
215/536-8026

Adams, V. "Remembering the First Drink." *Psychology Today* 17(5) (1983): 82.

Bashir, K.R., et al. "Brief Alcoholism Rating Scale: A New Test for Diagnosing." *Canadian Family Physician* 28 (1982): 987–90.

Begleiter, H., B. Porjesz, B. Bihari, et al. "Event-Related Brain Potentials in Boys at Risk for Alcoholism." *Science 1984*, 225:1493–95.

———. "Human Brain Electrophysiology and Alcoholism," in *Alcohol and the Brain*, Tarter, R., and D. Van Thiel, eds. New York: Plenum Press (in press).

Beresford, T., et al. "Computerized Biochemical Profile for Detection of Alcoholism." *Psychosomatics* 23(7) (1982): 713–14, 719–20.

Buehler, M.S. "Relative Hypoglycemia: A Clinical Review of 350 Cases." *Lancet,* July 1962: 289–92.

Burton, B.T. "The Significance of Serum B-1 and Magnesium in DT's and Alcoholism." *Journal of Clinical Psychiatry* 40 (1979): 476–79.

Cedarbaum, A.I., E. Dicker, C.S. Lieber, and E. Rubin. "Factors Contributing to the Adaptive Increase in Ethanol Metabolism

Due to Chronic Consumption of Ethanol." *Alcoholism* 1(1) (January, 1977): 27–31.

Cohen, G., and M.A. Collins. "Alkaloids from Catecholamines in Adrenal Tissue: Possible Role in Alcoholism." *Science* 167 (1970): 1749–51.

Davis, V.E., and M.J. Walsh. "Alcohol, Amines, Alkaloids: A Possible Biochemical Basis for Alcohol Addiction." *Science* 167 (1970): 1005–07.

de Lint, J., and W. Schmidt. *Biological Basis of Alcoholism.* New York: Wiley-Interscience, 1971.

Eckardt, M.J. et al. "Health Hazards Associated with Alcohol Consumption." *Journal of the American Medical Association.* 246(6) (1981): 648–66.

Elmasian, R., et al. "Event-Related Brain Potentials are Different in Individuals at High and Low Risk for Developing Alcoholism." *Proceedings of the National Academy of Sciences,* December 1982.

Emrick, C.D. "A Review of Psychologically Oriented Treatment of Alcoholism." *Quarterly Journal of Studies on Alcohol* 36 (1975): 88–108.

Filstead, W.J., J.J. Rossi, and M. Keller, eds. *Alcohol and Alcohol Problems: New Thinking and New Directions.* Cambridge: Ballinger, 1976.

Gelenberg, A. J., et al. "Tyrosine for the Treatment of Depression." *American Journal of Psychiatry* 137 (1980): 622.

Goldberg, I.K. "L-tyrosine for the Treatment of Depression." *Lancet* 2 (1980): 364.

Goldman, M.S., "Cognitive Impairment in Chronic Alcoholics: Some Cause for Optimism." *American Psychologist* 38(10) (1983): 1045–54.

Goleman, Daniel. "Matter Over Mind: The Big Issue Raised by Newly Discovered Brain Chemicals. *Psychology Today,* June 1980: 66–76.

Goodhart, R.S. "The Role of Nutritional Factors in the Cause, Prevention, and Cure of Alcoholism and Associated Affirmities." *American Journal of Clinical Nutrition* 5 (1957): 612.

Goodwin, D.W. *Chronic Effects of Alcohol and Other Psychoactive Drugs on Cerebral Function.* Toronto: Addiction Research Foundation Press, 1975.

————. "Genetic Aspects of Alcoholism." *Drug Therapy* October 1982.

Grant, M., and P. Guinner. *Alcoholism in Perspective.* Baltimore: University Park Press, 1979.

Growdon, J.H., and R.J. Wurtman. "Dietary Influence on the Synthesis of Neurotransmitters in the Brain." *Nutrition Reviews* 37 (1979): 129–36.

Guthrie, A., and W.A. Elliott. "Early Cerebral Impairment in Alcoholism." *Health Bulletin* 39(6) (1981): 384–92.

Hoes, M.J.A.J.M. "The Significance of B-1 and Magnesium in DT's and Alcoholism." *Journal of Clinical Psychiatry* 40 (1979): 476–79.

Hofmann, F.G. *A Handbook on Drug and Alcohol Abuse: The Biomedical Aspects.* New York: Oxford University Press, 1983.

Hudspeth, W.J., et al. "Neurobiology of the Hypoglycemia Syndrome." *Journal of Holistic Medicine* 3(1) (1981): 60.

Kissin, B., and H. Begleiter eds. *The Biology of Alcoholism* (5 volumes). New York: Plenum Press, 1971–76.

Kline, N.S., and B.K. Shah. "Comparable Therapeutic Efficacy of Tryptophan and Imipramine: Average Therapeutic Ratings Versus 'True' Equivalence and Important Differences." *Current Therapeutic Research* 15 (1973): 484.

Korsten, M.D., A. Mark, and C.S. Lieber. "Nutrition in the Alcoholic." *Medical Clinic of North America* 63:963–972, 1979.

Lieber, C.S. "Alcoholism and Nutrition: A Seminar." *Alcoholism Clinical and Experimental Research* 3(1979): 126.

———— "The Metabolic Basis of Alcohol's Toxicity." *Hospital Practice* 12(2) (February 1977): 73–80

————. "The Metabolism of Alcohol." *Scientific American* 234(3) (March 1976): 29.

———— (ed.). *Metabolic Aspects of Alcoholism.* Baltimore: University Park Press, 1976.

———. "Alcoholism and Nutrition: A Seminar." *Alcoholism Clinical and Experimental Research* 3 (1979): 125.

———. *Medical Disorders of Alcoholism: Pathogenesis and Treatment,* Philadelphia: Saunders 1982.

———. "Symposium: Interactions of Alcohol and Nutrition." *Alcoholism Clinical and Experimental Research* 7(1) (Winter 1983).

———. Y. Hasumara, R. Teschke, S. Matsuzaki, and M. Korsten. "The Effects of Chronic Ethanol Consumption on Acetaldehyde Metabolism," in *The Role of Acetaldehyde in the Actions of Ethanol.* vol. 3, K.O. Lindros and C.J.P. Ericksson, eds. Helsinki: Finnish Foundation for Alcohol Studies, 1975.

McLaughlin, E.J., L.A. Faillace, and J.E. Overall. "Alcohol Studies: Cognitive Status and Changes During 28-day Hospitalization." *Currents in Alcoholism: Biomedical Issues and Clinical Effects of Alcoholism* 5:378. New York: Grune and Stratton, 1979.

Marks, V. "Alcohol and Carbohydrate Metabolism." *Clinics in Endocrinology* 7 (1978): 333–49.

———, and J.W. Wright. "Endocrinological and Metabolic Effects of Alcohol." *Proceedings of the Royal Society of Medicine* 70 (1977): 337–44.

Meyer, J.G., and K. Urban. "Electrolyte Changes and Acid Base Balance after Alcohol Withdrawal, with Special Reference to Rum Fits and Magnesium Depletion. *Journal of Neurology* 215(2) (May 13, 1977): 135–40.

Milam, J.R., and K. Ketcham. *Under the Influence: A Guide to the Myths and Realities of Alcoholism.* Seattle: Madrona, 1981.

Philpott, W.H. "Allergy and Alcohol Addiction." *Texas Key Newsletter,* February 1975.

———, and D.K. Kalita. *Brain Allergies: The Psychonutrient Connection.* New Canaan: Keats Publishing, 1980.

Pristach, C.A., et al. "Alcohol Withdrawal Syndromes: Prediction from Detailed Medical and Drinking Histories." *Drug and Alcohol Dependence* 11 (1983): 177–99.

Register, U.D., S.R. Marsh, C.T. Thurston, B.J. Fields, M.C.

Hornning, M.G. Hardinge, and A. Sanchez. "Influence of Nutrients on Intake of Alcohol." *Journal of The American Dietetic Association.* 61(2) (1972): 159.

Rodgers, J.E. "Brain Triggers: Biochemistry and Behavior." *Science Digest,* January 1983.

Roe, D.A. *Alcohol and the Diet.* Westport: AVI Publishing, 1979.

Ryback, R., et al. "Biochemical and Hematological Correlates of Alcoholism. *Research Communications in Chemical Pathology and Pharmacology,* March 1980.

Schuckit, M.A. "Alcoholism and Genetics: Possible Biological Mediators." *Biological Psychiatry* 15(3) (1980): 437–47.

———. *Drug and Alcohol Abuse: A Clinical Guide to Diagnosis and Treatment.* New York: Plenum Press, 1984.

———. "Genetics and the Risk for Alcoholism." *Journal of the American Medical Association,* 254 (18) (November 8, 1985).

———. D.W. Goodwin, and G. Winokur. "A Study of Alcoholism in Half Siblings." *American Journal of Psychiatry* 128 (1972): 122–26.

———, and V. Rayses. "'Ethanol Ingestion: Differences in Blood Acetaldehyde Concentrations in Relatives of Alcoholics and Controls." *Science* 203 (1979): 54.

Scientific American (issue on "The Brain"), September 1979.

Sereny, G., L. Endrenzi and P. Devenyi. "Glucose Intolerance in Alcoholism. *Journal of Studies on Alcohol* 36 (1975): 359.

Sherin, K. "Screening for Alcoholism." *American Family Physician* 26(1) (1982): 178–89.

Snyder, S. *Biological Aspects of Mental Disorder,* New York: Oxford University Press, 1980.

Stockwell, T., D. Murphy and R. Hodgson. "Severity of Alcohol Dependence Questionnaire: Its Use, Reliability and Validity." *British Journal of Addiction* 78(2) (1983): 145–55.

Thompson, A.D. "Alcohol and Nutrition." *Clin. Endocrin. Metab* 7(2) (July 1978): 405–28.

Thompson, W.L. "Management of Alcohol Withdrawal Syndromes." *Archives of Internal Medicine* 138 (February 1978): 278–83.

Wallgren, H., and H. Barry. *Actions of Alcohol* (2 volumes). New York: Elsevier, 1970.

Watterlond, M. "The Telltale Metabolism of Alcoholics." *Science* 83: 72–102.

Williams, R.J. "Alcoholism as a Nutrition Problem." *Journal of Clinical Nutrition* 1 (1952–53): 32.

———. *You are Extraordinary.* New York: Pyramid Books, 1967.

———. *Nutrition Against Disease,* New York: Pittman, 1971.

———. *Physician's Handbook on Nutritional Science.* Springfield, IL : Charles C. Thomas, 1975.

———. *The Wonderful World Within You: Your Inner Nutritional Environment.* New York: Bantam Books, 1977.

———, and D.K. Kalita. *A Physician's Handbook on Orthomolecular Medicine.* New Canaan: Keats, 1979.

Wolff, P.H. "Ethnic Differences in Alcohol Sensitivity." *Science* 175 (1972): 449–50.

Worden, M., and G. Rosellini. "Applying Nutritional Concepts in Alcohol and Drug Counseling." *Journal of Psychedelic Drugs* 11 (3) (July–Sept 1979).

———. "Role of Diet in People Work: Use of Nutrition in Therapy with Substance Abusers." *The Journal of Orthomolecular Psychiatry* 7 (4) (1978): 249–57.

Wright, J. "Endocrine Effects of Alcoholism." *Clinics in Endocrinology* 7(1978): 351–67.

Research monographs from the U.S. Dept. of Health and Human Services, Alcohol, Drug Abuse and Mental Health Administration (Rockville, Maryland: DHHS)

No. 2, (1982) "Biomedical Processes and Consequences of Alcohol Use." 378.

No. 5, "Evaulation of the Alcoholic: Implications for Research, Theory and Treatment." Meyer, R. E., et al., eds., 409.

No. 9 (1983), "Biological/Genetic Factors in Alcoholism." Hessel-brock, V.M., E.G. Shaskan and R.E. Meyer, eds., 166.

No. 11 (1983), "Biological Approach to Alcoholism." C.S. Lieber, ed.

"Alcohol and Drug Abuse Curriculum Guide for Psychiatry Faculty. D.S. Gallant, 1982, 78.

Recommended Books

Personal Accounts

Harold Hughes: The Man from Ida Grove. Harold E. Hughes with Dick Schneider. Lincoln, VA: Chosen Books, 1979
Senator Hughes, the first politician to focus national attention on alcoholism, tells the story of his alcoholism, near-suicide, and eventual recovery and involvement in politics.

End of the Rainbow. Mary Ann Crenshaw. New York: Macmillan, 1981.
A graphic and exhaustive personal account of drug addiction, written by a former *New York Times* fashion reporter.

Five O'clock Comes Early. Bob Welch and George Vecsey. New York: William Morrow, 1982.
Twenty-three-year-old Bob Welch, former star pitcher for the Los Angeles Dodgers, details his treatment and the impact of his disease on his family, friends, and teammates.

The Quality of Mercy. Mercedes McCambridge. New York: Berkley, 1982.
Actress McCambridge (the voice of the devil in the movie *The Exorcist*), describes her life as an alcoholic.

Where Did Everybody Go? Paul Molloy. New York: Warner Books, 1982.
Syndicated *Chicago Sun* columnist describes his long battle with alcoholism and numerous attempts to recover.

A Private Practice. Patrick Reilly, M.D. New York: Macmillan, 1984.

Patrick Reilly is a pseudonym for a pediatrician from Cleveland, Ohio, who entered an in-patient treatment program in Toronto to overcome his addiction to sedatives (Valium, Dalmane, Doriden, Librium, Palicidy). The day-to-day descriptions of his treatment and his relationship to the other members of his therapy group are fascinating, as is his insight into his own attitude about alcoholism.

The Courage to Change. Dennis Wholey. Boston: Houghton Mifflin, 1984.

Reading this book is like attending a star-studded AA meeting where everyone has had a chance to polish up their stories beforehand. Taken as a whole, it's about as accurate a look at alcoholism from the inside out as we are likely to get.

Off the Sauce. Lewis Meyer. New York: Macmillan, 1967.

A funny, tough yet tender love song to AA, written by an author and television personality.

Prodigal Shepherd. Father Ralph Pfau, and Al Hirshberg. New York: Popular Library, 1958.

A priest's account of his addiction to alcohol and eventual recovery.

A Sensitive, Passionate Man. Barbara Mahoney. New York: David Mckay, 1974.

Barbara Mahoney's husband eventually died of alcoholism; this is her story of their last, agonizing years together.

The Times of My Life. Betty Ford with Chris Chase. New York: Ballantine Books, 1979.

Chapters 38 and 39 tell of the former First Lady's addiction to alcohol and prescription pills, her family's intervention, and her treatment and recovery.

The Lost Weekend. Charles Jackson. New York: Farrar and Rinehart, 1944.

Charles Jackson was an alcoholic and died of suicide; his accounts of fictional alcoholic Don Birnam's obsession with alcohol, his drinking binges, the withdrawal symptoms, and an overnight stay at a city hospital are harrowing and gut-wrenching.

Broken Promises, Mended Dreams. Richard Meryman. Boston: Little Brown, 1984.

A fictionalized, detailed account of a woman alcoholic (a composite of many women the author studied and spent time with), her treatment and recovery.

Bill W. Robert Thomsen. New York: Popular Library, 1975.
The autobiography of Bill Wilson, co-founder of AA.

I'm Dancing As Fast As I Can. Barbara Gordon. New York: Harper and Row, 1979.
Gordon, a TV producer, was addicted to Valium; one day she threw all her pills away and steeled herself for a rough couple of days. But as this nightmarish account reveals, the ordeal lasted for months.

Walker, Alexander, ed. *No Bells on Sunday: The Rachel Roberts Journals.* New York: Harper and Row, 1984.
British actress Rachel Roberts kept these journals for three years prior to her suicide; they provide a vivid description of her addiction to alcohol and other drugs.

Turnabout: New Help for the Woman Alcoholic. Kirkpatrick, Jean, Ph.D. Seattle: Madrona, 1986.
Written by the woman who founded Women for Sobriety, a self-help program for women and an alternative to AA.

A Rational Counseling Primer, Howard S. Young. New York: Institute for Rational Living, Inc., 1974.
A short (31 pages) and simple introduction to the concepts of rational motive therapy (RET).

General Interest

Alcohol Problems and Alcoholism: A Comprehensive Survey. James E. Royce. New York: Free Press, 1980.
An excellent overview of research in the field.

Alcoholics Anonymous. New York: AA World Services, 1955.
"The Big Book" is a real Bible for AA members. In the first part of the book the basic AA program is outlined; numerous personal histories form the second half of the book. AA literature is not available through bookstores but can be purchased through local AA offices or ordered from the General Services Board of AA, 468 Park Avenue South, New York, NY 10016.

Alcoholism: The Nutritional Approach. Roger J. Williams. Austin: University of Texas Press, 1959.

Roger Williams is a pioneer in the field of alcoholism and nutrition, and in this short, easy-to-read book, he presents his "genetotrophic" concept that alcoholism develops from a genetically determined nutritional disorder.

The Disease Concept of Alcoholism. E.M. Jellinek. New Haven: Hillhouse Press, 1960.

Jellinek was a pioneer in alcoholism theory and treatment, and with this book his "disease concept" of alcoholism was catapulted into public awareness.

Eating Right to Live Sober. Katherine Ketcham and L. Ann Mueller, M.D. Seattle: Madrona, 1983. (New American Library paperback edition, 1986.)

Explores the role of nutrition in recovery from alcoholism. Detailed meal plans and recipes are included.

Hypoglycemia: A Better Approach. Paavo Airola, Ph.D. Phoenix: Health Plus, 1977.

The causes, symptoms, and treatment of hypoglycemia are described in a book written for the layperson by a nutritionist whose controversial theories are often scoffed at by the medical establishment.

I'll Quit Tomorrow. Vernon E. Johnson. New York: Harper and Row, 1973.

The first book to detail the concept of intervention, in which the alcoholic is forced to confront the reality of his disease. Excellent sections are included on the symptoms of alcoholism, particularly rationalization and denial.

Is Alcoholism Hereditary? Donald Goodwin, M.D. New York: Oxford University Press, 1976.

The evidence that alcoholism is, indeed, hereditary (i.e., passed from parent to child through genes) is compellingly presented in this entertaining, clearly written book.

Marty Mann Answers Your Questions About Drinking and Alcoholism. Marty Mann. New York: Holt, Rinehart and Winston, 1981 (revised ed.).

Frequently asked questions about alcoholism are answered by Marty Mann, one of the first women members of AA, and a founding member of the National Council on Alcoholism.

The Natural History of Alcoholism: Causes, Patterns, and Paths to Recovery. George Vaillant. Cambridge: Harvard University Press, 1983.

Vaillant, a Harvard psychiatrist and researcher, makes some fascinating conclusions in this synopsis of a long-term study of six hundred alcoholics, including the fact that people are not predisposed by personality to become alcoholics and psychological approaches are useless in treating alcoholics.

The Neutral Spirit: A Portrait of Alcohol. Berton Roueche. Boston: Little, Brown & Co., 1960.

Alcohol and its use and abuse from ancient to modern man are described in entertaining, vivid prose by a veteran writer for *The New Yorker* magazine.

The Prevention of Alcoholism Through Nutrition. R.J. Williams. New York: Bantam Books, 1981.

Seven steps are presented for maintaining good health and protecting yourself against alcoholism.

Primer on Alcoholism. Marty Mann. New York: Rinehart & Co., 1950.

Written for both the alcoholic and the nonalcoholic, this book describes how to recognize alcoholism and what to do about getting help. Revised and updated in 1958 as *New Primer on Alcoholism.*

The Tranquilizing of America. Richard Hughes and Robert Brewin. New York: Warner Books, 1979.

An exhaustively researched, fascinating look at prescription-drug use in the U.S., with some troubling information about the federal government's role in regulating and overseeing the pharmaceutical industry.

Under the Influence: A Guide to the Myths and Realities of Alcoholism. James R. Milam and Katherine Ketcham. Seattle: Madrona, 1981. (Bantam paperback edition, 1983.)

A comprehensive and controversial look at the physiological factors determining alcoholism, with specific recommendations for treatment, recovery, and prevention of alcoholism.

800-Cocaine. Mark S. Gold, M.D., New York: Bantam Books, 1984.

800-Cocaine is a 24-hour-a-day nationwide referral and information service founded by author Gold; this book answers users' questions about cocaine use, addiction, and treatment.

Relaxation Techniques

Kicking Your Stress Habits: A Do-It-Yourself Guide for Coping with Stress. Donald A. Tubesing, Ph.D. New York: New American Library, 1981.
Managing stress by changing the way you cope with life.

Life After Stress. Martin Shaffer, Ph.D. Chicago: Contemporary Books, 1983.
An examination of what stress is, how to analyze it in yourself, and how to deal with it; excellent relaxation techniques included.

The Relaxation and Stress Reduction Workbook. Davis, Eshelman and McKay. Oakland: New Harbinger Publications, 1982.
Useful and informative sections on progressive relaxation, meditation, self-hypnosis, breathing, and managing your time.

Especially for the Family

Adult Children of Alcoholics. Janet Woititz. Pompano Beach, Fla.: Health Communications, 1986.

Another Chance: Hope and Health for the Alcoholic Family. Sharon Wegscheider. Palo Alto: Science and Behavior Books, 1981.

Getting Them Sober. Toby Rice Drews. Plainfield, N.J.: Bridge, 1980.

Not My Kid: A Family's Guide to Kids and Drugs. Beth Plson and Miller Newton, Ph.D. New York: Arbor House, 1984.

Sitting in the Bay Window: A Book for Parents of Young Alcoholics. Jack Mumey. Chicago: Contemporary Books, 1984.

Women Who Love Too Much. Robin Norwood. New York: Pocket Books, 1986.

Other Drugs

Cocaine: A Drug and Its Evolution. Lester Grinspoon and James Bakalar. New York: Basic Books, 1976.

Cocaine: Seduction and Solution. Stone, Fromme, and Kagan. New York: Crown, 1984.

The Coke Book. Chilnick, ed. New York: Berkeley, 1984.

Getting Tough on Gateway Drugs: A Guide for the Family. Robert L.DuPont, Jr., M.D. New York: American Psychiatric Press, 1984.

The All-American Cocaine Story: A Guide to the Realities of Cocaine. David R. Britt. CompCare Publications, 1984.

Chocolate to Morphine: Understanding Mind-Active Drugs. Weil and Rosen. Boston: Houghton Mifflin, 1983.

Marijuana Alert. Peggy Mann. New York: McGraw-Hill, 1985.

Alcoholism Information Services

Alcohol Awareness Service. A paid subscription service, published every other month, which includes the latest alcohol information and brief abstracts from major publications in the alcohol field. National Clearinghouse for Alcohol Information, PO Box 2345, Rockville, MD 20852. The Clearinghouse also provides a computer data base search for alcohol-related information, free of charge.

Rutgers Center of Alcohol Studies, Rutgers University Piscataway, NJ 18854. Extensive bibliographic references on specific alcohol-related topics are available for a fee. A complete list of topics and ordering information is available upon request. The Rutgers Center of Alcohol Studies Library also makes their library books and materials available through an interlibrary loan process.